Palgrave Studies in Classical Liberalism

Series Editors
David F. Hardwick, Department of Pathology and Laboratory Medicine, The University of British Columbia, Vancouver, Canada
Leslie Marsh, Department of Economics, Philosophy and Political Science, The University of British Columbia, Okanagan, Canada

This series offers a forum to writers concerned that the central presuppositions of the liberal tradition have been severely corroded, neglected, or misappropriated by overly rationalistic and constructivist approaches.

The hardest-won achievement of the liberal tradition has been the wrestling of epistemic independence from overwhelming concentrations of power, monopolies and capricious zealotries. The very precondition of knowledge is the exploitation of the epistemic virtues accorded by society's situated and distributed manifold of spontaneous orders, the DNA of the modern civil condition.

With the confluence of interest in situated and distributed liberalism emanating from the Scottish tradition, Austrian and behavioral economics, non-Cartesian philosophy and moral psychology, the editors are soliciting proposals that speak to this multidisciplinary constituency. Sole or joint authorship submissions are welcome as are edited collections, broadly theoretical or topical in nature.

Ben Burgis · Matthew McManus
Editors

Analytical Marxism and Democratic Socialism in the 21st Century

Revisiting G.A. Cohen

palgrave
macmillan

Editors
Ben Burgis
Rutgers University
Los Angeles, CA, USA

Matthew McManus
Spelman College
Atlanta, GA, USA

ISSN 2662-6470 ISSN 2662-6489 (electronic)
Palgrave Studies in Classical Liberalism
ISBN 978-3-032-02893-8 ISBN 978-3-032-02894-5 (eBook)
https://doi.org/10.1007/978-3-032-02894-5

This Palgrave Macmillan imprint is published by the registered company Springer Nature Switzerland AG
The registered company address is: Gewerbestrasse 11, 6330 Cham, Switzerland

In fact, the realm of freedom actually begins only where labour which is determined by necessity and mundane considerations ceases; thus in the very nature of things it lies beyond the sphere of actual material production. Just as the savage must wrestle with Nature to satisfy his wants, to maintain and reproduce life, so must civilised man, and he must do so in all social formations and under all possible modes of production. With his development this realm of physical necessity expands as a result of his wants; but, at the same time, the forces of production which satisfy these wants also increase. Freedom in this field can only consist in socialised man, the associated producers, rationally regulating their interchange with Nature, bringing it under their common control, instead of being ruled by it as by the blind forces of Nature; and achieving this with the least expenditure of energy and under conditions most favourable to, and worthy of, their human nature. But it nonetheless still remains a realm of necessity. Beyond it begins that development of human powers which is an end in itself, the true realm of freedom, which, however, can blossom forth only with this realm of necessity as its basis.

Karl Marx, *Capital: Volume Three*

Preface

The world has changed a lot since G.A. Cohen passed away in 2009. Back then, the prospects of a world without capitalism did indeed seem more remote than the end of the world itself. Neoliberalism was facing a massive test with the Great Recession but seemed set to survive through the implementation of harsh austerity measures and bailouts. The problems facing the system were fundamental but the solutions proposed by centrist politicians like Barak Obama, Angela Merkel, Gordon Brown, and Stephen Harper were anything but radical. Marxism hung on as the nominal official ideology of authoritarian states like China, Vietnam, and Cuba. But outside of these holdouts, which were themselves all moving toward some degree of market reform, few people thought Marx's ideas had much of a future.

The last sixteen years have seen a global ideological sea change. Large segments of the population of western nations are distrustful of liberal and neoliberal political elites. By and large, though, this has by and large not benefitted the left, which might seem like the natural vehicle for such anger. There have been flashes of possibility like Bernie Sanders's two campaigns for the American presidency and Jeremy Corbyn's short-live ascendancy as leader of the British Labour Party, but the liberal center has largely been depressingly successful in containing these insurgencies. Meanwhile, they've been far less successful in battling the Right. Center-left parties from the Canadian liberals to the German SPD and the American Democratic party have struggled mightily and lost ground impotently. As we write this in 2025 Donald Trump has returned to power in the United States. Canada, Cohen's home country, was saved at the last minute from electing its most conservative government in decades, not by the successes of a renewed socialist left, but by a wave of anti-Trump and anti-U.S. but fundamentally conservative Canadian nationalism. Crypto bros and Austrian influenced economists wield power in much of South America. In Europe, right wing populists attack many elements of neoliberal globalization and integration, even as they slash taxes for the wealthy *a la* Liz Truss or shift billions to their oligarchic backers like Victor Orban.

This is grim situation. It is, however, a very *different* kind of grim situation than the one that prevailed during the final period of Cohen's career.

Cohen was raised in a working-class Jewish community in Montreal where many members of his family were members or fellow travelers of Canada's Communist Party (back then temporarily reorganized as the Labour-Progressive Party to get around a ban on the original Communist Party of Canada under the Defense of Canada Regulations of 1939). Later in life, he would sometimes describe this upbringing by saying that he was raised as a "Stalinist Communist" the "same way some people are raised Roman Catholic or Muslim." Several of his relatives served time in Canadian jails for their "subversive" political activity.

Cohen spend his early years at attending the Morris Winchevsky School, where the day of instruction was divided between standard primary-school subjects taught in English by gentile non-communist teachers in the mornings and political education taught in Yiddish in the afternoon. His report cards were folded in half, with English subject on the left and Yiddish on the right, since Yiddish (like Hebrew) is written from right to left. Looking back on one such report card decades later, he was proud to note that he received a straight Aleph in *Geschichte fun Klassen Kamf* (History of Class Struggle), a subject that would later become central to some of his own most important academic work. He had to transfer to a non-communist school when Morris Winchevsky was shut down by the Monstreal police Red Squad, but the core of the worldview he imbibed there stayed within him to the end of his life.

That doesn't mean he didn't change his mind. He did, in large and small ways, at several points over the course of his career. The most politically important of these changes happened long before he started adding to the academic literature on Marxism. As a young man, like so many other left-wing intellectuals of his generation, he became disillusioned with Soviet authoritarianism. The disillusionment didn't come all at once, but a little bit at a time from Khruschev's speech revealing Stalin's crimes to the Soviet invasion of Czechoslovakia to crush an experiment in "socialism with a human face" in 1968. He had, by then, fundamentally lost his belief that anything going in the USSR and the supposed "people's democracies" in Eastern Europe represented a desirable model, but on the day Soviet tanks rolled into Prague, Cohen would recall telling his then-wife, "for the first time, I am *anti*-Soviet."

Unlike many intellectuals formerly aligned to the pro-Soviet mainstream of the Communist movement, though, it never seemed to occur to Cohen to react to all this by rejecting socialism itself as a "God that failed." Even after the fall of the Soviet Union two decades and change later, he chided those former socialists who prematurely concluded that the failure of "the first attempt to run a modern economy" outside of the brutal logic of capitalist markets should lead us to the conclusion that capitalism (even a form of capitalism softened by social welfare programs and a regulatory state) is the best humanity can do. We desperately needed, he thought—as the two of us, and almost all of the contributors to this volume still think—to go back to the drawing board and find a better, more humane, more democratic, and more economically viable way of organizing a post-capitalist society. Nor did the twisting of Karl Marx's ideas in the hands of Soviet apparatchiks lead Cohen to abandon Marxism as a theoretical framework for understanding the nature of capitalist exploitation, the historical progression that led to humanity here, or the future progression that could lead to something better. One of his earliest and most important academic mentors was Isaiah Berlin, with whom he fiercely disagreed on all of these subjects, but even in the forge of constant arguments with his friend and mentor, Cohen retained his conviction in the basic soundness of Marx's insights.

He did, however, significantly change the *way* he approached Marx's theory, and this second shift in his thinking, roughly coinciding with the first, was ultimately the more consequential of the two. There were, after all, no shortage of late twentieth-century western (and indeed eastern) intellectuals who rejected the Soviet model without rejecting Marxism or socialism. Cohen's importance lies in the trail he blazed in developing a specifically *analytical* version of Marxism, one where Marxism isn't seen as distinctive for any methodological reason. Rather, Marxist conclusions about such subjects as the Geschichte fun Klassen Kamf must, according to analytical Marxist, be advanced and defended by rigorous arguments made using the standard intellectual tools developed by non-Marxist social scientists and "analytic" philosophers.

In the introduction to the 2000 edition of his masterpiece *Karl Marx's Theory of History: A Defence*, Cohen recalls an early incident that set him on this road. He'd written a paper in the late 1960s on Marx's early work. Commenting on a passage about the power of money in Marx's *Economic and Philosophic Manuscripts of 1844*, Cohen claimed that Marx's view would be that "a rich capitalist's mistress does not love him because of his money" because what she loves is the money itself. He was taken to task by the American philosopher Isaac Levi, who wanted to know "exactly what that meant and/or how one was supposed to go about telling whether or not it was true" and "what, precisely, was the difference between loving someone just because of their money and loving that money itself?"

At the time, Cohen considered the interrogation to be "hostile and unhelpful." On his way out of the room, though, Levi told Cohen something that stuck with him—that he didn't mind thinking about things in a different way as long as he understood which "ground rules" were being assumed:

> That remark hit me hard and sunk in deep. In the aftermath of Levi's admonition, I stopped writing (at least partly) in the fashion of a poet who puts down what sounds good to him and who needn't defend his lines (either they resonate with the reader or they don't). Instead, I tried to

> ask myself, when writing: precisely what does this sentence contribute to the developing exposition or argument, and is it true? You become analytical when you practice that sort of (frequently painful) self-criticism. ([])

Those lessons are all over both Cohen's work on historical materialism and his normative work. The latter got going at about the same time as the former, with his brick-by-brick demolition of the libertarian philosophy of Robert Nozick. A second front later opened up with Cohen's complicated and rich socialist dialogues with the emerging school of liberal egalitarianism (particularly embodied in the work of John Rawls). As his normative work continued, he staked out increasingly radical egalitarian positions, which some critics have thought were in tension with some of his historical materialist commitments. Readers will find very different perspectives on that question in the contributions from the two of us. They've also find a defense of Cohen's version of historical materialism from his student Steve Paxton, as well as explorations of his normative philosophy by heavy hitters like Christine Sypnowich as well as a variety of established and up-and-coming thinkers. That includes a robust dissent by libertarian philosophy professor Chris Freiman, which is absolutely what Cohen himself would have wanted. Unlike those Marxists who too casually dismissed critiques of their fundamental assumptions as so much enemy propaganda, one of Cohen's characteristic virtues was that he took rigorous arguments from all quarters, Rawlsian-liberal or Nozickian-libertarian, deadly seriously. He was never satisfied with condemning or mocking these interlocutors. He needed to carefully refute them.

But as much as libertarian and bourgeois-liberal voices will always be part of serious discussion of Cohen's work, the primary reason for producing a book about Cohen in this historical moment is as an intellectual contribution to the resurgent socialist Left. When Cohen first started his two-fold project of defending historical materialism and propounding his egalitarian normative views in the late 1970s, what we now think of as the neoliberal turn had certainly kicked off, but it was far from clear how deep the damage would go. The victories of the workers' movement in previous generations, which had created modern welfare states and powerful industrial unions, could still seem to many (as they manifestly sometimes seemed to Cohen) to be permanent fixtures from which future progress could be launched. And as deeply flawed as the Soviet model of socialism may have, the existence of the Cold War rivalry between economic systems kept the basic question of how to organize the economic fundamentals of society on the historical agenda. By the last two decades of his life and career, things already looked very different. Cohen, like his fellow socialist stalwarts, was fighting ideological rearguard battles, arguing against the British Labour Party's removal of Clause IV (which committed the party to collective ownership of the means of production) from the party's constitution, and urging wavering socialist thinkers not to overreact to the Soviet failure by giving up on finding a better way to organize a noncapitalist economy.

As we've said, though, the world has changed again since his death, and what we face now a very different kind of grim situation. The defining ideological struggle between proverbially liberal capitalism and communism clearly didn't end with a definitive victory for a liberal capitalism that could triumphantly inaugurate the end of history. Instead, the victory was remarkably pyrrhic. Twenty-first-century capitalism has seen widening inequality and frequently stagnant or declining real incomes, the rule of plutocratic elites, and the enormous sense of nihilistic instability. All this has produced enormous discontent, which the far right has rode successfully to power and influence. Unless a better alternative, grounded in reason and upholding the principles of liberty, equality, and solidarity offers hope things are very likely to get worse. The unfulfilled promise of democratic socialism, killed by authoritarian betrayal and capitalist militancy alike, needs to become a promise kept. And the good news is that, while it's very far from the case that the good guys are winning, the toxic pseudo-populism of the militant Right hasn't been in the *only* response to worsening conditions. The situation is complex, and part of that complexity is that even in capitalism's North American heartland, we're in the middle of by far the biggest resurgence of popular and scholarly interest in socialism and Marxism in several decades. In his fascinating new book *Marx in America*, scholar Andrew Hartman traces the way that different generations of American thinkers have engaged with Marx's work, from the Gilded Age, when Marx was turned to for the light his work could shed on inequality, to the Great Depression, when he was received a prophet of capitalism's destructive contradictions, to the mid-century American liberalism that used Marx as a foil to…the 2020s, when Marxism is being rediscovered by new generations of radicals, raised in a world of endless wars in the Middle East (as this goes to print, yet another one may be starting in Iran), forced to accept lower living standards than their parents, and far more open than those parents to basic critiques of the system under which they live. Hartman thinks we're living through the "fourth Marx boom."

This is where the thinking of G.A. Cohen is of such vital importance. If we really are undergoing a "boom" in interest in Marx, then everyone will be better off if their Marxism gets a healthy injection of analytical rigor. Cohen isn't the only thinker who can be helpful in that regard. (Anyone inspired by this book to read Cohen might want to follow that up by looking into the analytical class analysis of Cohen's friend and colleague Erik Olin Wright, for example, or the more recent contributions of Wright's protégé Vivek Chibber.) But Cohen is an indispensable starting point.

Both of us are great admirers of Cohen's combination of analytical rigor, theoretical sweep, and lucidity. But more important of course is the substance of his arguments and ideas; long respected in the academy yet little known to the general public. Cohen was a veritable engine of intellectual imagination. There were few philosophical or political issues where he didn't bring his powerful intelligence to bear, and the results were always interesting and stimulating. Cohen was one of the great figures of late twentieth and early twentieth-century Marxism. His profoundly egalitarian instincts might have led him to dislike such a compliment. Yet, there's really no other way of describing the thought that emerged from such a combination of intellectual gravity, moral passion, and deep humanity.

Let us be clear though: we come here to talk about Cohen, not praise him the whole way down. The goal of this volume is to engage his thinking fruitfully from a number of different theoretical and political traditions to mine the rich veins of insight where they are there. Where they are not, many of the contributing authors are clear in saying so. To do otherwise would violate the whole animating spirit of analytical

Marxism. To quote, out of context, one of the analytic philosophers Cohen generally had the least time for, W.V.O. Quine, *everything* needs "open to revision." Everything is on the table, including Cohen's own ideas. And that's exactly how he would have wanted it.

Los Angeles, USA Ben Burgis
Atlanta, USA Matthew McManus

Acknowledgements

Nothing would be less egalitarian than taking undue credit for this volume, which owes an enormous amount to an enormous number. In the course of preparing it, we racked up more debts than it would ever be possible to acknowledge. So we'll just briefly single out some of the most important here.

Thanks a lot to the University of Michigan and Rutgers for keeping us gainfully employed during the writing. Solidarity with the crew of *Give Them An Argument* and *Academic Edgelords* for all their hard work. Much gratitude to Palgrave MacMillan for supporting the volume and giving us the time and resources to whip it into shape. Thanks to all our friends, family, and loved one without whom we'd never have written a thing. And finally: rest in power to all those who've struggled long and hard for egalitarian justice. This book is dedicated to them, starting of course with G.A. Cohen.

Contents

List of Contributors

Ben Burgis Rutgers University, Los Angeles, USA

Christopher Freiman John Chambers College of Business and Economics, West Virginia University, Morgantown, USA

Lesley A. Jacobs Ontario Tech University, Oshawa, ON, Canada

Michael Kates Saint Joseph's University, Philadelphia, USA

Michael Law-Smith Department of Philosophy and Faculty of Law, University of Toronto, Toronto, Canada

Matt McManus Spelman College, Atlanta, USA

Steve Paxton Aylesbury, UK

Igor Shoikhedbrod St. Francis Xavier University, Antigonish, Canada

Christine Sypnowich Department of Philosophy, Queen's University, Kingston, Canada

Part I

Marxism, History and Materialism

1

G.A. Cohen's Theory of History: A Defence

Steve Paxton

Such has been the impact of Cohen's work that no-one writing in the field in the last half-century has been able to ignore his contribution—even his critics acknowledge that "he cuts through a century of evasion and double-think, and forces us to think seriously, clearly and honestly about what are the central and distinctive claims of historical materialism" (Sayer, 1987, p. 5). Cohen's clarity and rigour are widely acknowledged but—as we'll see—some who praise his clear and unforgiving methodological approach also like to retain the option of not having to live with the conclusions such an approach delivers. In a similar vein, we'll cover more than one example of critics whose characterizations of Cohen's work remove all of his subtlety and nuance and who then complain that his work is too stark and simplistic, too black and white—lacking in subtlety and nuance.

S. Paxton (✉)
Aylesbury, UK
e-mail: steve@stevepaxton.co.uk

B. Burgis and M. McManus (eds.), *Analytical Marxism and Democratic Socialism in the 21st Century*, Palgrave Studies in Classical Liberalism,
https://doi.org/10.1007/978-3-032-02894-5_1

In his *Karl Marx's Theory of History—a Defence (KMTH)*, Cohen set out to "construct a tenable theory of history which is in broad accord with what Marx said on the subject" (Cohen, 2000, p. *ix*). Given the volume and range of Marx's writing, it would be strikingly optimistic to imagine such a project could be completed without having to resolve ambiguities and contradictions, and without having to dismiss propositions which are untenable in the face of the historical record. Cohen's application of the standards of analytical philosophy to this material necessarily involved a process of tidying-up, refining and updating Marx's work. This is sufficient for some to reject his approach on the grounds that he has deviated from *the Word*.[1] Others dismiss his work because he explicitly rejects the idea that there is a specifically dialectical method: "there is no such thing as a dialectical form of reasoning that can challenge analytical reasoning. Belief in dialectic as a *rival* to analysis thrives only in an atmosphere of unclear thought" (Cohen, 2000, p. *xviii*). Sean Sayers, for example, argues that "Cohen's use of the analytic method and his rejection of dialectics leads him to give a systematically distorted account of Marx's theory of history" (Sayers, 1984).[2]

While it's important to acknowledge these responses to Cohen's work, both flavours of criticism described so far object to the extent to which Cohen is supposed to have deviated from or misrepresented the work of Marx, rather than the extent to which the theory of history he develops is tenable or otherwise. It is this latter, more interesting question that will be the focus of this chapter. This approach reflects Cohen's own priorities, in which advancing our understanding of the world was always far more important than advancing our understanding of Marx. In the revised edition of *KMTH*, a quarter century after the original, Cohen stated that he now had doubts about his earlier position: "I have come to wonder whether the theory the book defends is true (though not whether, as I claimed, it was affirmed by Karl Marx). I do not now believe that historical materialism is false, but I am not sure how to tell whether or not it is true" (Cohen, 2000, p. 341). It's to Cohen's credit that he was

---

[1] See for example Rogers (1981a; 1981b) and PROYECT.

[2] Sayers' argument here relies on disingenuously selective quotations from *KMTH*.

able to doubt, and confront, long held convictions and to explore challenges to those convictions with the aim of understanding "what kind and degree of revision of [historical materialism], if any, they justify" (Cohen, 2000, p. 341).

The challenges to Cohen's understanding of historical materialism which I'll address in this paper centre around whether the theory is logically consistent, whether its assertions about human nature are tenable and whether its claims are compatible with the historical record. The first target of these critics is Cohen's 'development thesis', which states that *the productive forces tend to develop through history*, and that they do so because humans are sufficiently intelligent to be able to improve their material situation, and sufficiently rational to be disposed to do so, given their historical situation of scarcity (Cohen, 2000, p. 345).

Cohen anticipates a basic objection to the development thesis, namely the complaint that the thesis requires that human nature is constant throughout history—that the thesis denies that human nature itself can be modified by the historical circumstances in which humans find themselves. Andrew Levine and Erik Olin Wright are among those who make this objection, arguing in favour of "class-specific notions of scarcity and rationality" (Levine & Wright, 1980). Cohen certainly doesn't deny that many aspects of human nature may be shaped by material circumstances, but he also insists that there are certain trans-historical attributes which provide sufficient motivation for the requirements of the development thesis. For Cohen, "the proposition that human nature changes in history is importantly true in some important sense of 'human nature', but it is also true that there are *permanent attributes* of human nature in some equally important sense" (Cohen, 2000, p. 151).[3] What, then, are these permanent attributes, and are they sufficient to provide the impetus to technological progress which the development thesis requires? When Cohen says that people "in a certain respect are somewhat rational" (Cohen, 2000, p. 152), what exactly does this entail?

Firstly, it's not hard to imagine the aspects of human nature that are likely to manifest themselves in the face of scarcity, whatever other conditions might obtain. Even from our position of relative luxury in the

[3] My emphasis.

twenty-first century we ought to be able to conceive that, in the conditions of scarcity which have afflicted and continue to afflict most human lives, being hungry is rarely preferable to not being hungry, and being too cold is never preferable to being warm enough. Security is preferable to peril. Not wanting to be eaten by a crocodile, to die of bubonic plague or to be enslaved by a neighbouring society seem to me to be rational motivations to welcome the march of technology, an acceptance of which doesn't require us to disregard the complexity of the human condition.

Secondly, we should remember that the development thesis doesn't require that these rational impulses prevail in every person, in every circumstance of human history. The thesis requires only that when presented with an opportunity to make their lives easier people will not always reject it. There is no requirement that people will always accept such an opportunity, or even that they will often, or regularly do so. The minimum required acceptance rate, across human history, is such that net progress is achieved, despite the susceptibility of development to experience periods of stagnation or regression. Clearly net development *has happened*—the question is whether it has happened as a result of the combination of intelligence and rationality (in the face of scarcity) which the development thesis proposes. We might not be equipped to answer this question confidently at this stage, but as Cohen observes "whatever defects the argument for [the development thesis] has, its reliance on claims about what people are like in all times and places is not one of them" (Cohen, 2000, p. 152).

A related objection is that scarcity should not be considered a historically invariant condition. According to Marcus Roberts, for example, "the concept of scarcity is intelligible only relative to the (historically variable) needs and wants of human beings" (Roberts, 1996, pp. 82–83). Similarly, S.H. Rigby argues that both scarcity and human needs are relative concepts—as the necessities of life are catered for, new needs arise and the condition of scarcity is renewed (Rigby, 1987, p. 118). Of course, these observations are correct, but they don't inflict the damage on the development thesis which their proponents imagine. In addition to compelling wants such as status and authority (which may indeed vary considerably according to circumstance), the need for individual and group security stimulates significant desire to continually increase the efficiency of the production of use-values. When human rationality is seen as 'situated' in a context of competition within and between societies, then the need for security is manifested in the need for development. Societies which do not develop technologically will be at a significant disadvantage to those which do. Far from showing that the development thesis is false, Rigby's correct assertion supports it by providing a trans-historical rational basis for preferring development to its absence.

At first glance, it would appear that the rampant over-consumption of modern Western society—seemingly the polar opposite of scarcity—would provide fertile ground for arguments against the development thesis. However, most of Cohen's critics (from within the Historical Materialist camp, at least) recruit their counter-examples from pre-capitalist history. Levine and Wright, for example, contend that the relevant form of scarcity under feudal relations of production is the need of feudal barons to compete militarily with each other and therefore to continually grind increasing amounts of surplus out of the workforce. They argue that this means the incentive to development derives not from a trans-historical aspect of rationality, but from the specific class relations of pre-capitalist Europe. Aside from the spurious attempt to elevate one aspect of scarcity to the status of the sole "imperative to improve agrarian means of production" (Levine & Wright, 1980), this position mistakes the fact that the impact of scarcity will play out differently under various production relations for the idea that the impulse to overcome scarcity only exists *because of* the prevailing production relations. Levine and Wright argue that there was no rational basis for the peasants to want technological development, particularly as the price was feudal exploitation, suggesting that "most peasants would probably have preferred completely stagnant development of the productive forces without exploitation, to slowly developing productive forces with exploitation." They may well be right, but it's an absurd leap from that assertion to the idea that, had they managed to rid themselves of their oppressors, development would have come to an abrupt halt because no one would have wanted more food stored for next winter than last, or three meals a day instead of two. The prevailing production relations are the conduit of the rational desire for progress, not its source.

Levine and Wright do at least accept that there was an impulse to development in pre-capitalist societies. Robert Brenner, on the other hand, argues that the necessity to innovate in ways that create more output for less work is a unique feature of capitalism and berates everyone since (and including) Adam Smith for detecting any hint of progress under pre-capitalist structures. Brenner's argument is that pre-capitalist production relations ensured that both peasants and lords "found it rational to adopt patterns of economic action which, in the long run, prevented increases in aggregate *per capita* output" (Brenner, 1986, p. 28). The obvious limitations of Brenner's position are the actual existence of the per capita increases in output whose absence he's is trying to explain[4] and the adoption of economic actions which, in the long run, enabled those increases.[5]

There is no hint in the development thesis itself, or in the broader claims which Cohen requires the development thesis to support, that the rate of pre-capitalist development could come close to that achieved under capitalism. It is in the nature of capitalism to "constantly revolutionise the instruments of production" (Marx & Engels, 1967, p. 83). But the idea that there was no development before capitalism—as well as being contradicted by the empirical evidence—surely requires a more surprising view of human nature and human history than the development thesis itself.

[4] Labour productivity in the pre-capitalist era is notoriously difficult to quantify and must generally be inferred from indirect statistics, but (given insignificant import and export figures for the period) an increase in the non-agricultural population of England from 23% in 1520 to 39% in 1670 and 54% by 1750 would be difficult to explain without significant improvements in labour productivity (Wrigley, 1985, pp. 700–701). Robert C. Allen estimates that "labour productivity grew by about 40% between 1500 and 1700 and another 40% in the first half of the nineteenth century" (Allen, 2000, pp. 1–25, 2005). Evidence of improvements in land quality—a major influence in labour productivity increases—was, according to Overton, "commonplace from the mid-sixteenth century" (Overton, 1996, p. 89).

[5] Numerous advances increased labour productivity under pre-capitalist production relations. Horses, for example, had been replacing oxen as the main form of traction on farms since at least the Middle Ages, leading to an increase of labour productivity of up to a third. The number of horses exceeded the number of oxen in many eastern counties by the fifteenth century and in most areas by the middle of the eighteenth (Overton, 1996, pp. 126–7).

Brenner is fixated on the idea that the impulse to improve technology, or to adopt advances developed by others, can only possibly arise out of the necessity to compete in a capitalist marketplace: "Only under capitalism, as we have argued ad infinitum will the individual economic actors necessarily have the motivation (survival) to adopt new techniques; only under capitalism will there obtain a process of natural selection to weed out those who do not" (Brenner, 1986, p. 45). But however tirelessly Brenner repeats the same argument, he cannot magic away the actual, historical development which he claims could not have happened because no one wanted it or was in a position to enable it. If we tone down Brenner's position somewhat—to suggest perhaps that there was far less incentive to innovate (and to adopt innovations) under pre-capitalist production relations than there is under capitalism, then we arrive at a position supported by the historical record, but also one which is now entirely compatible with the development thesis (and with Cohen's broader approach). Even Brenner's insistence that pre-capitalist production relations not only failed to nurture development but actively worked against it can be easily accommodated by the development thesis, provided that, despite these difficulties, *some* net development occurred (which, as we've noted, was in fact the case).

Cohen anticipates an additional concern—that *even if* we accept that certain actions would be rational for individuals, that doesn't necessarily guarantee that those actions can be taken in the social context in which they are situated: "For it is not evident that societies are disposed to bring about what rationality would lead men to choose. There is some shadow between what reason suggests and what society does. Further considerations are required to show that the shadow is not unduly long" (Cohen, 2000, p. 153). For many of Cohen's critics, it is at this point that discussion of the validity of the development thesis itself often begins to stray into the territory of Cohen's 'primacy thesis'. Cohen is careful to separate out the arguments for (and objections to) each thesis because—as we'll see—the validity of the development thesis is part of the argument for the primacy thesis, and so an independent case must be made for the development thesis. The question—for now—is strictly related to whether advances in technology or technique which would be rational for certain individuals to adopt would actually be adopted. There could be any number of reasons why such advances may—in fact—not be adopted in certain circumstances. Perhaps they would be neglected because a society has a deep seated religious aversion to a particular element of a new technique. Perhaps a labour saving advance which labourers would rationally welcome would not be adopted because the non-labouring landowner has no productive use for more labour and therefore no interest in a labour saving contraption. There will be occasions when a development is clearly at odds with the interests of a ruling class (or any powerful group) and they are able to successfully prevent its adoption, or when a cultural inclination or religious tradition rules out progress of a certain type.[6] There are numerous possible scenarios in which potential developments could be thwarted, which means that the development thesis can only rely on all the occasions when that wasn't the case, which is, in fact, all the ones where development actually occurred—a not inconsiderable catalogue. We should bear in mind that the requirements of the development thesis in terms of what individuals may be *capable of adopting* are no more or less stringent than the requirements discussed earlier, relating to what they might *rationally prefer*. The development thesis requires only that when presented with an opportunity to make their lives easier people will not always be prevented from adopting it—or, more precisely, that the minimum required adoption rate, across human history, is such that net progress is achieved, despite the susceptibility of development to sometimes stagnate or regress.

This susceptibility to periods of (at least) stagnation does not in any way embarrass Cohen's approach (nor that of Marx). It is central to Cohen's interpretation of historical materialism that as the productive forces develop the production relations which once enabled or promoted that development will come to stifle further growth. It is the resolution of this conflict between the continued development of the forces and the existence of production relations which hinder such development that

[6] It will often be the case, though, that the ruling class don't identify a particular development as something that threatens their position. When farmers learnt that adding lime and marl to the soil would increase yields, the likely response of feudal barons would not have been to fear the potential for such a development to enable the rise of a new economic structure under which they would lose wealth, power and status, but to welcome a greater store of wheat for the coming winter.

constitutes the era of social revolution and ushers in a new economic structure. The way in which this process plays out is the crux of Cohen's primacy thesis and it's that to which we now turn. The primacy thesis states that that *the nature of a set of production relations is explained by the level of development of the productive forces embraced by it* (to a far greater extent than vice versa) (Cohen, 2000, p. 134).

Most serious criticisms of the primacy thesis revolve around the claim of explanatory primacy—either in terms of a competing candidate as 'prime mover' or by questioning the concept of a prime mover altogether—and therefore rejecting the validity of any primacy claim in historical explanation. Before considering such objections, though, it's worth looking at some criticisms upstream of the primacy thesis itself—objections to some of the conceptual components of the primacy thesis.

1.1 Intent

Are transformations from one economic structure to another the *intended* result of individual or group actions, or can they sometimes be *unintended* outcomes of actions designed to achieve quite different goals?

Vivek Chibber insists that "it is indisputable that Cohen does offer an intentional version of his argument, once he is forced to unpack it" (Chibber, 2011, p. 72 (fn 15)). In fact, Cohen offers an intentional version *as one possible elaboration among various possibilities.* In *KMTH* Cohen argues that the nature of the primacy of the productive forces is such that "the character of the forces functionally explains the character of the relations" (Cohen, 2000, p. 160) and provides a non-exhaustive classification of four possible elaborations of this form of explanation, only one of which could be described as 'intentional'. (The others he refers to as Darwinian, Lamarckian and self-deception) (Cohen, 2000, p. 288).[7] Later, in *History, Labour and Freedom*, Cohen (in addressing a criticism made by Levine and Wright) states that "being

[7] It's worth noting at this point that Cohen views functional explanation as "compatible with rejection of functionalism." See pp. 283–285.

rational, people retain and reject relations of production according as the latter do and do not allow productive improvement to continue" (Cohen, 1988, p. 91). Chibber interprets this as Cohen's acknowledgement that his theory *requires* intentional selection of production relations on behalf of individual economic actors. In fact, Chibber has mistaken Cohen's clarification of what it is that *people-who-choose* are choosing, for an acknowledgement by Cohen that choosing is what people must always do (Cohen's position is that *in some scenarios*, deliberate choices will play a role in advancing progressive change, and in such scenarios, their choices may apply more to relations of production than to the productive forces. Chibber's caricature implies that Cohen's position is that deliberate choices will always determine the character of progressive change). Chibber's initial error is to assume that this means there is no room for non-intentional outcomes in Cohen's approach. His further error, I think, is to imagine that by "choosing" Cohen literally means 'making a conscious decision to follow a particular path with the aim of achieving a particular outcome'. It is clear, though, from a broader reading of Cohen's work (in both *KMTH* and *History, Labour and Freedom*) that Cohen here means choosing as *selecting*—not necessarily in the sense of a conscious intentional decision, but via mechanisms similar to the Darwinian process of natural *selection* through chance variation. Relations of production may be 'chosen'—or *selected*—as society-wide outcomes of many individual decisions. There is nothing in Cohen's approach that excludes the idea that progress might arise through the aggregation of hundreds, thousands, millions of decisions, each aimed at improving the decision maker's immediate situation, but together delivering profound social change which none of the decision makers anticipated or necessarily wanted. Chibber's reading of Cohen is one-dimensional, attributing to him a wholly unrealistic model of historical change: "it is hardly warranted to presume that a menu of options is ever presented to social agents in the fashion required by Cohen's theory, allowing them, not only to simply choose from among its items, but also to reject one choice in favour of another. In other words, agents have to be aware, not only of the possibility of alternative production-relations, but also of their availability, and there is no reason to assume that this will be the case." Of course, Cohen's theory *requires* no such thing, though it does *accommodate* that possibility. (We might also note that agents rejecting one set of production relations in favour of another was in fact an important part of the consolidation of capitalism in England—was exactly what happened through the process of parliamentary enclosure from the late-seventeenth century to the mid-nineteenth century. Enclosing landlords consciously deprived tenants of any claims to occupancy, taking full ownership of land over which various groups had previously claimed an assortment of intertwined rights, and in doing so instituted a new set of production relations).[8]

1.2 Optimality

When one economic structure replaces another, must the succeeding structure be the *optimal* structure for further development of the productive forces, or simply one that is more suitable than the structure it succeeds?

Wright, Levine, and Sober claim that Cohen insists vehemently on optimality "even in the face of obvious counterexamples" though they don't avail us of the counterexamples they have in mind (Wright et al, 1992, p. 31). They refer briefly to pre-capitalist production relations, which "for the most part, can hardly be said to have encouraged the development of the productive forces" and note Cohen's observation that this doesn't rule out their optimality, but Wright, Levine and Sober don't see the need to furnish us with a counter argument against this. Chibber is equally convinced that "Cohen's version of canonical historical materialism thus appears to flounder, unable to bear the weight of the optimality-thesis" (Chibber, 2011, p. 71) despite Cohen's explicit rejection of optimality in this sense. Cohen even provides a relatively lengthy thought experiment about a society in which two forms of capitalist relations are available and although one form prevails "a different

[8] Even here, though, it would be fanciful to imagine that the enclosing landlords were doing so because they wanted to build a capitalist economic structure. The immediate benefits—to the landlords—of greater wealth and income with fewer obligations would have been a much more realistic incentive than the wholesale transformation of society.

structure could have obtained at the same level of productive development" (Cohen, 2000, p. 161). Given that the nature of optimality is that both structures could not have been optimal (and that they are not is explicitly stated in the scenario for good measure) it is clear that Cohen's position does not *require* optimality. Again, as with the question of intent, Cohen can *accommodate* optimality, but does not *require* it. There is nothing in Cohen's approach that requires any more than the conviction that an emerging economic structure will only survive if it's more suitable to develop the productive forces than the structure it supersedes. The level of development of the productive forces determines the range of economic structures which meet this condition, but the precise relations which develop will be influenced by the nature of the pre-existing relations and the roll of the historical dice.

Chibber suggests that this represents a retreat for Cohen: "The functional requirements of the productive forces now only explain the range of potential production-relations that can succeed…the one that actually succeeds… from within that range is to be explained by class-struggle. The explanatory work of the class-struggle…has dramatically expanded" (Chibber, 2011, p. 68). While the position outlined here is in conflict with the model which Chibber, Wright, Levine, and Sober all attribute to Cohen, it's entirely compatible with Cohen's actual position: "[Relations of production] help to determine the particular path development takes, and this restricts the independent explanatory power of the forces" (Cohen, 2000, p. 165). For Cohen, the primacy of the forces is qualified by the influence exerted by the economic structure over the rate and the specific details of development of the forces. These influences are greatly increased during the entire period of transition and particularly during the era of social revolution. The nature of the forces during this era is, to a significant extent, explained by the transitional character of the economic structure—development intermittently stalls and falters amid local (sectional) and sporadic bursts of growth as the relations adjust to meet the requirements of the existing and potential forces of production.

As we now move on to consider the primacy thesis proper, the debate about the role of class struggle in historical development takes centre stage. It's important to be careful here that we don't let wishful thinking cloud our judgment. We may all be inspired by tales of Wat Tyler and George Loveless, of resistance at Peterloo and Orgreave, but historical explanation isn't a matter of taste or preference. Brenner, Chibber, Wright, Levine, and Sober all seem keen to find a way to give class struggle more importance than they imagine it is accorded by Cohen. Historian (and veteran of the 'Transition Debate') Rodney Hilton admits as much: "If I seem to over-weight class-struggle as the 'motor' of history, it is not only because, in feudalism, it was of great significance for the determination of ruling-class incomes, but *because I want to emphasize the positive and creative role of the exploited*" (Hilton, 1984.).[9] Not only is it poor practice to go looking for empirical evidence to support your preconceptions, but it's also unnecessary—certainly for anyone whose concern is to evaluate Cohen's approach to historical change. Cohen clearly recognises that class struggle has an important place in history: "It is a banal but important truth that human beings on the whole prefer freedom to its opposite. That is why history records so much class struggle against the bondage which has been the usual condition of the mass of mankind" (Cohen, 2000, p. 204). The role of class struggle in Cohen's schema is limited only in that its potential to institute a successful transformation to a new economic structure relies on opportune timing with regard to the then existing level of development of the productive forces. We should also recognise, however, that there is nothing in Cohen's work that restricts the concept of class struggle to the expectations of the popular imagination. Transformation isn't always brought about by manning the barricades or storming the Winter Palace. The transition from feudalism to capitalism was largely accomplished by a section of feudal landowners changing their operations onto a capitalist footing. Yes, there was agitation from below, and the sacrifices on both sides in the conflicts in which the political world caught up with the economic transformation were disproportionately made by the exploited classes, but the actual, substantive change in production relations consisted largely in the process of enclosure—particularly parliamentary enclosure. The beneficiaries of this process were rarely the 'kulak' farmers who had risen from the rank of husbandman in the fifteenth and sixteenth centuries—the established landowning gentry

[9] My emphasis.

was the group that really gained from enclosure and related processes (Mingay, 1976, p. 59). This process fits the description outlined by Cohen under the term 'adaptive metamorphosis' (Cohen, 2000, p. 293).

The central criticism of the primacy thesis, from within the Historical Materialist camp, is that Cohen has the explanatory primacy back-to-front—that social transformation is driven by particular features of the class structure of societies. From this perspective, the speed and character of the development of the productive forces are determined by the nature of the production relations—that is, by the class structure, and in particular, the process of class struggle. As we've noted above, Cohen's approach allows for—in fact, insists upon—the influence of production relations on the rate and character of the development of the productive forces. It's a central tenet of historical materialism that the production relations act on the development of the productive forces—it's also explicitly stated, albeit in brackets, in Cohen's statement of the primacy thesis.[10]

Cohen is clear, though, that *explanatory primacy* resides in the development of the productive forces—the expansion of productive capacity. Brenner's challenge to this position is more convincing than his objections to the development thesis, though still, ultimately, unsuccessful. Brenner argues that while the level of development of the productive forces in early modern England was comparable to that of both France and Poland, only England saw the emergence of capitalist production relations and the subsequent (and consequent) rapid acceleration of productive capacity. If the level of development of the productive forces was more or less similar in each case, but the outcome was different then—according to Brenner—the cause of that outcome could not have been that level of development. Brenner argues that the class structures of England, France and Poland each had particular features which explain why capitalism emerged in England, while in France the nascent bourgeoisie was too weak to overcome the *Ancien Regime* and Poland fully regressed to a 'second serfdom'. Jon Roemer responds to Brenner's criticism with the argument that, in time, both France and Poland

[10] The primacy thesis states that that "the nature of a set of production relations is explained by the level of development of the productive forces embraced by it (*to a far greater extent than* vice versa)" (Cohen, 2000, p. 134). (My emphasis—Cohen adds the note that "some such qualifying phrase is always to be understood whenever the primacy thesis is asserted").

experienced the emergence of capitalism and that a difference of a few centuries should not be considered a problem for Cohen's approach. (Roemer, 1988, p. 123)[11] Although I tend to agree with Roemer that—in a world historical context—a few centuries isn't as significant as it might sound, I also think there's a different argument that is far more relevant to the correct understanding of Cohen's position. Firstly, we should note that a successful transition from feudalism to capitalism requires both a certain level of development of the Productive Forces *and* a set of additional circumstances, including various factors relating to the nature of the prevailing production relations—namely the willingness and capacity of economic actors or classes to bring about a transformation of the economic structure (This latter concept is more intricate than it may, at first, appear and we'll address some of its complexities later, but for the purpose of this particular issue, we can simply conceive of—for example—an emerging revolutionary capitalist class willing and able to overthrow an oppressive feudal economic structure).

Thus, we arrive at a pair of conditions relevant to the possibility of a successful transition from one economic structure to another:

1. a level of development of the productive forces conducive to such a transition
2. an exploited (or frustrated) class, willing and able to impose a new set of production relations upon society.

Individually, each of (1) and (2) is a necessary but insufficient condition for the revolutionary transition.[12] Given this seeming equality of status, why should (1) be awarded explanatory primacy over (2)? Brenner frames this question with reference to the historical record—if (1) was present in England, France and Poland, and (2) was only present in England, then the development of capitalism in England, but not in

[11] Ellen Meiksins Wood ridiculed Roemer's suggestion and seemingly found it so obviously flawed as to not require any reason or evidence to be brought to the table in support of her position. See Meikskins Wood (1989).

[12] On Cohen's account, an instance of (1) without (2) would lead to stagnation of the development of the productive forces, whereas (2) without (1) would result in an unsuccessful, because premature, revolution—such as that which occurred in Russia in 1917.

France or Poland must mean—according to Brenner—that explanatory primacy resides with (2). For Brenner and his supporters, the historical record establishes explanatory primacy—the job is done. But in fact, this—on its own—is only half of the required argument. Later I'll make the case that Brenner's terms are not the terms relevant to Cohen's form of explanation, but even on Brenner's own terms, his explanation is incomplete and his conclusion premature. Consider the analogy of a petrol engine in which two conditions (a correct fuel mixture and a well-timed spark) are required to create the explosion which powers the piston. If English, French, and Polish engines all have the right mixture but only the English model has the properly timed spark should we conclude that the timing of the spark *explains* the successful operation of the English engine? Or might we set up an experiment in which all three engines have a well-timed spark but only the English one has the correct mixture? If we did so, and found that the English engine was still the only one that worked, then it would make no sense to claim that this time the mixture *explains* the successful outcome. Logical consistency would require us to conclude that causal primacy between two necessary but insufficient conditions cannot be established by this line of reasoning. Of course, Brenner can't set up such an experiment, and historians are justifiably reluctant to engage in counter-factual thought experiments, but the point is that Brenner's case is far from a conclusive case for the primacy of production relations—the primacy of the particular class composition of the economic structure of early modern England. His case needs at least a plausible argument as to why capitalism would not have developed in England alone had the requisite class composition existed in all three countries while only England enjoyed the required level of development. In the absence of such an argument, Brenner's conclusion isn't justified by the historical evidence he relies upon.

Levine and Wright take a more theoretical approach, and level two main criticisms against the primacy thesis, both intended to give class struggle the central role they believe Cohen to have shifted elsewhere. Firstly, they suggest that "Cohen's account neglects what is crucial for any adequate account of revolutionary social transformations: the question of class capacities. Thus the theory of history Cohen defends is, at best, partial and one-sided; and in consequence, defective both theoretically and politically" (Levine & Wright, 1980). Levine and Wright's objection here is that, for them, Cohen doesn't assign sufficient importance to the concept of class capacity—to the idea that even with sufficient technological development and a class willing to instigate a revolutionary transformation, that such a transformation cannot succeed in the absence of *the capacity of that class* to carry out its programme. There is no sense, however, in which Cohen diminishes the importance of this element of the recipe for social transformation. Class capacity is a necessary component of (2), above, and as such a requirement for revolutionary transformation. If we split (2) into two separate clauses, such that one clause (2a) requires a willing class and the other (2b) a class that is able to (has the capacity to) transform the economic structure, we are now confronted with three (rather than two) necessary, but insufficient conditions for a successful transformation, but substantively nothing has changed. A successful transformation remains impossible without a class willing *and able* to mount and sustain a successful revolution.

Levine and Wright (this time in collaboration with Elliott Sober) mount a second objection to the primacy thesis, from a more abstract, theoretical position, in which they explore different kinds of causal explanation and suggest that as each of (1) and (2) are equally necessary it follows that Cohen's position is merely a claim of "relative causal potency" (Wright et al, 1992, p. 159). But that is not Cohen's claim. Cohen ascribes explanatory primacy to the productive forces, not because their causal dynamic is like that of the production relations but more so—but because their explanatory capacity is more fundamental than that of production relations. It is here that the primacy thesis leans heavily—decisively—on the development thesis. Explanatory primacy resides with the productive forces because their development is driven by an autonomous tendency in a way that the development of production relations is not. The autonomy of the tendency of the productive forces to develop is certainly not absolute, but is "just its independence of social structure, its rootedness in fundamental material facts of human nature and the human situation" (Cohen, 1988, p. 84). The crucial point here is that the tendency of the productive forces to develop is not dependent on any particular set or range of production relations, but on "sub-social facts about humanity" (Cohen, 1988, p. 90). The claim is that the productive forces will have a tendency to develop *whatever the production relations*. Of course, any particular set of production relations will influence the style, pace, and extent of the development of the productive forces, but no set of production relations can subvert development indefinitely.

It has not been possible here to address all of the criticisms of Cohen's interpretation of historical materialism, but I have tried to confront the complaints which seem to gain most traction among those following the debate. In my view, none of these criticisms inflict serious damage on Cohen's approach, but that's not to say there are no problems or questions arising from his understanding of historical materialism. One vulnerability that might demand further attention is Cohen's 'four epochs' classification of history in which he combines all societies between pre-class societies and capitalism as a single economic structure—or at least a single family of related economic structures under an overarching category he describes as "pre-capitalist class society" (Cohen, 2000, p. 198). Rigby complains that that this category "takes up rather a large slice of human history" and includes "a variety of forms of class relations" (Rigby, 1987, p. 79). However, these various forms of class relations share significant, differentiating features. They involve exploitation of non-free immediate producers via non-contractual relations for the production of use-values. They produce some surplus, but not enough to allow the emergence of capitalism. If these features obtain throughout a large slice of human history, then it is to be expected that the category which defines them also does so. Marcus Roberts raises a more insightful objection to Cohen's 'four epochs' formulation. Roberts notes that if we accept Cohen's classification, then the explanatory credentials of his interpretation of historical materialism are weakened because there is now only "a single transition…to serve as a test for this thesis: the transition from feudalism to capitalism" (Roberts, 1996, p. 86). Even if left unanswered, this charge does not deal a fatal blow to Cohen's approach, but it does make it harder to tell whether his schema is merely a description of the transition from feudalism to capitalism or a more widely applicable account of how historical change progresses. The nature of this charge against Cohen means that it cannot be resolved by theory alone. There is no theoretical mechanism by which the 'four epochs' aspect of Cohen's approach can be made to apply to more than one transition, so we need to either accept that as sufficient, or to explore the contours of pre-capitalist class societies to discover whether the wider model accommodates other potential transitions. Either way, having brought us to this point, Cohen's work on historical materialism should be appreciated—not only for his rigour and honesty, but also for his substantive contribution to our understanding of the mechanisms of historical change.

References

Allen, R. C. (2005). *English and Welsh agriculture, 1300–1850: Output, inputs, and income*. Nuffield College, University of Oxford.

Allen, R. C. (2000). Economic structure and agricultural productivity in Europe, 1300–1800. *European Review of Economic History, 4*, 1.

Brenner, R. (1986). The social basis of economic development in ROEMER. J. *Analytical Marxism*. Cambridge University Press, London.

Chibber, V. (2011). What is living and what is dead in the Marxist theory of history? *Historical Materialism, 19*(2), 60–91.

Cohen, G. A. (1988). *History, labour, and freedom—Themes from Marx*. Clarendon Press.

Cohen, G. A. (2000). *Karl Marx's theory of history—A defence* (2nd ed.). Princeton University Press.

Hilton, R. (1984). Feudalism in Europe: Problems for historical materialists. *New Left Review*, I/147. Sept/Oct.

Levine, A., & Wright, E. O. (1980). Rationality and class struggle. *New Left Review*, I/123, September–October.

Marx, K., & Engels, F. (1967). *The communist manifesto*. Penguin.

Meiksins Wood, E. (1989). Rational choice Marxism: Is the game worth the candle? *New left review* I/177, September–October.

Mingay, G. E. (1976). *The Gentry: The rise and fall of a ruling class*. Longman.

Overton, M. (1996). *Agricultural revolution in England—The transformation of the agrarian economy 1500–1850*. Cambridge University Press.

PROYECT, L. *G.A. Cohen*. Retrieved July 21, 2025, from https://www.columbia.edu/~lnp3/mydocs/analytical_marxism/cohen.htm. Undated.

Rigby, S. H. (1987). *Marxism and history—A critical introduction* (p. 118). Manchester University Press.
Roberts, M. (1996). *Analytical marxism—A critique*. Verso.
Roemer, J. (1988). *Free to lose—An introduction to Marxist economic philosophy*. Radius.
Rogers, A. (1981). *Review of G. Cohen's Karl Marx's theory of history—A defence*. Retrieved July 21, 2025, from https://www.marxists.org/history/etol/newspape/isj2/1981/isj2-012/rogers.html.
Sayer, D. (1987). *The violence of abstraction—The analytical foundations of historical materialism*. Basil Blackwell.
Sayers, S. (1984). Marxism and the dialectical method: A critique of G.A. Cohen. *Radical Philosophy, 36*, 4–13.
Wright, E. O., Levine, A., & Sober, E. (1992). *Reconstructing Marxism—Essays on explanation and the theory of history*. Verso.
Wrigley, E. A. (1985). Urban growth and agricultural change—England and the continent in the early modern period. *Journal of Interdisciplinary History*, 15.

Online Resources

PROYECT, L. *G.A. Cohen*. https://www.columbia.edu/~lnp3/mydocs/analytical_marxism/cohen.htm
Rogers, A. (1981). *Review of G. Cohen's Karl Marx's theory of history—A defence*. https://www.marxists.org/history/etol/newspape/isj2/1981/isj2-012/rogers.html

2

History and Freedom in Marx and Cohen

Ben Burgis

2.1 Introduction

G.A. Cohen first rose to prominence at the of the 1970s with *Karl Marx's Theory of History* (henceforth KMTH), a precise and rigorous defense of historical materialism. This was a key event in launching "analytical" (or sometimes, more abrasively, "no-bullshit") Marxism as a distinct intellectual trend.[1] Later in his career, Cohen was largely preoccupied

[1] Cohen himself (perhaps playfully) dates the birth of "analytical Marxism" to 2 years after the publication of KMTH, when the first meeting of what would later become the "September Group" took place in London (Cohen, 2000, p. xix). It's worth throwing in a note of caution here, since the September Group wasn't some philosophical faction that developed their views together, but rather a motely group of philosophers and social scientists who routinely and constantly disagreed with one another about nearly every imaginable point of Marxist theory. A general interest in 'doing' Marxism in broadly methodologically similar ways brought them together once a year to hang out in hotel rooms and tear each other's papers to shreds.

B. Burgis (✉)
Rutgers University, Los Angeles, USA
e-mail: benburgis@gmail.com

B. Burgis and M. McManus (eds.), *Analytical Marxism and Democratic Socialism in the 21st Century*, Palgrave Studies in Classical Liberalism,
https://doi.org/10.1007/978-3-032-02894-5_2

with normative political philosophy. *Rescuing Justice and Equality*, for example, was published during the last full year of his life, and he died while *Why Not Socialism?*, which makes an unabashedly moral case for socialism, was being prepared for publication. Some casual observers of his career have seen this change of focus as indicative of the failure of his original project (or perhaps just his failure to see it through). A sympathetic version of this story would be that Cohen abandoned his attempt to defend hide-worn Marxist dogmas in favor of asking more interesting questions. An unsympathetic one (from the left) would be that his attempt to do real Marxist materialism "without dialectics" was doomed to failure, and that this resulted in a degeneration into un-Marxist moralism. An equally unsympathetic version of the story (from the right) would be that attempting to extract the "bullshit" from Marxist thought just proved that it was bullshit all the way down.

In what follows, I'll argue that this narrative (in all its iterations) is fundamentally misguided. I certainly wouldn't deny that Cohen changed his mind about many things in the three decades between the first edition of KMTH and his death 30 years later. While there's far more consistency in his views throughout that period than is often realized, it would have taken a particularly dull intellect to have gone through decades of constant engagement with sharp and interesting critics without *any* alteration to any detail of his positions. My claim isn't that he was static. Rather, I argue that (a) Cohen left us with plenty of gas in the tank of an analytical defense of historical materialism, (b) all the main normative views that characterized Cohen's later work were present much earlier in his career, and (c) there's no deep conflict or tension between his historical materialism and (at least the main lines of) his normative case for socialism,[2] although (d) that normative case, at least in the form in which Cohen tended to present it in his final years, is importantly incomplete.

[2] The parenthetical is important because *some* of his fine-grained normative claims may not be covered by this defense. I press yjsy worry in my essay, "Analytical Marxism, Marx's Marxism, and the Future of Scientific Socialism: Reflections on G.A. Cohen's Contributions to Socialist Thought" (in McManus & Hamilton, 2025). My interest here, to repeat, is in defending the main lines of his normative views, so I'll put aside the kind of finer-grained criticism I make there.

One way of thinking our way into this bundle of questions would be to start with the introduction to the 2000 edition of KMTH, in which Cohen takes up Engels's use of "scientific socialism" as an alternate name for the Marxist project. Echoing his comrade Erik Olin Wright's term "emancipatory social science," Cohen parses "scientific socialism" as, "at least among other things, the study of the nature of, and the route to, socialism, using the most advanced resources of social science, and within the frame of a socialist commitment."[3] That may be the best summary Cohen would ever give of how the different strands of his lifelong project of marshalling the intellectual resources of analytic philosophy for Marx-inspired ends connected to one another. Historical materialism is a set of factual claims about both the internal workings of various "modes of production" (e.g. feudalism, capitalism or, if all goes well, socialism) and how these systems rise and fall and reshape other social institutions around them over the course of history. It is, to whatever extent that it can claim to be truly "scientific," a matter of applied science like engineering or medicine. Someone *could* become an expert in medical science without the slightest interest in helping anyone live a longer and healthier life, but in practice medicine operates within that normative frame. Marxism, understood as "scientific socialism," similarly operates "within a frame of socialist commitment."

As we'll see below, it's simply a chronological fact that neither Cohen's interest in studying the frame itself nor the key normative conclusions he defended in his late work could have been downstream of any sort of failure of the project of analytically reconstructing and defending historical materialism. But even once that's been established, there's still the matter of establishing that Cohen's simultaneous pursuit of both of these sides of his project didn't involve any sort of conceptual incoherence. Finally, we can examine what's left out of his understanding of the normative frame. I'll do my best to check all of these boxes as I go on. First, though, we need to examine a more basic question. Even if Cohen's normative philosophizing didn't result from the failure of his defense of historical materialism, did the latter in fact fail?

[3] Cohen (2000, p. xxvii).

2.2 Marx and Cohen on Historical Progress

Cohen starts KMTH with a chapter on Hegel. While Cohen is often caricatured as unbendingly hostile to and incurious about any sort of philosophical work done in a "continental" (rather than analytic) way, he's a notably careful and sympathetic reader of Hegel. His interpretations are far from uncontroversial, but throughout that chapter, he distills Hegel's arguments into carefully delineated premises and conclusions, and goes out of his way to look for reasons why Hegel's premises might be at least somewhat plausible and push back against overly hasty skepticism. Cohen's own (Marxist) understanding of history is very different, of course, but he also clearly thinks understanding Hegel can help us understand Marx.

In Hegel's hands, Cohen writes, history "is no miscellany of mighty deeds and catastrophes." (Cohen, 2000, p. 3) Rather, Hegel affirms a much more general picture of historical progress. This much, at least, is going to be true as well about Marx's theory of history. Where Hegel sees history as "the increase, now gradual, then sudden, in the self-awareness of the world spirit," Marx's picture emphasizes "material" factors.

Marxism is "materialist" in two senses. One, although Cohen never quite puts it this way, is that while of course human psychology is complicated and often involves a messy combination of disparate motives, we can at least be confident that *enough* people will be *sufficiently* motivated by pursuing their economic interests that this fact can ground various kinds of interesting and substantive predictions about history and sociology.[4] The other, which is a special case of this more

[4] The failure of global proletarian revolution to arrive is often seen by non-Marxists (and even by Marxists themselves) as naturally giving rise to some degree of doubt about either this claim at the level of generality in which I've given it or the particular analysis Marxists have traditionally given according to which socialism is in the economic interests of the working class. This is one basis, for example, for the widespread belief that Marxism needs to be supplemented by insights about ideology derived from psychoanalysis. A plausible contrary story is told, though, by possibly the most important contemporary Marxist academic working in a recognizably "analytical" vein, Vivek Chibber, who argues in Chibber (2022) that Marxist class theory contains within itself the resources for an explanation of working-class non-resistance to capitalism, but that in order to see it, we need to zoom in on the *individual* interests of workers due to their position within the class structure. The difficulties of effective socialist organizing may ultimately revolve around frustratingly simple collective action problems. If so,

general point, narrower claim about how the various ways human society has been organized over the course of history, how these historical stages work, and how and when old ones pass away and new ones are born, can be understood in terms of basic facts about how production goes on at the base of society.

The standard explanation of the relationship between the Hegelian and Marxist theories of history is that both are "dialectical" but Marx turned Hegel's dialectic on its head to make it materialist. But what does that actually *mean*?

One problem with this has been vividly diagnosed by Michael Heinrich (a prominent contemporary Marxist of a not particularly "analytical" type). "More often than not," Heinrich has written, Marxists' "grandiose rhetoric about dialectics" is "reducible to the simple fact that everything is dependent upon everything else and is in a state of interaction and that it's all rather complicated—which is true in most cases, but doesn't really say anything."[5]

The same suspicion informs Cohen's approach to the subject. "Dialectics," "the dialectic," or things really or allegedly being "dialectical" get precious few mentions in the body of KMTH. In the preface to the book's 2000 edition, though, Cohen takes on the issue head-on.

> The fateful operation that created analytical Marxism was the rejection of the claim that Marxism possesses valuable intellectual methods of its own. Rejection of that claim enabled an appropriation of a rich mainstream methodology that Marxism, to its detriment, had shunned.[6]

This is often parsed by careless critics as Cohen and his fellow analytical Marxists 'rejecting dialectics' (such that any sort of claim made in dialectical language is automatically rejected as 'bullshit') but that's

---

the answer lies in the often slow and maddeningly difficult work of organizers in building up a culture of solidarity. For a relatively deep dive into this debate and my own position on it, see Burgis (2025a).

[5] Heinrich (2012, pp. 36–37). Thanks to Steve Sidawi in my Los Angeles *Capital* class for bringing this passage to my attention!

[6] Cohen (2000, p. xvii).

importantly not quite right. Just a few pages later, we see Cohen offering a much more nuanced perspective.

> I said…that analytical Marxists do not think that Marxism possesses a distinctive and valuable method. Others believe that it has such a method, which they call 'dialectical'. But we believe that, although the word 'dialectical' has not always been used without clear meaning, it has never been used with clear meaning to denote a method rival to the analytical one: *there is no such thing* as a dialectical form of reasoning that can challenge analytical reasoning. Belief in dialectic as a rival to analysis thrives only in an atmosphere of unclear thought.[7]

This rules out uses of "dialectics"-talk in order to avoid the necessity of being clear and precise, getting clear on what the evidence is supposed to be for empirical premises, and so on. So, for example, Cohen has little patience with saying that the relationship between A and B is "dialectical" as an excuse to avoid getting clear on whether A causes B or vice versa (or, if it's a bit of both, *exactly* what the sense is in which A causes B vs. *exactly* the sense in which things are the other way around). But it does leave the door well open for interpreting dialectics-talk in ways that *don't* make it a rival to more standard methods of analysis.

The most important analytical Marxist book on historical materialism and related subjects to be written *after* KMTH is Andrew Levine, Elliott Sober, and Erik Olin Wright's *Reconstructing Marxism.* In there, they take a few tentative steps through this door.

> [It] does seem that the skillful use of dialectical metaphors can serve worthwhile heuristic purposes. But it is one thing to be fluent in a suggestive idiom, something else to deploy a distinctive methodology.
> This is not to say that all of the specific elements traditionally subsumed under the expression "Marxist method" should be rejected out of hand. The point is that in order to be useful, such elements have to be translated into a language of causes, mechanisms and effects, rather than left as elusive philosophical principles. Take the notion of "contradiction", a key element of the purported dialectical method. One way of explicating

[7] Cohen (2000, pp. xxii–xxiii).

> this concept in conventional causal language is to treat a contradiction as a situation in which there are multiple conditions for the reproduction of a system which cannot all be simultaneously satisfied. Alternatively, a contradiction can be viewed as a situation in which the unintended consequences of a strategy subvert the accomplishment of its intended goals. Or finally, a contradiction can be viewed as an underlying social antagonism that produces conflicts: if a social relation has certain properties, which have an intrinsic tendency to generate conflict, one might say that the conflict is generated by a contradiction. There may be advantages or disadvantages to each of these formulations. In all of these cases, however, "contradiction" is not treated as a philosophically driven way of interpreting the essence of a process, but as a way of explicating the interactions among a set of causal mechanisms. This kind of translation of an element of Marxist method into a language of causal mechanisms is essential if the explanations generated using the element are to be scientifically intelligible.[8]

This is pretty much what Cohen himself does in translating the picture of history sometimes understood as "dialectical" materialism into straightforward causal mechanisms.[9] The canonical statement of this picture is Marx's, 1859 preface to *A Contribution to the Critique of Political Economy* (henceforth, "the 1859 preface"). There, Marx writes:

> In the social production of their existence, men inevitably enter into definite relations, which are independent of their will, namely relations of production appropriate to a given stage in the development of their

[8] Wright et al., (1992, pp. 6–7).

[9] The phrase "dialectical materialism" is ambiguous. Sometimes, especially when *contrasted* to "historical" materialism, it refers to a Theory of Absolutely Everything, which would apply to biology and chemistry no less than politics and economics. This is the direction Engels took things in *Anti-Dühring* and *The Dialectics of Nature*. I tend to find this about as plausible as any other Theory of Absolutely Everything, and to think this sort of thing is something of a black mark on Engels's otherwise impressive intellectual record, as well as the records of those later Marxists like Trotsky who enthusiastically embraced "dialectical materialism" in this sense. The alternate sense in which I'm using it here, though, is just the sense in which "dialectical materialism" is an alternate name for "historical materialism" which is used to direct our attention to the "dialectical" aspects of the theory—the way that, for example, the rise and fall of different modes of production can be understood in terms of the working out of "contradictions" (which can in turn be understood in the way suggested in *Reconstructing Marxism*).

> material forces of production. The totality of these relations of production constitutes the economic structure of society, the real foundation, on which arises a legal and political superstructure and to which correspond definite forms of social consciousness. The mode of production of material life conditions the general process of social, political and intellectual life. It is not the consciousness of men that determines their existence, but their social existence that determines their consciousness. At a certain stage of development, the material productive forces of society come into conflict with the existing relations of production or – this merely expresses the same thing in legal terms – with the property relations within the framework of which they have operated hitherto. From forms of development of the productive forces these relations turn into their fetters. Then begins an era of social revolution. The changes in the economic foundation lead sooner or later to the transformation of the whole immense superstructure.... No social order is ever destroyed before all the productive forces for which it is sufficient have been developed, and new superior relations of production never replace older ones before the material conditions for their existence have matured within the framework of the old society.[10]

There are three levels here. At the 'top' level, there's the legal and political superstructure. Some later Marxists have talked about an "ideological" superstructure. Marx himself never talks this way, and Cohen treats relatively lightly on the whole issue of how ideology relates to this picture. (We'll return to that issue in Sect. 4.) Instead, following Marx, Cohen sees the superstructure as a set of legal and political institutions that stabilize the productive relations, most obviously by giving them legal warrant (but also by, for example, maintaining the necessary background conditions of day-to-day social order as production goes on). Beneath that, there are relations of production (which are the "base" underlying that superstructure). For example, the foundational production relation of a society might relate masters and slaves, or lords and serfs, or capitalists and proletarians. Or, if things go very well, the production relations of a socialist future would be relations among freely associated

[10] Marx (1859).

workers. Finally, below even that level, there are the 'forces' of production (roughly, the capacity of a society to produce goods and services).

Eschewing any sort of vague "zig-zag 'dialectic' between forces and relations, with priority on neither side" (and approach that, he notes with some frustration, is "widely favored") Cohen opts for a straightforward interpretation of Marx's meaning according to which, while of course there will be some causation in both directions, the forces are at least *primarily* seen as the cause rather than the effect of the relations, and these in turn are primarily seen as the cause rather than the effect of the superstructure. In both cases, the relationship will be at least somewhat analogous to the way environments select for traits (or, on some interpretations, genes) in evolutionary biology. The forces tend to select for relations that are better at developing them, and the relations in turn tend to select for superstructures that are better at stabilizing them. Questions about how *exactly* that might work, what the mechanisms are, whether this involves causation in implausible directions, and so on, take up some of the most interesting parts of KMTH. In very broad strokes, though, and primarily focusing, as Cohen does, on the primacy of the forces over the relations, Cohen reconstructs Marx's claim as a combination of two theses, both of which he defends.

(a) The productive forces tend to develop throughout history (the Development Thesis).
(b) The nature of the production relations of a society is explained by the level of development of its productive forces (the Primacy Thesis proper).[11]

In *Reconstructing Marxism*, which remains the state of the art (largely because analytical reconstruction of historical materialism is a project to which far too little intellectual attention has been paid since), Wright, Levine, and Sober defend (a) on the reasonable grounds that the only assumption we need to make sense of (a) is that the level of development of the productive forces will be "sticky downward."[12] In other words, in a

[11] Cohen (2000, p. 134).
[12] Wright et al., (1992, p. 79).

broad, transhistorical sense, it's easier to come up with innovations that increase the productive capacity of a society than for old innovations to disappear.[13] This asymmetrical stickiness is all you need to get (a) holding over any sufficiently long period of time. I've seen some particularly stubborn critics hold the line against the stickiness claim, but it's hard to see how it can be rejected without this devolving into a degree of skepticism it would be difficult to take seriously in any other context. No one thinks, for example, that it's mysterious how or why the general tendency of mathematical knowledge is to grow over time. Manifestly, it's easier for mathematicians to prove new things than for old results to be totally lost by the global community of mathematicians. Once the parallel point is admitted for productive developments, you've got the Development Thesis.

What about the Primacy Thesis? This in turn can be subdivided into two claims. The first, which we can call the Constraint Thesis, is the idea that a certain level of development of the productive forces is a necessary condition for the rise of each new mode of production. The second, which we can call the Causation Thesis, is that new modes of production triumph over old ones *because* they're better at developing the productive forces.

The Constraint Thesis is what the Marxist theorist Walter Daum was affirming, with considerable frustration, in his book *The Life and Death of Stalinism*, when he grumbled about Maoists who thought that with sufficient ideological fervor China could leap from semi-feudal conditions such as held in 1949 a socialist society without having to pass through capitalism. "By this logic," he wrote, "human misery could have been avoided from the start—if only Adam and Eve had found a Little Red Book instead of an apple."[14]

This may be the part of historical materialism that remains most politically relevant, not just for arguments with the handful of Stalinist and Maoist dead-enders who persist in the twenty-first century, but for cutting edge debates with those ecosocialists who think the path out

13 We can think of this as a sort of 'walking speed' of the growth of the forces, prior to the forces-developing properties of various particular modes of production speeding things up to a run, or perhaps even to something best analogized to a faster-than-light spaceship.

14 Daum (1990, p. 12).

of global climate change lies not through a green technological revolution but through the planned "degrowth" of the global productive forces. It's also much easier and more straightforward to defend the Constraint Thesis than the Causation Thesis. Wright, Levine and Sober duly sign off on it.[15]

They seem fairly skeptical about the Causation Thesis, though, as are a great many other critics. There could be many reasons for this skepticism, but I don't think I can be accused of cherry-picking objections which are easy to answer if I restrict myself here to two. Both have motivated many skeptics. The first arises from the "Brenner debate" about the rise of capitalism in England, covered by Steve Paxton in his contribution to this volume. Many participants in that debate held that this transition between modes of production, so canonically important for Marxism, is better explained by local and contingent factors rather than any grand historical narrative about progress in the forces of production giving rise to new relations. The second has to do with the difficulty in identifying a single clear engine of upward causation (i.e. of the selection of relations by forces).

Plausibly, both can be dealt with at one blow by reframing the Causation Thesis as a claim, not about transitions in particular countries, but about global transitions. Why capitalism got its first foothold in England, for example, is precisely the sort of question whose answer we should *expect* to revolve around local and contingent factors about how the class struggle played out in a particular place at a particular time. Why capitalism became the overwhelmingly dominant global mode of production, on the other hand, is the sort of question about which general facts like 'capitalism does a much better job than pre-capitalist arrangements did of developing the productive forces' look *highly* relevant. Similarly, the reasons for the success of the Bolshevik Revolution in 1917 seem explicable only in terms of the particular contingencies of politics in Petrograd during the First World War, but the fact that this first foothold of a new

[15] I'd argue that the Causation Thesis is also politically relevant, if only in that it should spur us to think harder about how to design a feasible socialism, not saddled with unacceptable economic inefficiencies. If socialism can't compete with capitalism in the way it further develops the productive forces (and do a better job, at the very least, in developing them in directions that improve the lives of the majority of society), it won't and can't triumph.

system didn't lead to Soviet-style state socialism becoming the world's dominant mode of production seems to be non-coincidentally related to the deep failures of that system to do as well as capitalism in developing the productive forces, never mind fulfilling Khruschev's dream of "catching up and overtaking" the development of the West.[16]

Nor is it even clear that this move departs from Marxist orthodoxy. An interpretation of not only the Causation Thesis but even the Constraint Thesis in global rather than local terms seems implicit in Marx's own late-in-life musings on the possibilities for socialism in Russia. He didn't think Russians could leap-frog across historical stages and build socialism in a single backward country on the steam of their own ideological fervor, but he and Engels wrote in their preface to the 1882 Russian edition of *The Communist Manifesto* that *if* "the Russian Revolution becomes the signal for a proletarian revolution in the West, so that both complement each other," Russia might not have to pass through capitalism.[17]

When looked at from this level analysis, the demand for a *single* causal mechanism by which forces select relations that better develop them begins to look misplaced. When we start thinking about the forms in which systems of production jostle against each other on a global scale, it becomes apparent that a new set of relations' ability to develop the forces better than its predecessor did can give it a multiplicity of advantages. William Clare Roberts puts this point very crisply.[18]

> [M]ore productive class relations are more powerful class relations, which tend to win out in comparison with other, less productive class relations. The mechanism of this winning out can vary. It might be that more productive class relations outspread less productive, which would remain in place but only as an ever more miniscule fragment of production. Instead, they might developmentally outstrip them, making the

---

[16] Connecting this to the point about the USSR in Sect. 2.3 below, it's plausible that the Soviet failure was overdetermined in ways predicted by both the Constraint and Causation Theses.

[17] Marx and Engels (1882).

[18] These passages occur in an essay I dislike very intensely, since it's largely devoted to accusing various people (including yours truly and several of my friends) of something called "class abstractionism," which updates the more familiar charge of "class reductionism." For a response to *that*, see Burgis (2025b; 2025c). On points Roberts gets right, though, he can be very good.

> less productive relations literally impossible by, say, replacing the infrastructure upon which they rely. The more productive relation might also lead to military overmatching, such that the less productive relations are scrapped at gunpoint, as it were.[19]

Moreover:

> [A] tendency is just a tendency, and will be more notable and stable at a large scale and over a long time than it is locally and at any given moment. Historical materialism is supposed to be explanatory and predictive, but it is not a species of determinism. The United States, with far-and-away the most powerful economy and military in the world, lost its war against the Democratic Republic of Vietnam and the Viet Cong, representing a population of peasants living at or barely above subsistence. By 2018, however, the economy of Vietnam could be touted as a "miracle" by the World Economic Forum. Privately-owned firms account for 43% of GDP and employ 85% of the workforce. The long-term tendency of capitalist relations of production to win out could not determine the outcome of the war. The intransigence of the Vietnamese people could defeat the US on the battlefield, but holding the line against more powerful relations of production would have entailed levels of sacrifice that no people should be expected to bear.[20]

It seems to me that the Development Thesis and the Constraint Thesis are quite easy to defend, and if there's more room for debate about the Causation Thesis, the sorts of considerations Roberts points to in these passages should at least give us some reason for optimism there too. Put more programmatically, there's simply far more gas in the tank of the project of analytically reconstructing and defending historical materialism than Cohen's critics sometimes admit. But how does this relate to the *normative* philosophizing that so dominated the later stages of his career?

---

19 Roberts (2023, p. 252).

20 Roberts (2023, pp. 252–253).

2.3 Getting the Chronology Straight

Consider the core claims of the posthumously published *Why Not Socialism?* (henceforth WNS). There, Cohen holds up a totally marketless version of socialism as his ultimate ideal. He grounds this in a commitment to luck-egalitarianism, unpacked in quasi-popularized terms in WNS as "socialist equality of opportunity."

This ideal contrasts with two weaker forms of equal opportunity.[21] "Bourgeois equal opportunity" forbids as unjust inequalities in outcome resulting from legal barriers to advancement such as those characteristic of slavery, serfdom, South African apartheid, and so on. This is nothing to sneeze at. The achievement of this kind of equality, to the extent that it has been (unevenly) achieved in the world around us, has been the longest step in the right direction in human history. But it leaves a lot to be desired. The improved ideal of "left-liberal equality of opportunity" starts where bourgeois equality of opportunity leaves off and additionally forbids inequalities rooted in social disadvantage. Cohen gives the example of Head Start programs as an attempt to implement this second ideal. But even if we could somehow rigorously implement left-liberal opportunity within a capitalist society, making it exactly as easy for the children of janitors and the children of stockbrokers to prosper, this would still leave intuitively unacceptable inequalities in place.[22] Cohen's

[21] Cohen (2009, pp. 14–18).

[22] My own view, for the record, is that it would be impossible (and indeed *very obviously* impossible) to even approximately implement left-liberal equal opportunity without overcoming capitalist property relations. To pick the most glaring problem, a standard component of property rights in the means of production is the right to pass on that ownership to one's children. But even if we expand our imaginations to envision a form of capitalism or quasi-capitalism where the ownership etch-a-sketch was somehow shaken each generation (and private schools and private tutors were abolished while we were at it), numerous other obstacles to "left-liberal" equal opportunity would remain. Short of abolishing private child-rearing entirely (thus reconciling capitalism with equal opportunity at the cost of enacting something out of Ayn Rand's most lurid nightmares), I can't for the life of me see how we're supposed to neutralize the social advantages of the children of college-educated middle managers with an abundance of energy and free time to devote to helping their sons or daughters advance through life over the children of warehouse workers who come home drained and exhausted every night. One generation's social outcomes are the next generation's opportunities, and there may simply be no (even remotely acceptable) way to achieve even approximate "left-liberal" equal opportunities among children in the face of sufficiently large material disparities between parents. As such, what Cohen labels "left-liberal" and "socialist" equality of opportunity might be given

especially demanding ideal of "socialist equality of opportunity" forbids inequalities in outcome linked to factors outside the control of whoever gets the short end of the stick, whether social (e.g. being born into a poor family rather than a rich one) or internal-but-still-involuntary (like not testing well). Whatever one makes of the compatibility of left-liberal equal opportunity with socialism, it's clear that overcoming capitalism is the only way to get anywhere within ten thousand miles of fully realized socialist equal opportunity.

Take the ambitiously radical agenda for what my co-authors Mike Beggs and Bhaskar Sunkara and I elsewhere call Full Democratic Socialism (henceforth FDS).[23] This would begin where the partial kind of "democratic socialism" that's advanced farthest in places like Norway and Sweden leaves off, with an expansive public sector and a generous, universalistic welfare state, keeping all of that in place (and indeed expand it farther than any entrenched class of capitalists would allow) while abolishing the class division between workers and capitalists, partly by expanding the public sector even further, where doing so makes sense, but partly by replacing the capitalist private sector with a market sector of worker-controlled firms financed by grants from nationalized banks. This model takes into account the hard lessons of twentieth-century experiments in totally marketless planning (which we sadly have economic reasons to suspect wouldn't be easily overcome by participatory-democratic feedback, cybernetics, or anything else we've managed to come up with at this stage of history[24]) while still seeking to achieve the core historical socialist objectives of class abolition, workplace democracy, and removal of the obstacles posed to human flourishing by significant material inequality.

How would it fare on the "socialist equality of opportunity" test? It would be a significant advance in that direction relative to capitalism,

the less aesthetically pleasing but more accurate names "socialist" and "ultra-socialist" equality of opportunity.

23 We outline this in detail in *The Blueprint: Life After Capitalism* (forthcoming from Verso), but for early versions see Sunkara (2019, pp. 5–31), which presents an intuitively vivid picture of how it might work, or Beggs (2022), which deals with a variety of technical issues and possible objections.

24 See Burgis (2024a) for an exploration of this point, with a heavy assist from Beggs (2022).

certainly. No one would inherit a factory from his father and thus be in a position to give orders all day on the basis of sheer genetic luck, and no one would inherit poverty or have and thus have to spend all day taking orders at work as a being born into the wrong kind of family. Similarly, in a world where delivery businesses were worker-owned, and warehouse workers thus got to vote on wage scales, people who through no fault of their own lack the "internal" talents helpful for climbing various kinds of educational and career ladders would have something far *closer* to an absolutely equal slice of the pie than their counterparts enjoy under capitalism.

Even so, the persistence of market mechanisms would mean that FDS would fall well short of what could be achieved by a totally marketless socialism that somehow solved the logistical problems that afflicted earlier attempts at central planning (while also, of course, protecting human and democratic rights trampled by those authoritarian socialist experiments). Some sectors would inevitably be more profitable than others, as would some firms within those sectors, so the dramatic reduction in intra-firm inequality would co-exist with persistent inter-firm inequality, even if maximalist welfare-state mechanisms could at least partially address the latter. And even some forms of intra-firm inequality would surely fail to meet Cohen's standards. Really existing worker cooperatives don't have totally flat wage scales (or even wages scales that are flat in every respect that touches on matters of luck), and it's unlikely that even worker-controlled firms in a market socialist economy would either. No one would be able to accumulate brain-meltingly vast piles of wealth like Jeff Bezos or Elon Musk, but individuals with rare and desirable skills they were able to acquire in large part because of their greater innate talents would no doubt still be able to negotiate better compensation packages for themselves than those without comparable advantages.

Likely, even if a previously unimagined logistical breakthrough eliminated the allocation problems afflicting previous planning experiments enabled us to completely eliminate markets in an advanced socialist future, even this wouldn't *entirely* eliminate such discrepancies. But, even if it did, it doesn't follow that Cohen would consider all remaining inequalities acceptable. In WNS, he tends to reserve the word "justice" for the achievement of equality, but he thinks his equality principle needs to be supplemented with a "principle of community."[25] He says much less about this than he does about socialist equal opportunity, but the basic motivating intuition is clear enough. If someone makes "regrettable" but free decisions (or suffers from bad "option luck" after freely choosing to take a rational risk), the resulting decline in their quality of life might be consistent with socialist equal opportunity. Nevertheless, if someone is part of the circle of our human concern (our "community") there's only so far we'd let them sink. In the language of France's bourgeois-democratic revolutionaries at the end of the eighteenth century, the socialist version of *égalité* needs to be supplemented with a socialist version of *fraternité*.

If you found your brother sleeping on a park bench, even if you knew he'd gotten there by foolishly frittering away his life savings in poker games, you wouldn't just let him stay there. It may not be realistic (or perhaps even desirable on a deep human level) to think that all the citizens of any society would care as much about every other random citizen as they would about their own sibling (which would be the most literal way to parse social "fraternity") but Cohen suggests that a decent society wouldn't let anyone sink, even as a result of their own bad choices, to a level where some citizens were making ten times the income of others.

Many of Cohen's critics, ranging from a certain kind of hard-headed Marxist who might roll her eyes at an excessive concern with moral questions to the many libertarians who esteem Cohen as a sharp and interesting interlocutor but have little time for his central conclusions, might find the level of utopianism on display in WNS exasperating for all sorts of reasons. Even market socialism isn't good enough? A notion of equality so demanding that even totally marketless socialism (of a kind Cohen himself acknowledges we don't yet know how to implement) would be merely necessary but not sufficient to achieve it? A vision of a good society that not even somehow-total implementation of that ideal of equality doesn't suffice without a communitarian backup principle? *Why not demand oceans of lemonade while you're at it, Jerry?*

[25] Cohen (2009, p. 34).

A tempting narrative for these critics might be that, having given up on a material analysis of history, within which socialism might emerge realistically from capitalism, Cohen pivoted to seeing socialism as a purely moral imperative, and thereupon he got lost in daydreams of perfect justice totally unmoored from the real world. But there are two stubborn problems for any such story. The first is that Cohen's demanding standards for what would count as absolute justice co-exist with an unabashed pragmatism about the progress we can make in real history. He acknowledges that justice needs to be balanced against competing considerations, among which he explicitly counts economic efficiency. His view in WNS is that, if we don't know how to "turn the wheel of the economy" in a totally marketless way[26], and thus wall-to-wall economic planning isn't (yet) on the agenda, we should at least push for market socialism as our medium-term political aspiration. He just doesn't want us to stop trying to figure out how to design institutions that could take us even farther in a marketless direction. Nor does he turn up his nose at social progress short of a full break with capitalist property relations. The man campaigned for the Labour Party.

The second and much more basic problem is that the chronology simply doesn't work for any such story. In his essay "John Rawls and the Death of Western Marxism," philosopher Joseph Heath writes:

> Back when I was an undergraduate, during the final years of the cold war, by far the most exciting thing going on in political philosophy was the powerful resurgence of Marxism in the English-speaking world. Most of this work was being done under the banner of "analytical Marxism" (aka "no-bullshit Marxism"), following the publication of Gerald Cohen's *Karl Marx's Theory of History: A Defence* (and his subsequent elevation to the Chichele Professorship in Social and Political Philosophy at Oxford). Meanwhile in Germany, Jürgen Habermas's incredibly compact *Legitimationsprobleme im Spätkapitalismus* promised to reinvigorate Marx's analysis of capitalist crises in the language of contemporary systems theory. It was an exciting time to be a young radical. One could say, without exaggeration, that many of the smartest and most important people working in political philosophy were Marxists of some description.

[26] Cohen (2009, p. 55).

> So what happened to all this ferment and excitement, all of the high-powered theory being done under the banner of Western Marxism? It's the damndest thing, but all of those smart, important Marxists and neo-Marxists, doing all that high-powered work, became liberals. Every single one of the theorists at the core of the analytic Marxism movement – not just Cohen, but Philippe van Parijs, John Roemer, Allen Buchanan, and Jon Elster – as well as inheritors of the Frankfurt School like Habermas, wound up embracing some variant of the view that came to be known as "liberal egalitarianism." Of course, this was not a capitulation to the old-fashioned "classical liberalism" of the 19th century, it was rather a defection to the style of modern liberalism that found its canonical expression in the work of John Rawls.
>
> If one felt like putting the point polemically, one might say that the "no-bullshit" Marxists, after having removed all of the bullshit from Marxism, discovered that there was nothing left but liberalism. This is not quite right though, because what they actually discovered was that the new, modernized, reinvigorated liberalism propounded by Rawls was both expressively and rhetorically superior to the reconstructed Marxism they had been trying to defend. So they switched allegiances (sometimes with fanfare, more often without).[27]

When this essay was published, I saw it widely celebrated not just by anti-Marxist liberals like Heath but by many readers who see themselves as hardened anti-liberal Marxists, and would put plusses where Heath puts minuses and vice versa. Perhaps agreeing with Leon Trotsky's classic admonition that Marxism without the dialectical method is "a clock without a spring"[28], they conclude that trying to reconstruct Marxism without its spring, Cohen inevitably degenerated into a contemptible liberal. (As an analytical Marxist in good standing, I can't resist pointing out that these days most clocks are constructed using significantly more advanced technology. Just about *all of them* lack springs.) But putting all such competing judgments of whether analytical Marxism purges Marxism of mere "bullshit" or vital insights, Heath and the Marxist admirers of his essay agree about the basic facts of the case.

---

[27] Heath (2024).

[28] Trotsky (1973, p. 43).

Are they right?

That Habermas, for example, drifted away from Marxism is undeniable. Some of his other examples (e.g. John Roemer) are more dubious. Sticking with Cohen, though, the timeline simply can't be made to work for (any version of) this story.

I've spent so much time belaboring the details of the normative views Cohen had at the very end of very end of his life (again, he died just *before* WNS saw print) because these would have to be the views that critics like Heath have in mind when they claim that Cohen ended his life as an advocate of something recognizable as a version of "liberal egalitarianism." They're certainly *egalitarian* views, and whether they count as "liberal" depends on which of the many importantly different senses of the l-word you have in mind, some of which might or might not be incompatible with socialism and/or Marxism.[29] Certainly, the idea that caring about equality is foreign to socialist politics would be a great surprise to the most socialists, past and present, including Karl Marx, who explicitly objects to capitalist exploitation in both *Capital* and *Critique of the Gotha Program* on the ground (among others) that it produces deep distributive inequality. At any rate, if Cohen shifted *from* Marxism to something else, the "something else" would have to be represented by what we just finished exploring in some depth.

With that in mind, let's take a look at when this shift would have had to happen. Anyone who reads WNS to the end will find an Acknowledgment page noting that an earlier version of the essay appeared in *Democratic Equality: What Went Wrong?*, an anthology edited by the late great Canadian democratic socialist politician Ed Broadbent. That came out in 2001, and while it's highly likely that Cohen's essay would have been finished by sometime before that, we can start by setting 2001 as the latest date this great ideological transition could have occurred. If so, it must have been as abrupt as Paul's conversion on the Road to Damascus (and lacking in even the slightest trace of "fanfare"), because just the year before, Cohen came out with a second edition of KMTH in which,

[29] I explore this ambiguity, as well as the specific relation between Marx's theory of history and Rawls's theory of justice (which I argue are quite compatible) in Burgis (2024b).

while he now added various reservations and caveats, he still enthusiastically endorsed both the main lines of the original project, and Marxism more generally.

But the idea of Cohen waking up as a "liberal egalitarian" sometime between his finalization of the 2000 edition of KMTH and his sending off the original version of WNS to Broadbent doesn't work either. In 1994, Cohen wrote an essay for *New Left Review* called "Back to Socialist Basics" in which every single component of the combination of normative views he expresses in WNS is unambiguously present.

There, he writes:

> If one person produces more than others that is because he is more talented or because he expends more effort or because he is lucky in his circumstances of production, which is to say that he is lucky with respect to whom and what he produces with. The last reason for greater productivity, lucky circumstance, is morally (as opposed to economically) unintelligible as a reason for greater reward. And whereas rewarding productivity which is due to greater inherent talent is indeed morally intelligible, from certain ethical standpoints, it is nevertheless a profoundly anti-socialist idea, correctly stigmatized by J. S. Mill as an instance of 'giving to those who have', since greater talent is itself a piece of fortune that calls for no further reward.

> Effort might be a different matter…

> So:Socialist equality of opportunity? Check.

Supplementing this principle of equality with a socialist principle of community? Check.

> I mean, here, by 'community', the anti-market principle according to which I serve you not because of what I can get out of doing so but because you need my service. That is anti-market because the market motivates productive contribution not on the basis of commitment to one's fellow human beings and a desire to serve them while being served by them, but on the basis of impersonal cash reward.

Granting that all of this needs to be balanced against other considerations, including economic efficiency? Granting that market socialism may be the best we know how to design at this stage of history? Nevertheless insisting that we hold to the north star of marketless socialism as our long-term ideal? Check, check, and check.

> In the famous statement in which Adam Smith justified market relations, he pointed out that we place our faith not in the butcher's generosity but on his self-interest when we rely on him to provision us. Smith thereby propounded a wholly extrinsic justification of market motivation, in face of what he acknowledged to be its unattractive intrinsic character. Traditional socialists have often ignored Smith's point, in a moralistic condemnation of market motivation which fails to address its extrinsic justification. Certain contemporary over-enthusiastic market socialists tend, contrariwise, to forget that the market is intrinsically repugnant, because they are blinded by their belated discovery of the market's extrinsic value.[30]

If we ignore the powerful evidence on every page of the 2000 edition of KMTH that Cohen remained a committed Marxist, we can perhaps postulate that his conversion from Marxism to liberal egalitarianism happened sometimes between the first edition of KMTH (where, remember, Heath begins his timeline) and the issue of *New Left Review* that included "Back to Socialist Basics." That gives us a 14-year window. Perhaps we could speculate that it had something to do with the fall of the Soviet Union refuting Marx's theory of history and forcing Cohen to retreat to an abstract moral case for socialism. Or we could, that is, if this too wasn't flatly contradicted by the evidence. As the Soviet Union was on the brink of falling (the final act mere months away), Cohen wrote a different *New Left Review* essay, "The Future of a Disillusion" explaining why it would be foolish to stop pushing for socialism on the basis of the failure of this deeply flawed experiment.[31] And while he *could* have come to this conclusion despite giving up on any historical-materialist grounds for hope about the matter, he didn't. The 2000

30 Cohen (1993).

31 Cohen (1991).

edition of KMTH contains a whole chapter (Ch. XV, "Marxism After the Collapse of the Soviet Union"), in which he explicitly argues that the fall of the USSR *vindicates* historical materialism, a key prediction of which is that it would be impossible to establish a flourishing socialism on the basis of an insufficient level of development of the productive forces (which is certainly what the Bolsheviks inherited from the semi-feudal Russian Empire in 1917).[32] In the chapter, he credits the contributions of his student Steve Paxton, who went on to write an entire short book expanding on this point.[33] With characteristic wit and insight, Cohen writes:

> If the Soviet Union had succeeded in building an attractive socialism, then that would have been wonderful for socialism and for humanity, but bad for the credibility of historical materialism. Of course, since human beings are the sorts of creatures that, fortunately or unfortunately, they are, they might have been more willing to believe historical materialism had the Soviet Union succeeded. But by 'credibility', here, I mean what it could be rational to believe, so the stated infirmity of human nature does not affect what I have said.[34]

So, if the conversion Health postulates happened, it had nothing to do with the fall of the USSR. It must have been a result of purely intellectual developments of some sort. And it must have happened, remember, *after* the publication of KMTH in 1979, which is Heath's kickoff point for "by far the most exciting thing going on in political philosophy" being "the powerful resurgence of Marxism."

But even this can't be made to work. Two years *before* the publication of KMTH, we have Cohen's paper "Robert Nozick and Wilt Chamberlain: How Patterns Preserve Liberty."[35] There, his explicit concern throughout is defending the importance of normative egalitarianism per se. Over and over again in that paper, we see him invoking "equality" as the value with which he's most concerned. He also writes about the

[32] Cohen (2000, pp. 389–395).

[33] Paxton (2021).

[34] Cohen (2000, pp. 394–395).

[35] Cohen (1977).

importance in a better society of fostering a "desire for community, an unqualified relish of cooperation, and an unqualified aversion to being on either side of a master/servant relationship." That sounds a whole lot like the socialist principle of community in WNS (and "Back to Socialist Basics"). Even more strikingly, we find Cohen saying:

> [A]ssigning a certain role to unregulated transactions in the determination of holdings is compatible with using an egalitarian principle to decide the major distribution of goods and to limit, for example by taxation, how much more or less than what he would get under that principle alone a person may come to have in virtue of transactions which escape its writ. I think socialists do well to concede that an egalitarian principle should not be the only guide to the justice of holdings, or, if it is, then justice should not be the only guide to the moral legitimacy of holdings.[36]

...and, in the endnote attached to that passage:

> I prefer the second formulation, being convinced that justice, very roughly, *is* equality.[37]

So, we have (a) a strong identification of egalitarian distribution with justice per se, (b) the view that justice needs to be pragmatically balanced against other considerations that might allow for some degree of inequality, and (c) a concern that fostering a "sense of community" be somewhere in this mix. If all that adds up to "liberal egalitarianism," then Cohen's staunch commitment to "liberal egalitarianism" *preceded* the book which kicks off the period of Marxist intellectual ferment which Heath has somehow convinced himself ended with a conversion *from* Marxism *to* liberal egalitarianism. In fact, in the 1977 paper, KMTH is referred to as a work-in-progress. He'd already signed the contract with Oxford and Princeton, but it was still far enough from publication to have an entirely different name. Cohen calls it *[A] Philosophical Defense of Karl Marx's Theory of History.*

---

[36] Cohen (1977, p. 10).

[37] Cohen (1977, p. 22 n. 8).

2.4 Ww Were Cohen's Commitment to Historical Materialism and Egalitarian Justice Jointly Coherent?

As a last, desperate maneuver, someone trying to make a Heath-like story about Cohen's development work might try to argue that the missing element in 1977 was the tolerance of market rather than marketless socialism is the best we currently know how to design. Perhaps the inefficiencies of the Soviet economy, and the in-principle calculation worries of economists, hadn't yet kicked in for Cohen in the late 70s. The philosopher Brandon Warmke seems to be suggesting something along these lines in a social media posts defending the Heath essay, where he wonders whether "contemporary Marxists feel betrayed" because Cohen, "who provided the Great Hope of defending historical materialism in the 1970s" had, by in WNS, "admitted that socialist planning couldn't beat the information function of markets and the price system."[38] But on the face of it, this is a *non sequitur*. Historical materialism is an intellectual framework for thinking about how historical change works. How a post-capitalist society can be most optimally designed doesn't even look like the same question. If the two subjects are even linked, the direction of this link *undermines* any sort of Heath/Warmke story. Both the "socialist calculation debate" among economists and the manifest failures of Gosplan to efficiently coordinate production with consumer needs in the USSR obviously postdated Marx, but the idea that there are pragmatic limitations on how closely socialist ideals can be approximated at any given historical moment is not a *departure* from historical materialism but its key themes. This is exactly why we have Marx, in *The Critique of the Gotha Program*, explicitly arguing that certain kinds of luck-based inequalities (some workers may be able to work harder than others, for example, and thus will be rewarded more) are (i) unfortunate but (ii) must nevertheless be tolerated in the early stage of a post-capitalist society when a socialist economy hasn't yet achieved runaway material abundance, for the sake of providing appropriate incentives. "Right," he argues, "can never be higher" than the level of economic

[38] Warmke 2024

development permits.[39] In the same spirit, many of the *most prominent* "contemporary Marxists" (such as Bhaskar Sunkara and Richard Wolff) seem to have attitudes *at least* as friendly as Cohen's to market socialism. Why would they "feel betrayed" by Cohen agreeing with their conclusion?

Even if none of this is promising, though, persistent critics might still insist that Heath and Warmke are on to *something*. Even when it's acknowledged that Cohen pursued his defenses of historical materialism and egalitarian justice simultaneously (that much being a simple fact), it could be maintained that this was always an incoherent combination. Perhaps, to whatever extent that Cohen's primary *emphasis* decisively shifted to the second project later in life, this was a belated (if only implicit) acknowledgment of this incoherence.

If we could hold a séance in which Cohen's ghost could be fed some sort of (perhaps ectoplasm-based) truth serum, we might find out if there was any level on which the man himself agreed with this narrative. Lacking such a breakthrough in paranormal research, we're left to judge him by the actual words he wrote, which don't lend much support to the idea that he thought his earlier views had been incoherent. Whether he *realized* he was being incoherent or not, though, it's still possible to argue that he was incoherent as a matter of fact.

In its strongest form, the incoherence claim might boil down to the claim that *any* concern with normative ideals is un-materialist. But this strongest form of the claim is also by far the least promising, for two reasons. First, on its face, it flies in the face of Hume's Law (the logical impossibility of factual premises entailing normative conclusions in the absence of assistance from relevant normative premises).[40] Historical materialism is a set of claims about historical causation. Such claims *can't* entail anything one way or the other about moral questions. They can't entail any particular view about justice and it equally can't entail the negation of *all* views about justice. Second, even if we water down the incoherence claim to the idea that historical materialism contradicts any sort of concern with normative ideals not because its core factual

[39] Marx (1875).

[40] Exploration of this principle is one of the primary themes of Burgis (2019).

claims are truly incompatible with normative conclusions but *because historical materialism itself builds in fact/value slippage*, this strikes me as unwarrantedly uncharitable to Marx.

An incoherence claim a step weaker than that might revolve around the idea that historical materialism entails sweeping skepticism about moral epistemology. The idea here might be that whatever we think about morality can only be a result of economic conditions at any given time, so Marxists should be generally skeptical of any arguments based on present-day moral intuitions.[41]

The passage most commonly cited in support of this idea is the one omitted from the quote we looked at in Sect. 2 from the 1859 preface:

> In studying such transformations it is always necessary to distinguish between the material transformation of the economic conditions of production, which can be determined with the precision of natural science, and the legal, political, religious, artistic or philosophic – in short, ideological forms in which men become conscious of this conflict and fight it out. Just as one does not judge an individual by what he thinks about himself, so one cannot judge such a period of transformation by its consciousness, but, on the contrary, this consciousness must be explained from the contradictions of material life, from the conflict existing between the social forces of production and the relations of production.[42]

Some Marxists, it's true, read sweeping claims into this, such that everything going on in any given society at a "political, religious, artistic or philosophic" level must flow from more basic economic facts. But this isn't what Marx said. His claim isn't that all of politics, philosophy, art, religion, and so on reflect nothing but economic facts, but merely that the aspects of politics, philosophy, art, religion, and so on "in which men become conscious" of economic conflicts and transitions are downstream of the transitions themselves. Bluntly, a given mode of production's

[41] This seems to be what's suggested in, for example, Rossi (2025), though it should be noted that Rossi doesn't discuss Marx exegesis there and so it would be unfair to attribute to him the common misunderstanding of Marx discussed below. See Burgis (2025d) for an exploration of where I think his argument goes wrong (even without bringing Marx into it).

[42] Marx (1859).

nonsense about itself doesn't *explain* the existence of the mode of production. It comes along later as a rationalization. John Locke didn't create capitalism. He just used his philosophical and rhetorical powers to tell a story that justified what was emerging.[43]

A more cautious version of the claim of tension between Cohen's normative views and his historical materialism comes, elsewhere in this collection, from my very good friend and co-editor Matt McManus. His target isn't Cohen's general willingness to make moral claims, or even his willingness to rely on moral intuitions experienced by chronological natives of the capitalist epoch, but the particulars of Cohen's critique of Rawls's theory of justice. Rawls thinks what counts as "just" can vary according to conditions on the ground, such that inequalities aren't morally unjust if (among other conditions) they're necessary to provide economic incentives that work out to the benefit of the least well-off.

---

[43] Confusion on this point leads some Marxists to all sorts of strange places. William Clare Roberts, in a far less defensible part of the essay quoted above, goes as far as to say this: "The underlying notion that class struggle has been or can be displaced or replaced by culture wars is not so much mistaken as it is confused. It cannot be the case that 'culture wars have displaced class struggle as the engine of politics,' because class struggle has only ever been – could only ever be – the engine of politics insofar as it takes the form of a culture war. A basic tenet of Marxism is that we must 'distinguish between the material transformation of the economic conditions of production' and 'the legal, political, religious, artistic or philosophic – in short, ideological forms in which men become conscious of this conflict and fight it out.' It is puzzling, then, that those who wish to uphold the tradition of hard-headed Marxian class analysis are abandoning this distinction in favor of the self-defeating belief that ideological struggle – for this is what 'culture war' amounts to in the older idiom – could displace class struggle, that the lived experience of class struggle could displace the class struggle of which it is the lived experience" (Roberts, 2023, p. 256). This is hopelessly confused from start to finish. It's true that, given basic Marxist claims about history, whatever the "engine" of politics is must have to do with class struggle in order for that engine *to take us from one mode of production to another*, but very obviously no Marxist critic of progressive preoccupation with culture wars thinks that culture war can get us to a new mode of production. If they thought that, they wouldn't be critics! If we remove the 'taking us to a new mode of production' restriction and say that culture wars can't be the engine of politics in any sense for any period of time without simply being an "ideological struggle" with reducible to the "lived experience" of the class struggle, this amounts to a deeply implausible claim about human history being monocausally driven by economics that, again, it would be extraordinarily uncharitable to attribute to Marx. Let's assume for the argument that Marx really did think this, though. If so, it seems to me that any Marxist who wants to preserve those insights from Marx that are actually worth preserving should be hard at work purging their Marxism of this monumental implausibility. Finally, even if we bite the immense bullet of reducing all of cultural conflict (or even all of cultural conflict that can dominate the politics of a given society at a given time) to the reflection of class struggle, Roberts's suggestion that this reflection can be *what drives historical change* precisely reverses Marx's point in the passage he's quoting.

Cohen is willing to make the same tradeoff but, given the strictly egalitarian understanding of "justice" discussed above, he sees this is a matter of sacrificing some degree of justice because the pursuit of justice has to be balanced against other considerations.[44] McManus sees a conflict between this inflexible, transhistorical conception of justice and Cohen's historical materialism. After all, as we've seen, Marx's historical materialism led Marx to the conclusion that "right" can't rise hire than the underlying economic circumstances. Doesn't a transhistorical "Platonic" notion of justice contradict that claim?

Happily, on this point we don't need to hold a séance to see Cohen himself reply to the objection. He does it in his fascinating essay on Isaiah Berlin ("Isaiah's Marx and Mine") at the beginning of *Finding Oneself in the Other*. There, Cohen discusses the attribution of a historical relativism about what counts as just to Marx.

> A famous sentence in the Critique of the Gotha Programme which is frequently cited in substantiation of some such attribution to him in fact subverts it. The sentence is preceded by a morally informed critique of the norm of distributive justice ("to each according to his contribution") which Marx thought would perforce govern the initial, immediately post-capitalist, stage of communism. Having displayed the "defects" of that norm, Marx says that they are unsurprising, since "right can never be higher than the economic structure of society and its cultural development conditioned thereby." The sentence presupposes—it is amazing that in the vast realms of Marxology this is never, to my knowledge, remarked—an antirelativist contrast between lower and higher forms of right or justice.[45]

In other words, the insight that *how much* justice can be achieved in a particular society at a particular time is limited by economic conditions is incomprehensible *without* a historically invariant standard by which

[44] See Burgis (2023) for a discussion of whether this is ultimately best understood as a semantic dispute about how to *talk* about "justice."

[45] Cohen (2013, p. 15).

we can evaluate the direction of historical change. We can only (coherently) talk about how far "right" can rise if we can measure its height in different times and places by the same transhistorical yardstick.

2.5 Is Cohen's Normative Case for Socialism *Complete*?

If Cohen is right about all of this (which I think he is), which *particular* yardstick should we use? As we saw in Sect. 3, Cohen's presentation of the moral case for socialism tended to come very close to a socialist update of the classical slogans of the bourgeois revolution. He spends a lot of time on socialism's *égalité* (luck-egalitarianism) and socialism's *fraternité* (the socialist value of community). But *liberté* gets somewhat short shrift. And this, I think, is a serious mistake. While it doesn't and (given the fact/value barrier) *can't* contradict historical materialism per se, it creates distance between Cohen's views and Marx's way of framing the wide sweep of historical change in terms of the growth of human *freedom*. Indeed, as Cohen himself alludes to in that chapter on Hegel at the beginning of KMTH, Marx and Hegel had very different notions of what human freedom and/or independence from nature were all about, but the general importance of these themes connected their very different philosophies of history.

Of course, you might (quite reasonably) shrug this off on the grounds that Cohen's views should be evaluated on their own merits, and that dissimilarity to the ideas of a long-dead philosopher (even one as important as Marx is to the socialist Left) needn't be seen as a strike against him. The philosophically important question, of course, is whether Marx was *right* to emphasize freedom. I think he was. And I'd also point out that, *especially* in a nation as obsessed with freedom as the one I live in (the United States), the socialist Left can only benefit on a pragmatic rhetorical level from a renewed emphasis on the case for socialism from the value of *liberté*.

I wouldn't want to overstate this criticism of Cohen. He has a great many interesting and valuable things to say about freedom throughout his career. He brilliantly defends Marx's claim that the working class is forced to submit to capitalist exploitation in his essay "The Structure of Proletarian Unfreedom."[46] He adds interesting layers to this analysis in ""Are disadvantaged workers who take hazardous jobs forced to take hazardous jobs?"[47] He makes a thoroughly convincing case for the inseparability of distributive inequality from inequality in freedom from interference in his essay "Freedom and Money."[48] And in many other places, he's very concerned to refute libertarian arguments that caring about freedom gives us a reason to favor capitalism. He's also attuned throughout his work on egalitarianism to situations in which a good society might be justified in sacrificing some degree of equality in order to avoid infringing on various kinds of important freedom. So, he can't stand accused of indifference to freedom or obliviousness to ways in which the value of freedom might intersect with the normative debates with which he was preoccupied. Nevertheless, it remains the case that freedom was mostly an afterthought *when he was making his case for socialism.* It tends to enter the equation when there's a libertarian argument from freedom to rebut (or a moderate-liberal claim about it, as in "Freedom and Money"), or a claim made by Marx about capitalist unfreedom to defend (as in "The Structure of Proletarian Unfreedom"), or when it's just in the mix as one of those values (like economic efficiency) we need to carefully weigh in the balance when figuring out how exactly to pursue the north star of egalitarian justice at any given time. At best, as in the pre-KMTH essay quoted above ("Robert Nozick and Wilt Chamberlain: How Patterns Preserve Liberty"), it's there, as the title suggests, as a clever way of turning the tables on his ideological opponents while mostly running a defense of the importance of equality. He's not, for the most part, putting freedom front and center in his positive case for socialism.

My best guess about why not is that, while he's concerned with various kinds of freedom and unfreedom in various contexts, he isn't straightforwardly committed to one central account of what kind of *liberté*

[46] Cohen (1983).
[47] Cohen (1987).
[48] Cohen (1995).

we should be most concerned with, in the way that he centers luck-egalitarianism as an account of the most important kind of *égalité* and the anti-market value of "community" as the notion of *fraternité* that's most relevant to his purposes.

And here, I suspect, Cohen's work might be usefully supplemented by the burgeoning literature on the connection between Marxism and republicanism. In Bruno Leipold's *Citizen Marx* (Leipold, 2024), for example, Leipold makes a persuasive case that a commitment to some version of the republican notion of freedom (where the relevant dimension is freedom from domination, or from "arbitrary power") is an important through-line in Marx's socialism.[49] As Leipold emphasizes, "antipathy to relations of dependency" is an important theme running through Marx's early writings like those later published as the *Economic and Philosophical Manuscripts of 1844*.[50] While Leipold is mostly thinking like a historian about the influence of the republican tradition on Marx's socialism rather than thinking like a normative political philosopher about the case for emphasis on the kind of freedom republicans emphasize, literature on the latter has flourished in recent years, and Leipold's book signposts important ways in which this renewed philosophical republicanism could connect with concerns central to both Marx and post-Marx socialists. Sticking for a moment with the 1844 *Manuscripts*, for example, Marx is concerned with various forms of alienation, and in multiple cases, Leipold points out, Marx "makes an explicit connection" between "alienation and domination."[51] Workers are alienated from the product of their labor and from the process of production itself by their domination by the capitalist class. And even the capitalists are dominated by impersonal economic forces.

Nor are these concerns of the young Marx that can be plausibly held to disappear in some Althusserian rupture (the opposite of the transformation Heath thinks was undergone by Cohen!) in which humanistic concerns give way to a monomaniacal preoccupation with unsentimental questions of material analysis. Any reader of *Capital* who got to Ch.

[49] A similar emphasis is one of the most laudable aspects of Roberts (2016).

[50] Leipold (2024, p. 176).

[51] Leipold (2024, p. 179).

15 knows how concerned Marx is with the ugly mechanics of capitalist domination in the workplace. When he discusses factory codes, his language explicitly centers republican concerns about arbitrariness and domination.

> In the factory code, the capitalist formulates his autocratic power over his workers like a private legislator, and purely as an emanation of his own will, unaccompanied by either that division of responsibility otherwise so much approved of by the bourgeoisie, or the still more approved representative system.[52]

Indeed, one of the primary themes of *Capital* is that the profits of capitalists are extracted from workers by virtue of class relations of domination, and the primary analogy he goes back to again and again and again in making this case is to various forms of pre-capitalist extraction that, by the time of *Capital*'s publication in 1867, would have been very widely understood as unacceptable infringements on human freedom. Usually, the analogy is to the feudal *corvée*, where Marx wants to show that just like the feudal serf, the modern worker has no realistic choice is made to work hours of "surplus labor" in addition to the nature-imposed hours of "necessary labor" to meet his own needs (the time a serf spends farming his own little plot of land, or the hours of the working day the proletarian spends reproducing his own wages), even if the serf is forced at the point of a sword while the "silent compulsion" of economic necessity (due to the underlying division of property) is what "sets the seal on the domination of the capitalist over the worker."[53] Sometimes, Marx goes much further back than the Middle Ages, harkening back to the kind of extraction practiced by the Roman Empire, as when he talks about the extraction of surplus-value as "the tribute annual extracted from the working class to the capitalist class."[54] In all cases, the point is the same.

Republican philosophers don't deny that freedom from interference is often quite important. But they think that freedom from domination is

---

[52] Marx (1976, pp. 549–550).

[53] Marx (1976, p. 899).

[54] Marx (1976, p. 728).

more fundamental. (The classic example is that a slave who's whipped every day is more interfered with than one with a kind master, but the latter is no more *free*.) If they're right, the work on exploitation that formed such a massive portion of Marx's most important output (as well as forming, for example, such a massive portion of the class analysis produced by Cohen's friend and comrade in the trenches of analytical Marxism, Erik Olin Wright) doesn't just shed light on the sociological and economic *mechanics* of capitalism, but is centrally relevant to the normative case against that system and for transitioning to a socialist world in which we can break free of the "autocratic" personal domination of capitalists at the workplace, the "mute compulsion" of capitalist property relations, and in the long run perhaps also the impersonal domination of market imperatives as they would impact even worker-controlled firms. If traditional socialist predictions about automation, of the kind Marx makes in Ch. 15, pan out, such that the kinds of developments that lead under capitalism to some people being thrown into unemployment and desperation while some are worked as hard as ever would lead under conditions of workers' control of production to less work being spread out more evenly among the whole working population, with no concomitant loss of consumption, then as this process plays out, we have (at least) an important partial advance in freedom even from the nature-imposed requirement of "necessary labor."

This is central to Marx's notion of historical progress, and Cohen's own case for socialism becomes even more formidable when we supplement his (already powerful) arguments regarding equality and social solidarity with Marx's own emphasis on the deep importance of republican freedom.

References

Beggs, M. (2022). The market and workplace in a democratic socialism. *Catalyst*, 6(3). https://catalyst-journal.com/2023/01/the-market-and-workplace-in-a-democratic-socialism

Burgis, B. (2019). *Give them an argument: Logic for the left*. Zero Books.

Burgis, B. (2023). Thinking harder about justice: Rawls vs. Cohen vs. Marx. *Philosophy for the People*. https://benburgis.substack.com/p/thinking-harder-about-justice-rawls

Burgis, B. (2024a). Mike Beggs on how a viable socialism might work. *Philosophy for the People*. https://benburgis.substack.com/p/mike-beggs-on-how-a-viable-socialism

Burgis, B. (2024b). Did Rawls kill analytical Marxism? *Philosophy for the People*. https://benburgis.substack.com/p/did-rawls-kill-analytical-marxism

Burgis, B. (2025a) Taking the red pill? William Clare Roberts vs. Vivek Chibber on the class matrix. *Philosophy for the People*. https://benburgis.substack.com/p/taking-the-red-pill-william-clare

Burgis, B. (2025b). On the charge of class abstractionism. *Philosophy for the People*. https://benburgis.substack.com/p/on-the-charge-of-class-abstractionism

Burgis, B. (2025c). 'Class reductionism' is a straw man. So is 'class abstractionism.' *Philosophy for the People*. https://benburgis.substack.com/p/class-reductionism-is-a-straw-man

Burgis, B. (2025d). Matt McManus vs. Enzo Rossi on socialism, liberalism, and moral reasoning. *Philosophy for the People*. https://benburgis.substack.com/p/matt-mcmanus-vs-enzo-rossi-on-socialism

Chibber, V. (2022). *The class matrix: Social theory after the cultural turn*. Harvard University Press.

Cohen, G. A. (1977). Robert Nozick and Wilt Chamberlain: How patterns preserve liberty. *Erkenntnis*, 11(1, Social Ethics, Part 1).

Cohen, G. A. (1983). The structure of proletarian unfreedom. *Philosophy and Public Affairs, 12*(1), 3–33.

Cohen, G. A. (1991). The future of a disillusion. *New Left Review*, 1/190 (November–December 1991). https://newleftreview.org/issues/i190/articles/g-a-cohen-the-future-of-a-disillusion

Cohen, G. A. (1994). Back to socialist basics. *New Left Review* I/207 (September–October 1994). https://newleftreview.org/issues/i207/articles/g-a-cohen-back-to-socialist-basics

Cohen, G. A. (2000). *Karl Marx's theory of history—A defense* (Expanded). Princeton University Press.

Cohen, G. A. (2008). *Rescuing justice and equality*. Harvard University Press.

Cohen, G. A. (2009). *Why not socialism?* Princeton University Press.

Cohen, G. A. (2013). *Finding oneself in the other*. Princeton University Press.

Daum, W. (1990). *The life and death of stalinism*. Socialist Voice.

Hamilton, C., & McManus, M. (Eds.). (2025). *Flowers for Marx*. Revol Press.

Heath, J. (2024). John Rawls and the death of Western Marxism. In: *Due course*. https://josephheath.substack.com/p/john-rawls-and-the-death-of-western

Heinrich, M. (2012). *An introduction to the three volumes of Karl Marx's capital*. Monthly Review Press.

Leipold, B. (2024). *Citizen Marx: Republicanism and the Formation of Karl Marx's Social and Political Thought*. Princeton University Press.

Marx, K. *A contribution to the critique of political economy* (Marxist Internet Archive, 1859). https://www.marxists.org/archive/marx/works/1859/critique-pol-economy/preface.htm

Marx, K. (1875). *A critique of the Gotha program* (Marxist Internet Archive, 1875) https://www.marxists.org/archive/marx/works/1875/gotha/ch01.htm

Marx, K. (1882). Russian edition preface, *The Communist Manifesto* (Marxist Internet Archive, 1882) https://www.marxists.org/archive/marx/works/1848/communist-manifesto/preface.htm#preface-1882

Marx, K. (1992). *Capital: A critique of political economy*, Volume 1. Translated by Ben Fowkes. Penguin.

Paxton, S. (2021). *Unlearning Marx: Why the Soviet Failure was a Triumph for Marx*. Zer0 Books.

Roberts, W. C. (2017). *Marx's inferno: The political theory of capital*. Princeton University Press.

Roberts, W. C. (2023). Class in theory, class in practice. *Crisis and Critique, 10*(1), 248–262.

Rossi, E. (2025). Socialism is not liberal moralism on steroids. *Damage*.

Sunkara, B. (2019). *The socialist manifesto: The case for radical politics in an era of extreme inequality*. Basic Books.

Trotsky, L. (1973). *In defense of Marxism: The social and political contradictions of the Soviet Union*. Pathfinder Press.

Warmke, B. @BrandonWarmke Twitter (December 7th, 2024), "I've often wondered if contemporary Marxists feel betrayed by Cohen. The man who provided the Great Hope of defending historical materialism in the 1970s had, by 2009, admitted that socialist planning couldn't beat the information function of markets and the price system." https://x.com/BrandonWarmke/status/1872693874944286760

Wright, E. O., Levine, A., & Sober, E. (1992). *Reconstructing Marxism: Essays on explanation and the theory of history*. Verso.

Part II

Radical Socialism, Liberal Egalitarianism and Liberal Socialism?

3
Radical Socialist and Liberal Socialist Equality

Matt McManus

3.1 Introduction

G.A Cohen developed one of the most sustained critiques of liberal egalitarianism from the left. This became especially pronounced after the post-Soviet "turn" in his thinking away from the philosophy of history and towards moral and political philosophy. While his debates with Ronald Dworkin on the topic of expensive tastes[1] was instructive, it is of

[1] I've always found it very difficult to be invested in the debate about expensive tastes. Not because it is technically uninteresting, but because it is so far removed from more practical concerns about the kind of society we should instantiate. In a world defined by expansive and impactful inequality, debating whether a man who develops a taste for plovers eggs should have that catered to in a super-egalitarian society struck a Marxist chord in me as almost literally writing recipe books for the cook shops of the future.

M. McManus (✉)
Spelman College, Atlanta, USA
e-mail: mattmcmanus300@gmail.com

B. Burgis and M. McManus (eds.), *Analytical Marxism and Democratic Socialism in the 21st Century*, Palgrave Studies in Classical Liberalism,
https://doi.org/10.1007/978-3-032-02894-5_3

course Cohen's attack on Rawls and Rawlsianism, which is most significant. Cohen advances numerous objections against liberal egalitarianism, which range from an insistence that we should provision a more expansive socialist equality of opportunity to claiming that the demands of justice extend beyond the "basic structure" and should govern personal morality. These objections will undoubtedly be appealing to many on the left; especially those who are instinctively or habitually inclined (sometimes with good reason) to be wary of liberal egalitarianism generally and Rawlsianism particularly. This is despite a growing appreciation that liberal egalitarianism generally, and Rawlsianism in particular, can be quite radically egalitarian. This is especially true of liberal socialist variant of liberal egalitarianism, which are on the hard left wing liberalism(s). This paper will respond to Cohen by arguing his objections to liberal egalitarianism can largely be answered by Rawlsian liberal socialism. In cases where we face a choice between liberal socialism and Cohenean radical democratic socialism, it isn't clear to me that the latter should triumph.

The paper will be broken into three parts. Part One will focus on Cohen's critique of various liberalisms; paying special attention to his objections to Rawlsian liberal egalitarianism. Cohen tends to read Rawls as defending an insufficiently egalitarian position, which would be an improvement on capitalism, but falls short of the ideal of full socialist justice. Consequently, Cohen thinks we should reject liberal egalitarianism for his more satisfactory form of radical democratic socialism. In Part Two, I will draw on more recent scholarship to argue that a more radical form of Rawlsian "liberal socialism" can very easily be derived from Rawls' arguments. I will briefly discuss liberal socialism in its Rawlsian and generic forms, highlighting its core principles and modes of argumentation. Part Two will conclude with a defense of this form of liberal socialism against Cohen's forceful criticisms of liberal egalitarianism. Especially important will be my claim that socialists should follow Marx in focusing more on the free and largely equal flourishing of each rather than stringent and formalistic equality. This point was also recognized by the early Rawls in his discussion of the Aristotelean principle in *Theory of Justice.* Part Three of the paper will offer an olive branch to

Cohen by arguing liberal socialist theory is deficient in a deep way Coheneans can assist, to but these deficiencies aren't at the level of ideal moral theory. Instead, the more forceful Cohenean objection to liberal socialism response should be directed against its ideal-theoretic disinterest in questions of history and power. These are issues which Cohen's analytical Marxism took more seriously than liberal egalitarianism, suggesting that Cohen's strongest political objections to liberal egalitarian should in fact be descriptive rather than normative. Liberal socialists have much to learn from him on these issues.

3.2 Part One: Cohen's Moral Objections to Liberal Egalitarianism

3.2.1 The Normative Turn

Cohen's work took a well-known turn towards normative political and moral philosophy in the 1990s. Much of this was inspired by his ambivalent feelings about the fall of the Soviet Union, which Cohen had criticized throughout its life but which he felt instinctively protective of in its dying moments. This led Cohen to shift away from emphasizing the defense of Marxist historical materialism, where he had made his philosophical name with the publication of *Karl Marx's Theory of History: A Defense* in 1978. In particular, Cohen came to reject the Marxist doctrine of "inevitabilism" which held that historical materialist "science" demonstrated how the downfall of capitalism and the emergence and ultimate triumph of socialism were preordained. From an orthodox Marxist standpoint, this made offering normative arguments for the superiority of socialism unnecessary and perhaps even pre-scientific. As Cohen routinely noted, this outlook was very rarely held with deep consistency by Marxists, whose language clearly demonstrated they took the normative superiority of socialism over capitalism for granted.

Whatever the case, the failure of inevitablism evidenced by the collapse of the Soviet Union made this mode of Marxist arrogance seem outdated and more than a little funny. As Cohen put it, we can "no longer believe the factual premises of {Marxism's} conclusions about the practical [ir[relevance of the study of norms. We cannot share Marx's optimism about material possibility, but we therefore also cannot share his pessimism about social possibility, if we wish to sustain a socialist commitment…Marxism thought that equality would be delivered to us, by abundance, but we have to seek equality for the context of scarcity, and we consequently have to be far clearer than we were about what we are seeking, why we are justified in seeking it, and how it can be implemented, institutionally" (Cohen, 1995, pp. 11–12).

This turn contributed to Cohen's well known dialogues with political and moral philosophers across the spectrum. The most agonistic, and I'd argue important of these, was Cohen's near book length debate with libertarianism ala Robert Nozick in *Self-Ownership, Freedom, and Equality.* Alongside geopolitical events, Cohen credits Nozick with awakening him from his "dogmatic socialist slumber" and inspiring his more extensive engagement with liberal political philosophy. Cohen objects that "libertarianism" is not committed to "freedom as such, but freedom of a certain type, whose shape is delineated by the thesis of self-ownership" (Cohen, 1995, p. 67). The major liberty respecting rights defended by Nozick are derivative from this more basic conception of self-ownership, which means he is dismissive of the "propertyless proletarian" who is a "counter-example to his view that freedom prevails in capitalist society" (Cohen, 1995, p. 68).

3.2.2 How Equal Should We Be?

But it is Cohen's debate with liberal egalitarianism, rather than the libertarian tradition, that occupied the lion's share of his attention post-turn. This included debates with Dworkin and Sen amongst others. But without a doubt, Cohen's chief foil was John Rawls. His critique of Rawls sprawled across several books and articles, finally culminating in 2008's *Rescuing Justice and Equality.* To be clear, this debate was by no means mean spirited or dismissive. In the Introduction to *Rescuing Justice* Cohen claimed that "at most two books in the history of Western political philosophy have a claim to be regarded as greater than *A Theory of*

Justice: Plato's *Republic* and Hobbes's *Leviathan*" (Cohen, 2008, p. 11). Surprisingly for someone so identified with analytical Marxism, Cohen even claims that if one were disposed to "call me a left-Rawlsian, I would neither disavow nor dislike the description. There is a strong egalitarian element in Rawlsianism that I try to train against its inegalitarian conclusions" (Cohen, 2008, p. 12).

These "inegalitarian conclusions" are best reflected in the Rawlsian difference principle, chosen behind the veil of ignorance in the original position to govern the "basic structure" of society. The difference principle holds that inequalities are permissible to the extent they work to the benefit of the least well off by incentivizing greater efforts, especially by the talented. It has many unique characteristics that have, needless to say, been extensively studied. Perhaps the most important for Cohen's purposes is its apparent fact sensitivity. The correct application of the difference principle, and indeed the correct political regime to instantiate justice as fairness as a whole, is empirically sensitive to which distributive scheme would make the least well off better off. The claim is that where a more egalitarian distribution of resources may result in the least well off being worse off, say by disincentivizing the talented from working hard since they will not be rewarded, that scheme should be rejected for one which is more inegalitarian but "proven" to deliver the goods for the least well off.

As Cohen notes at various points in his debates with liberal egalitarians, there are clear bourgeois assumptions about human nature baked into these arguments in favor of a heavily ameliorated inequality. In the Rawlsian case, Cohen notes how Rawls seems to "agree with Bernard Mandeville (and Adam Smith) that 'private vices' make for 'publick benefits'-that (in other words) human selfishness can be made to benefit everyone-but that the Rawls of 1971 is unwilling to acknowledge that it is indeed vices which are in question" (Cohen, 2000a, 2000b, p. 122). Rawls' view is that individuals are too self-interested to work unless they expect to be rewarded, even if it's the case that justice does not entitle to them to such a reward. For Cohen, these assumptions are insufficiently interrogated, because if they were it would reveal that certain claims about our need to offer concessions to "human nature" are in fact claims that we must make a pact with human sinfulness.

Something similar can be said of Ronald Dworkin, whose own liberal egalitarianism is quite robust and sophisticated. In various writings, Dworkin argues for an equality of resources between citizens, except where inequalities are the result of non-morally arbitrary choices (Dworkin, 2002). For Dworkin, contingent social circumstances and the spread of natural talents are too arbitrary for a just distribution of resources to emerge from a pure market society. Instead he proposes an insurance based model of distributive justice, where citizens would guarantee themselves against brute bad luck. However, Dworkin does hold that inequalities which are the result of non-arbitrary choices, for instance, the pursuit of artistic ambition by starving but bohemian artists, are just and needn't be offset by a redistribution of resources through the state. While taking Dworkinean liberal egalitarianism seriously would also result in a considerably more equal society than we have now, it is telling that Dworkin is unable to fully give up a last residue of the liberal-meritocratic notion that inequities which result from choice must are acceptable. Cohen objects that this would leave the "undeserving poor" whose lot was the result of bad choices with little to no succor (Vrousalis, 2015, p. 65). I'd go further and suggest such a Dworkinean scheme could be unusually damaging to the social bases of self-respect defended by someone like Rawls. Imagine that the "undeserving poor" were made to feel that all the contingent external facts of society and the natural endowment of talents had been compensated for. This would mean that their bad lot would have to be internalized as feelings of guilt by the "undeserving poor," who would in effect be told they deserved to be poor because of crappy choices.

3.2.3 Cohen's Objections to Liberal Egalitarianism

Cohen levels several objections against these liberal egalitarian arguments in support of a qualified inequality. The most systematic of these are directed against Rawls. I will not be able to address all of Cohen's objections here, so will instead focus on the three most important: the incentives argument, the basic structure argument, and the freedom argument.[2] All are linked in important ways by Cohen's contention that the proper "site of distributive justice" must include individual choices and action. Put broadly, egalitarian distributive norms must govern more than institutions, economic policies, and political principles. They must permeate to the core of our relations with other people (Cohen, 2000a, 2000b, p. 134).

The incentives objection takes aim at Rawls' claim that allowing inequalities may be necessary to induce people to work harder, and so generate the wealth which is necessary to ameliorate the conditions of the least well off. As described by Cohen "left wing liberals, whose chief representative in philosophy is John Rawls" argue that inequality is justified if the rich's "high level of income cause unusually productive people to produce more than they otherwise would; and, as a result of the incentives enjoyed by those at the top, the people who end up near the bottom are better off than they would be in a more equal society" (Cohen, 2008, pp. 30–31). The problem with this argument is how the "unusually productive people" are allowed to be derelict in their duties to work to the benefit of the least well off in the absence of such incentivizing advantages. This is often abstracted away from by framing the argument about incentives as a third-person empirical claim about economic laws, rather than a first person claim about people's unwillingness to do their duty in the absence of incentivizing motivations. Cohen asks us to imagine the following thought experiment. Imagine a kidnapper demands a ransom to return a stolen child to its parents. Many of us would accept a third person argument that the parents should pay the kidnapper. But now imagine the kidnapper himself calls, argues that unless you pay him he will not return the child, and then claims you have a moral obligation to do so. We would immediately object that the kidnapper's first person argument that you have a moral argument to pay him to return your child falls very flat, since he could choose to do so in the absence of such a reward but would prefer to make off with ill gotten gains (Cohen, 2008, pp. 38–39). Cohen argues that same reasoning applies to those

[2] For reasons of space I do not discuss the Pareto argument of Brian Barry, to which Cohen dedicates a chapter of *Rescuing Justice and Equality*.

who accept the arguments for greater equality, but refuse to apply them to their personal actions and demand incentives to work harder.

The basic structure argument follows a similar pattern. Rawls' argument is that the principles of justice, including the difference principle, are not intended to apply to individual action. They instead govern only the basic structure of society, including the state, economic systems, civil society and (later) the family. The "later" bit is important since as Cohen notes Rawls "wobbles" on whether to include under pressure from a variety of feminist critics (Cohen, 2008, p. 117). From a feminist standpoint this initial Rawlsian "wobble" about the family might appear little more than an echo of the longstanding liberal failure to take seriously the injustice experienced by women in the so called "private sphere"-a failure Rawls largely set right when he included the family in the basic structure (Nussbaum, 2006, pp. 105–106). Cohen derives another set of conclusions from this "wobble." On his reading Rawls' was uncomfortable with including the family within the basic structure, because upon doing so the clean distinction between distributive principles applied to the basic structure and those which govern individual actions begins to collapse. If we take seriously the feminist idea that the "personal is the political" why should a political theory committed to egalitarian distributive justice insist its core principle apply only to the basic structure and not to relations between individuals, both within the family and beyond. As Cohen asks why "should we care so disproportionately bout the coercive basic structure, when the major reason for caring about it, its impact on people's lives, is also a reason for caring about informal structure and patterns of personal choice? To the extent that we care about coercive structure because it is fateful with regard to benefits and burdens, we must care equally about the ethos that sustains gender inequality and inegalitarian incentives" (Cohen, 2008, p. 138).

Finally, the "freedom objection" concerns the extent to which concerns about personal liberty, especially freedom to choose one's occupation, should bear on our commitment to egalitarianism. Imagine Janet would choose to be a doctor if she were to earn \$250,000 a year. Janet being a doctor would relevantly increase the Pareto optimality of the community. But in a hyper-egalitarian world, being a doctor would only be renumerated at \$50,000. Janet decides she would rather avoid the strains of a long education and take up gardening instead, which is also renumerated at $50,000. This would lead to a loss of welfare for the community-including the least well off-which needs doctors more than gardeners. But it is reflective of her choices under egalitarian distributive conditions. For the liberal egalitarian on Cohen's telling, these kinds of scenarios demonstrate a serious problem with an excessive concern about equality. It lead to a "trilemma" where stringently realizing egalitarian ambitions come at the cost of Pareto optimizing welfare if someone who could become a doctor takes up gardening instead and/or personal liberty if we compel Janet to go to medical school even though she would not have gone under freely chosen circumstances at the current level of compensation.[3] Cohen's response to this is to reaffirm that individuals committed to the "egalitarian ethos" of justice can choose to work for equal pay in tougher but potentially necessary jobs. If they choose not to do so that would constitute an abnegation of their moral duties, even if that choice must be respected and the alternative should not be coerced (Cohen, 2008, p. 203).

Cohen's objections are undoubtedly forceful to anyone with an egalitarian bent; especially the arguments about incentives and the basic structure which raise foundational questions about the extent to which a political philosophy focused on the right can cleanly demarcate itself from considerations of the good in terms of and individual's efforts and personal commitments to equality.

3.3 Part Two: Can Liberal Socialism Be Sufficiently Equal?

3.3.1 The Appeal of Liberal Socialism

Taken together, Cohen thinks his objections (and others!) demonstrate why liberal egalitarianism of Rawls and the rest of the team is not committed to a muscular enough version of equality. Muscular is an

[3] The thought experiment given here is not Cohen's, though it is inspired by him. I have compressed it for the sake of space.

appropriate term, since the spirit of Cohen's objections is that liberal egalitarians acknowledge the need for distributive equality but fear that going too far in this direction would make too many demands of ordinary people and be unrealistic. Liberal egalitarians aim at a "realistic utopia," not the kind of radical democratic socialism which Cohen thinks would truly conform with justice. So committed is Cohen to this that he even adopts the remarkably anti-materialist view that facts have no necessary relationship to the normative principles we have reason to adopt. Principles at the "summit of our conviction are grounded in no facts whatsoever" (Cohen, 2008, p. 229). Given this, even were it the case that the liberal egalitarians (or market socialists for that matter) are right that full socialist justice cannot not be achieved, that wouldn't be a reason to embrace liberal egalitarianism as true justice. It would just be a hollow approximation of the real deal. In this second section, I am going to argue that Cohen's grim interpretation of liberal egalitarianism understates the latter's radicalism. I am also going to argue that even where some of Cohen's objections highlight limitations to liberal egalitarianism, we shouldn't necessarily prefer his approach.

Cohen frequently, if sometimes waveringly, homologizes Rawls and liberal egalitarian philosophy generally with support for a specific kind of political regime and policies: namely the moderate welfarism advanced by center-left (and some conservative!) politicians and parties throughout the mid-twentieth century. In the opening chapter of *Rescuing Justice and Equality,* Cohen discusses the infamous "Lawson tax cut" to the wealthy introduced by the Thatcher regime. Many conservatives defended it on the basis of meritocratic arguments, which of course liberal egalitarians would reject. But Cohen chastises Rawls for being unable to effectively oppose the Lawson tax cuts on principle, since if they empirically work to benefit the least well off as many conservatives claimed then Rawlsians would feel compelled to defend them. Socialist egalitarians find this troubling in a way "left-wing" liberals do not, which is why the former are "to the left of left-wing liberals" (Cohen, 2008, pp. 29–30). In his classic "Freedom and Money" essay, Cohen aligns Rawls (and Berlin) with a variation of Roosevelt style social democracy and the New Deal. He goes on the criticize Rawls for still acceding to the "right-wing conceptualization of freedom" by thinking there are trade-offs between freedom and "economic security" for the poor (Cohen, 2011, p. 172). In *If You're an Egalitarian, How Come You're So Rich,* Cohen describes Rawls as committed to achieving moderate equality through taxation and redistribution. He argues the "standard (and in my view misguided) Rawlsian application of the difference principle can be modeled as follows. There is a market economy in which all agents seek to maximize their own gains, and there is a Rawlsian state that selects a tax function on income that maximizes the income return to the worst off people, within the constraint that, because of the self-seeking motivation of the talented, a fully equalizing taxation system would make everyone worse off than one which is less than fully equalizing" (Cohen, 2000a, 2000b, p. 127). And in *Why Not Socialism,* Cohen aligns "left-liberal equality of opportunity" with policies like "head start education for children from deprived backgrounds" which corrects for "social disadvantage, but not for native, or inborn, disadvantage" unlike "socialist equality of opportunity" (Cohen, 2009, pp. 11–12).

My main case for the radicalness of liberal egalitarianism lies through the careful reinterpretations of the tradition's egalitarian ambitions which has rightly come into vogue in recent political philosophy. These include reinterpretations of the socialist sympathies of such quintessential liberals as Mill and Rawls. Here, I will focus on Rawls, who is the main target of Cohen's polemics.

Rawls' work has been interpreted, defended, and critiqued as an apologia for mid-century welfarism so often it is not surprising Cohen would read it as such. But as far back as the original edition of *Theory of Justice* Rawls suggested, this more moderate reading was problematic. He noted that a (social) democratic regime where "land and capital are widely though not presumable equally held" would be able to answer "many socialist criticisms of the market economy..." But he went on to argue it was "clear that, in theory anyway, a liberal socialist regime can also answer to the two principles of justice. We have only to suppose that the means of production are publicly owned and that firms are managed by worker's councils say, or by agents appointed by them. Collective decisions made democratically under the constitution determine the general features of the economy, such as the rate of saving and the proportion of society's production devoted to essential public goods" (Rawls, 2005, p. 280).

Rawls' argument for a more radical form of liberal egalitarianism by instituting a regime of property owning democracy or liberal socialism only became more pronounced over time. In his final work *Justice as Fairness; A Restatement,* Rawls argues that welfare state capitalism must be rejected because it does not secure the "fair value of the political liberties, and while it has some concern for equality of opportunity, the policies necessary to achieve that are not followed. It permits very large inequalities in the ownership of real property (productive assets and natural resources) so that the control of the economy and much of political life rests in a few hands." Here we also see how Cohen was wrong to accuse Rawls of accepting the "right wing" view of freedom wherein we must accept a trade-off between liberty and economic security for the poor. One of the key Rawlsian arguments for rejecting *welfare state capitalism* is precisely that it constrains the political liberties of the poor. Rawls goes on to argue that only a property owning democracy or liberal socialist regime could "satisfy the two principles of justice" (Rawls, 2001, pp. 137–138). Either would be more radically egalitarian than welfare state capitalism/social democracy. Because I am interested in defending a liberal socialist regime rather than property owning democracy against Cohen's objections to liberal egalitarianism, I will discuss Rawls approach to liberal socialism exclusively.[4]

Rawls wrote comparatively little about liberal socialism, though as mentioned he described it approvingly as far back as the original *Theory of Justice.* In *Justice as Fairness* Rawls argues that a liberal socialist regime would "set up a constitutional framework for democratic politics, guarantee the basic liberties with the fair value of the political liberties and fair equality of opportunity, and regulate economic and social inequalities by a principle of mutuality, if not by the difference principle." In contrast with state socialism "firms under liberal socialism carry on their activities within a system of free and workably competitive markets. Free choice of occupation is also assured" (Rawls, 2001, p. 138). By far, Rawls' most

[4] I follow Edmundson in thinking that ultimately, in a choice between property owning democracy and liberal socialism, Rawls own arguments push in favor of the latter. See Edmundson (2017).

suggestive discussion of liberal socialism occurs in the Marx sections of his *Lectures on the History of Political Philosophy* (where Rawls calls Marx a "heroic" figure amongst other compliments). Rawls rightly observed that "central command socialism" as reigned in the Soviet Union is discredited, but points out the "same is not true of liberal socialism. This illuminating and worthwhile view has four elements:

- A constitutional democratic political regime, with the fair value of the political liberties
- A system of free competitive markets, ensured by law as necessary
- A scheme of worker-owned business, or, in part, also public-owned through stock shares, and managed by elected of firm-chosen managers
- A property system establishing a widespread and more or less even distribution of the means of production and natural resources..." (Rawls, 2008, p. 323)

Taken together, we can see how a liberal socialist regime is far radical than Cohen sometimes suggests in his polemics against liberal egalitarianism. Firstly, liberal socialism ala Rawls is committed to what should be the most important form of equality for a Marxist; namely, a "more or less even distribution of the means of production and natural resources." Secondly, the "standard" view that Rawls is simply calling for taxation and redistribution is uncharitable. Liberal socialism would require the introduction of "worker-owned businesses" as a form of workplace democracy. Thirdly, Rawls is not committed to the "right wing" view of freedom while thinking some forms of market liberty can be traded off to secure economic security of the least well off. This understates the importance of the political liberties for Rawls, and their connection to inequitable distributions of economic power. Fair value of the political liberties requires going beyond welfare state capitalism. Fourthly, liberal socialism must secure "fair equality of opportunity" for all. Contra the sharp demarcation Cohen makes between "left-liberal" and "socialist" equality of opportunity this does involve correcting for "native disadvantage." Indeed, given the extraordinary extent to which nature endowments are a pure expression of moral arbitrariness, it would be strange if Rawls did not address them. In *Justice as Fairness* Rawls reiterates that *Theory* showed how we "do not deserve (in the sense of moral desert) our place in the distribution of native endowments." The difference principle "represents an agreement to regard the distribution of native endowments as a common asset." This does not mean that society owns individual's native endowments "taken separately" but instead the common asset is the "distribution of native endowments, the differences among persons." People are to be encouraged to develop whatever happens to be their nature endowments, if necessary through incentives, so as "to contribute to others' good as well as their own" (Rawls, 2001, p. 75).

3.3.2 Can Liberal Socialists Respond to Cohen's Objections?

To what extent could Rawlsian liberal socialism answer the force of Cohen's three objections to liberal egalitarianism raised in Part One?

Firstly, on the point about incentives and the morality of market systems more generally it is very clear that Cohen would be unwilling to budge. His argument has force in the sense that permitting inequalities to incentivize efforts, even if those work for the benefit of the least well off, should be highly problematic for egalitarians. It reifies as third-person economic laws what are in fact the results of individual first person decisions: namely a decision not to produce in the absence of advantageous incentives. But the force of Cohen's objection would be considerably blunted in a more democratic and solidaristic economic context. In a liberal socialist economic dominated by worker owned firms, individuals would neither be alienating their labor for capital or purely adopting an individualistically acquisitive rather than solidaristically egalitarian ethic. They would be producing for their own sake *and* those of their fellow workers in a cooperative setting where the free development of one is a precondition for the free development of all. Now as Rawls stresses, a market economy with worker owned firms-even one accompanied by a "more or less even" distribution of the means of production-would still be oriented by incentive structures. But it would be a form of market socialism rather than market capitalism.

Cohen himself was notably wary of such a possibility. He acknowledged that "market socialism is called 'socialist' because it abolishes the division between capital and labor" since there is "no class of capitalists facing workers who own no capital, since workers themselves, that is, the whole population, own the capital of firms…" However, Cohen goes on to note that in market socialism equality would remain "prejudiced because market competition leads to inequality between winners and losers." "Community" would also be prejudiced because "market exchange is no less market exchange than it is under capitalism." What Cohen calls "true" reciprocity cannot be achieved (Cohen, 2009, pp. 68–69). But one needn't have such an expansive "true" reciprocity to answer Cohen's objection that a hyper-emphasis on incentives concedes too much to the possessive acquisitiveness of bourgeois individualism. Reciprocity within the workplace of a democratically managed firm would still constitute a regular form of other-oriented activity in which our own success was bound up with that of our comrades. It aligns bourgeois self-interest with the call for socialist community in a way that is respectful of each, and above all achievable. This may not be full and "true" reciprocity of the utopian sort envisioned, but even Cohen acknowledges that such a market socialism "scores far better" by the standards of socialist justice that market capitalism (Cohen, 2009, p. 74). And such a liberal market socialism is entirely consistent with Rawlsian liberalism more generally.

Secondly, we will discuss the "basic structure" objection. The "basic structure" objection is an unusual one for Rawlsian liberal socialists to respond to for a variety of reasons. Perhaps the most unusual is that it demonstrates the true gap between Cohen's early work as an analytical Marxist and his mature period developing normative socialist philosophy. Explaining why will require a partial segue into talking about more meta-ethical considerations, so I request the readers patience. The payoff will be that my meta-ethical argument against Cohen's basic structure objection will segue into the more interesting argument about his freedom objection, which of course is where a lot of the real normative action is.

By the time of *Rescuing Justice and Equality* Cohen takes a truly stunning position (for a Marxist) of denying that principles are grounded in "facts of human nature and the human situation" (Cohen, 2008, p. 229). Indeed, Cohen goes so far as to agree with Plato that "justice is the self-same thing across, and independently of, history" (Cohen, 2008, p. 291). For the mature Cohen principles of justice are transhistorical, fact-insensitive, and apply to individual actions as well as the basic structure of society. This is a staggering position for a Marxist to take. Marx undoubtedly held the view that there were normative universals, but a core thesis of his Hegelian inspired system qua the *Critique of the Gotha Project* is that "right" can only be as high as the economic structure of society in a given historical epoch (Marx, 1994, p. 321). Cohen's Platonic and anti-historicist meta-ethics also looks strikingly less materialist than Rawls' insistence that "conceptions of justice must be justified by the conditions of our life as we know it or not at all" (Cohen, 2008, p. 229). Rawls holds that the social facts of a society at a given point in its history have bearing on which conception of justice can be adopted, including his own. Justice as fairness cannot simply be fitted to any society regardless of circumstance.

This bears heavily on the "basic structure" debate between Cohen and Rawlsian liberal socialism. In his *Lectures on the History of Moral Philosophy*, Rawls argues that that he followed Hegel in taking "the basic structure of society as the first subject of justice. People start as rooted in society and the first principles of justice they select are to apply to the basic structure" (Rawls, 2000, p. 366). This decision to take the basic structure as the first subject of justice is not just Hegelian but Marxist. For Marx, questions of moral duties to induce egalitarianism would seem painfully abstract next to the need to describe and critique the economic base and superstructure present at any given time. For Rawls, we must prioritize the application of principles of justice to the basic structure because individuals are "rooted" in society and any conception of justice likely to be stable and subject to overlapping consensus must be respectful of the social facts of the time. If a conception of justice instantiated in the basic structure is too far removed from the social facts at a time it will be unlikely to be accepted and stable over time, even if it would appealing to the transhistorical Platonic intellect.

As far as I know, Cohen never accounted for how this extraordinary shift towards a transhistorical, fact-insensitive, meta-ethics troubled his

Marxism. In later editions of *Karl Marx's Theory of History*, published close to *Rescuing Justice and Equality*, Cohen still tips his hat to the descriptive accuracy of historical materialism without acknowledging the disjunction it posed for the direction of his normative theorizing (Cohen, 2000a, 2000b). And of course he does not apply these meta-ethical considerations to his basic structure objection in the way I have. So on this point we're in the odd position where Rawls is much more faithful to Marx's materialism and historicism than the mature Cohen is. Ironically by insisting on a Platonic ideal indifferent to history and social facts Cohen emulates the utopian socialism Marx condemned, while Rawls' "realistic utopia" at least tries to be sensitive to the kinds of concerns raised by traditional Marxism. This is a heavy price for Cohen to pay, and not just in fidelity to what is best in Marx from a socialist standpoint. A political theory which becomes so abstracted from the materiality of social life runs the risk of becoming a merely speculative project.

But a defender of Cohen might respond that I've missed the point about the basic structure objection. If its form deviates from Marx and Rawls more fact and history sensitive meta-ethics, then so much the worse for Marx and Rawls. What's important is the actual normative force of the basic structure objection. Why should we draw a clean normative line between the basic structure of society—whether in its Rawlsian forms as the state, the economy, civil society and the family or its Marxist forms as the economic base and legal/ideological superstructure—and more seemingly informal structures which can just as "profoundly affect people's life chances…" (Cohen, 2008, p. 137). Haven't feminists shown in their objections to Rawls (and for that matter Marx) that the personal should be the political the whole way down? And, qua Cohen, doesn't this mean that we shouldn't shunt egalitarian concerns to some arbitrarily defined basic structure, but instead also take them seriously at the individual level?

My response here bleeds into Cohen's third objection, which is concerned with the implications of his radical egalitarianism for liberal freedom. The price Cohen pays for his Platonizing move isn't just to meta-ethically sever his political philosophy from history and social facts.[5] It also comes at a high price to personal liberties. One of the costs in extending egalitarian principles from basic structure to individual actions is to raise potentially insolvable questions about how free one can be when the content of our choices is to be so circumscribed by an enormously demanding account of the egalitarian good. Rawls, and Rawlsian liberal socialists, focus on the basic structure for more than just meta-ethical reasons. Defining the basic structure is also a key task in delineating the space between the right and the good, and in so doing leaving individuals extensive space to pursue their life plans and interests in relative liberty. Liberty meaning non-coercion by the state of course, but also in the deeper sense of being able to formulate a life plan in line with one's conception of the good and execute it to the best of one's ability. Insisting that Platonic principles of justice extend beyond the basic structure to all individual actions would severely curtail that.[6] Indeed in a way Cohen himself struggled to live up to, as the title of *If You're An Egalitarian, How Come You're So Rich* indicates.

Now it is always available to the radical egalitarian socialist to baptise equality with such a weighty lexical priority that they can say "so much the worse then for liberal freedom." But beyond just being undesirable and ominous given the history of socialist authoritarian regimes, this option is not entirely available to Cohen if he wants to remain consistent. While equality is undoubtedly Cohen's most sacred principle, it is not the only one. His work is, as Vrousalis reminds us, multi-principled: equality is important, but so too is community, and of course liberty (Vrousalis, 2015). Some of Cohen's most well known writing is concerned to show how the commodification of life enacted under capitalism profoundly constrains freedom (Cohen, 2011). It is very unclear to me how such

[5] There is of course a further philosophical problem of how to reconcile liberty with a meta-ethics which is sensitive to social facts and history. This problem has haunted many versions of Hegelianism and Marxism, which critics point out always risk becoming deterministic. They also haunt Rawlsianism to a great degree, with many claiming Rawls' theory so emphasizes the external determinants of our lives to exonerate the least well off from moral responsibility for their plight that they virtually cease to be responsible agents. While all these questions are important I will not address them here.

[6] This is a problem that has haunted modern political and moral philosophy since at least when Kant declared that the free individual was to be an end in themselves, and then proceeded to show how a rational understanding of freedom would lead individuals to obey a peculiarly puritanical moral law.

a commitment to liberty can be meaningfully squared with a corresponding commitment to equality so demanding one's personal choice not work a job in the absence of higher compensation is taken to be a serious moral failing. This is true even if we are talking about uncoerced actions, since individuals choices are intended to be so highly determined by their egalitarian duties that the range of morally permissible decisions narrows very considerably. Indeed, Cohen's arguments border on the calls for a grim self-sacrificing altruism of the sort socialism's enemies have always accused it of.

By contrast, Rawlsian liberal socialism can adopt a pluralism of principled commitments to liberty, equality, and solidarity while specifying the relationship between them through a lexical ordering. These can then be applied to a basic structure which individuals endorse, beyond which they are left at liberty to pursue their vision of the good life in relative peace. What the contours of such a liberal socialist basic structure would look like I cannot say here, though I agree with Cohen that it would almost certainly have to be more expansive than those given by Rawls in order to meet important feminist objections.

This view is one that has long been shared by both liberal egalitarians and Marxists, and it is appealing. For instance, John Stuart Mill, who himself identified as a socialist, thought that a combination of respecting personal liberties and the development of human capacities through the institution of economic freedom would enable all individuals to flourish more effectively. They would also be able to more fully develop their individuality, becoming like a living tree that grew to its natural extent in conjunction with others. Marx felt that in a communist society the realm of necessity would be overcome, domination would cease, and the development of human powers would become an end in itself for the first time, since individuals would finally be free of the tyranny of economic necessity. Given a more equal distribution of goods they may well decide to spend some days hunting in the morning, fish in the afternoon, rear cattle in the evening and philosophize after dinner without needing to worry about whether their hunting, fishing, farming, or philosophizing is sufficiently conducive to broader egalitarian goals. From a liberal socialist standpoint, there must be limitations on the extent of our rightful duties, circumscribing them to the basic structure. A just society is one where there are limits to what justice demands of us.

3.3.3 The Appeals of Liberal Socialism

I think that Rawlsian-inspired liberal socialists can answer many of Cohen's objections. A transition to workplace democracy and market socialism would retain valuable incentive structures in an economic context which is far more reciprocal, egalitarian, and solidaristic. Applying the principles of justice primarily to an expanded basic structure is more meta-ethically faithful to the Marxist view that it is society that must fundamentally be changed to enable a more egalitarian society free of domination to emerge. It also permits a broader range of personal freedoms for individuals where they can choose to develop their human capacities without being unduly burdened by duties of egalitarian right. This of course reflects a left-liberal view that granting individuals personal liberties to pursue their conception of the good life, or in Rawlsian terms to follow the Aristotelean principle of self-expressing through the exercise of their realized capacities, is a valuable pursuit (Rawls, 1999a, b, pp. 372–380).

Where liberal socialism doesn't comprehensively answer Cohen's objections, it isn't clear to me that we should side with him for two reasons. The first is the very strident utopianism demonstrated in the mature Cohen's work, with its references to transhistorical Platonic justice and insistence that "true" reciprocity cannot be achieved even in a system that does much better than contemporary capitalism. The second is that Cohen himself concedes that he does not have a superior alternative ready to hand. In *Why Not Socialism?* Cohen acknowledges that he does not "know, speaking more generally, whether the full socialist ideal is feasible" and that we "socialists don't now know how to replicate camping trip procedures on a nationwide scale, amid the complexity and variety that comes with nationwide size. We don't now know how to give collective ownership and equality the real meaning that it has in the camping trip story but which it didn't have in the Soviet Union and similarly ordered states" (Cohen, 2009, pp. 75–76). I would add it is unlikely that we will learn how to do these things if we move to the kind of radically transhistorical meta-ethics Cohen does, since my own preference is we should be Marxist enough to enable room for social facts to be suasive of our principles and praxis. Though of course if we do so learn that would count as a very significant point in favor of moving from a more realistic liberal socialism to a purer version of Cohen's radical democratic socialism.

3.4 Part Three: What Can Liberal Socialists Learn From Cohen?

3.4.1 Recovering Analytical Marxism

The question then becomes what do contemporary Rawlsian liberal socialists have to learn from Cohen's work? Obviously I think an enormous amount in normative theory; not least how to engage in a longstanding and rich debate between alternative positions. Very few interlocutors were as skilled at getting to the heart of a disagreement as Cohen. But in this closing section, I'd like to reverse engineer Cohen's debate with liberal egalitarianism and Rawlsian liberal socialism by saying it is actually his earlier work on analytical Marxism that is of most relevance. This is because analytical Marxism offers a richer account of history, society, and above all power and domination than what is normally found in the writings of liberal egalitarians, including Rawls.

Liberal egalitarianism is a rich tradition in political philosophy, but it has been enormously handicapped by a failure to develop a sophisticated theory of history and power that goes much beyond what is found in the classical liberals. As Tony Smith points out, we need to tread cautiously here since liberal egalitarians are typically aware of the way society shapes individual life outcomes, and do take seriously the integration of economic and political power in a way classical liberal rarely do (Smith, 2017 and Anderson, 2017). The social ontology of liberal egalitarians is more advanced in this respect than that of the classical liberals in the heyday of possessive individualism, as is their appreciation for the various forms that power and domination can take (Macpherson,

1962). But liberal egalitarian insights into this social ontology have never been adequately systematized; indeed, until recently they rarely rose above intuitions like Rawls' that inequities in economic power must lead to unfair value of the political liberties for those who are less affluent (Anderson, 2023). Sheldon Wolin is no doubt right to chastise Rawls, and liberal egalitarians generally, for superficiality on these issues.

"…Reluctance to undertake the political analyses necessary to demonstrate that justice is an urgent matter is the direct consequence of its failure to offer a coherent theory of power. Rawls's political world is all rules, law, and principles, never (in his words) 'mere politics.' Especially striking is his failure to comprehend that an 'advanced' economic is both an internal structure of power and influence and an external one affecting not only domestic but also foreign and military policies. Rather Rawlsian justice prefers a setting undisfigured by the power formations represented in domestic concentrations of economic power and wealth, corporate globalization, and Superpower" (Wolin, 2016, p. 533).

This is where Cohen's analytical Marxism can be of great value to Rawlsian liberal socialists. Cohen's epic book *Karl Marx's Theory of History* is a rich mine of insights into the nature of power in a historically contingent capitalist society, whose style of argumentation and lucidity makes it uniquely well equipped to inspire deeper theorization on these issues by liberal egalitarians. Of particular note are two core analyses from the book.

The first is Cohen's unusually clear discussion of commodity fetishism and its importance for Marx's understanding of capitalist society as a whole. It has too rarely been acknowledged that Marx's core project was a "critique" of political economy, in the German idealist sense. Marxism was not intended to supplant bourgeois economics, but to demonstrate how the modes of cognition through which it apprehended the world emerged historically. These modes of cognition enter into a recursive relationship with practice, as individuals come to perceive the social world through the categories of bourgeois thought, act upon those categories, and so in turn legitimate their epistemic plausibility as an explanation for the makeup of the social world. Marx's point was not that bourgeois economic categories are wrong, since when individuals act upon things like price mechanisms in a capitalist society they are indeed acting rationally given the arrangement of contemporary material circumstances. The key mistake lies in ascribing a metaphysical, transhistorical necessity to either the categories of bourgeois economics or the society they are meant to describe.

We are in fact free to think and act in other ways, though conditions must be ripe to do so. But this freedom is occluded by the forms of fetishism and alienation that emerge within capitalism, which Cohen powerfully describes in *Karl Marx's Theory of History.* Cohen points out how the "social form is thus alienated from the productive content, and it dominates it. Social relations between things assert themselves against material relations between persons who lack direct social relations…Men do not recognize their own authorship of the value through which alone they relate, and which therefore regulates their lives as producers. They are thus in a quite specific sense alienated from their own power, which has passed into things" (Cohen, 2000a, 2000b, p. 120). This awareness of how human powers become alienated and subdued through social relations which become domineering, and which our own categories of thought and action contribute to this unknowingly, is a key insight of the Marxist tradition which liberal egalitarians have too often simply ignored. It tells us a lot about why forms of domination persist even in contexts (like our own) where millions wish to overcome them, but don't know how to even recognize domination let alone how to think of a socialist alternative (Sypynowich, 1990).

Secondly, Cohen offers a very lucid take on the more transparent forms of domination that persist within the capitalist system and workplace in particular. That is, why it is that the working classes in capitalism are not free despite being legally at liberty to work for whomever they wish. As Cohen notes the "proletarian is constrained to offer his labour power not to any particular capitalist, but to some capitalist or other. If he wishes to survive, he must present himself on the labour market to the capitalist class, and he is forced to serve that class. This accords well with Marx's frequent statement that the proletarian is owned noy by any given capitalist, but by the capitalist class as a whole" (Cohen, 2000a, 2000b, p. 223). In his helpful discussion of analytical Marxism, Tom Mayer connects this situation to enabling exploitation in a capitalist economy, even linking it to the availability of leisure time for workers and capitalists. Some "people are able to work less precisely because other people…must work more" (Mayer, 1994, p. 61). Liberal egalitarians like Elizabeth Anderson are only recently beginning to make this case, as when she stresses how the workplace is akin to a kind of tyrannical "private government" where workers are often dominated in ways that rival domination by state actors. And while workers may be able to move from firm to firm, they are likely to encounter the same kind of domineering Bezoseque conditions everywhere (Anderson, 2017).

3.5 Conclusion

There are of course many other valuable insights in Cohen's analytical Marxism that might be of value to liberal socialists. This little section barely scratched the surface. I simply highlight these two observations in particular because they relate back to the most glaring gaps in liberal egalitarianism's take on power: its inability to understand how forms of domination can emerge from modes of cognition and practices that individuals instantiate and which crystalize into social relations which can be ascribed a necessity they do not warrant, and more straightforwardly how the working class remains unfree in a capitalist system where they must sell their labour power to one capitalist or another since the alternative is probably starvation. There is much more to be said.

My point in this essay has been to show that liberal socialism can live up to many of Cohen's aspirations, even if very imperfectly. Where it cannot its not clear to me that Cohen is right to demand more. But liberal socialists still have much to learn from Cohen, particularly on how to think through the forms of power and domination operative in capitalist society. We live in a world where the rule of capital is more ubiquitous, inequitable, and (given the state of the environment) threatening than ever before. Cohen believed that ordinary people deserved a better world. Liberal socialists think he's right.

References

Anderson, E. (2023). *Hijacked: How neoliberalism turned the work-ethic against workers and how workers can take it back*. Cambridge University Press.

Anderson, E. (2017). *Private government: How employers rule our lives (and why we don't talk about it*. Princeton University Press.

Cohen, G. A. (2000a). *If you're an egalitarian, how come you're so rich?* Harvard University Press.

Cohen, G. A. (2000b). *Karl Marx's theory of history—A defense* (Expanded). Princeton University Press.

Cohen, G. A. (2011). *On the currency of egalitarian justice and other essays in political philosophy*. Princeton University Press.

Cohen, G. A. (2008). *Rescuing justice and equality*. Harvard University Press.

Cohen, G. A. (1995). *Self-ownership, freedom, and equality*. Cambridge University Press.

Cohen, G. A. (2009). *Why not socialism?* Princeton University Press.

Dworkin, R. (2002). *Sovereign virtue: The theory and practice of equality*. Harvard University Press.

Edmundson, W. A. (2017). *John Rawls: Reticent socialist*. Cambridge University Press.

Macpherson, C. B. (1962). *The political theory of possessive individualism: Hobbes to Locke*. Oxford University Press.

Marx, K. (1994). In L. H. Simon (Ed.) *Selected writings*. Hackett Publishing.

Mayer, T. (1994). *Analytical marxism*. SAGE Publications.

Nussbaum, M. C. (2006). *Frontiers of justice: Disability, nationality, species membership*. Belknap Press of Harvard University Press.

Rawls, J. (1999a). In: S. Freeman (Ed.) *Collected papers*. Harvard University Press

Rawls, J. (1999b). *A theory of justice: Revised edition*. Harvard University Press.

Rawls, J. (2000). *Lectures on the history of moral philosophy*. Harvard University Press.

Rawls, J. (2001). *Justice as fairness: A restatement*. The Belknap Press of Harvard University Press.

Rawls, J. (2005). *A theory of justice: Original edition*. Harvard University Press.

Rawls, J. (2008). *Lectures on the history of political philosophy*. The Belknap Press of Harvard University Press.

Smith, T. (2017). *Beyond liberal egalitarianism: Marx and normative social theory in the twenty-first century*. Haymarket Books.

Spynowich, C. (1990). *The concept of socialist law: First edition.* Clarendon Press of Oxford University Press.

Vrousalis, N. (2015). *The political philosophy of G.A. Cohen: Back to socialist basics.* Bloomsbury Academic.

Wolin, S. (2016). *Politics and vision. Continuity and innovation in western political thought-expanded edition.* Princeton University Press.

4

The Scope of Justice: Cohen's Challenge to Rawlsian Liberalism

Michael Law-Smith

"If, as I now believe, how selfish people are affects the prospects for equality and justice, then that is partly because, as I now also believe, justice cannot be a matter only of the state-legislated structure in which people act but is also a matter of the acts they choose within that structure, the personal choices of their daily lives. I have come to think, in the words of a recently familiar slogan, that the personal is political."

G.A. Cohen, If You're an Egalitarian, How Come You're So Rich? (Cohen, 2002, p. 122)

M. Law-Smith (✉)
Department of Philosophy and Faculty of Law, University of Toronto, Toronto, Canada
e-mail: michael.lawsmith@mail.utoronto.ca

B. Burgis and M. McManus (eds.), *Analytical Marxism and Democratic Socialism in the 21st Century*, Palgrave Studies in Classical Liberalism,
https://doi.org/10.1007/978-3-032-02894-5_4

4.1 Introduction

In this chapter, I explore G.A. Cohen's famous challenge to John Rawls's theory of justice. Rawls was the most influential Anglo-American political philosopher of the twentieth century. And Cohen was one of his most influential critics. Rawls set the terms for many of the major debates in analytic political philosophy for the last fifty years, especially on questions of distributive justice and equality. Cohen made profound contributions to these debates. These debates evolved in response to Rawls's groundbreaking 1971 book *A Theory of Justice* (Rawls, 1971). A self-proclaimed champion of what he would later come to call "political liberalism," Rawls was challenged from both the left and the right (Rawls, 1993). From the right, Rawls was challenged by libertarians, most notably by Robert Nozick (Nozick, 1974). From the left, he was challenged by socialists and egalitarians, most notably by Cohen.

Cohen developed his challenge to Rawls over three decades, beginning with early lectures such as *Incentives, Inequality, and Community* (1992), through articles like "The Pareto Argument for Inequality" (1995) and "Where the Action Is: On the Site of Distributive Justice" (1997) and culminating in his book-length treatment of Rawls in *Rescuing Justice and Equality* (2008). At the heart of Cohen's challenge is his claim that Rawls construes the scope of political justice too narrowly. Cohen argued that by limiting the application of the principles of distributive justice to the basic structure of society, Rawls's theory permits inequality-generating personal decisions that compromise justice. In Cohen's view, the principles of justice must apply not only to institutions, but also to the decisions individuals make within those institutions. That is, Cohen held that the principles of justice must inform and guide everyday personal choices in addition to society's basic economic and legal institutions. Justice, Cohen concluded, requires that people act from an ethos of egalitarian justice in their personal lives.

While Cohen formulated this challenge in various ways over the years, I focus here on the version framed in terms of the scope of justice—that is, in terms of whether and to what extent the principles of justice apply beyond state institutions. It's worth noting at the outset, however, that although Cohen was unwavering in his criticism of this aspect of Rawls's theory of justice, he held Rawls's work in the highest regard. Cohen described Rawls's *A Theory of Justice* as one of the three greatest works in the history of Western political philosophy, alongside Plato's *Republic* and Hobbes's *Leviathan* (Cohen, 2008, p. 11). Moreover, as we will see, the difference between Rawls and Cohen's substantive visions of the just society is smaller than Cohen's critical stance might initially suggest.

In reconstructing Cohen's challenge to Rawls, I hope to bring out some themes in Cohen's work and the broader analytical Marxist movement of which he was a pioneering member. Perhaps most obviously, the substance of Cohen's challenge shows the extent to which he departed from Marxist orthodoxy by embracing robust normative theory. Cohen not only dismissed a strict focus on the norms governing the institutions and structure of society, but he waded even deeper into individualist and moralist waters than most contemporary political theorists by emphasizing the significance of personal choices for social justice. Another theme is that although Cohen was notable for conceptualizing justice and equality in largely distributive terms, his challenge to Rawls appears to appeal to a kind of principle of relational equality. These threads and others discussed in this chapter help clarify but by no means resolve Cohen's complicated relationship to liberal thought.

I develop these ideas over four sections. In the first part, I briefly sketch Rawls's theory, focusing on his claim that the principles of political justice apply to the basic structure of society. In the second part, I present Cohen's core challenge to Rawls concerning whether the principles of justice should also apply to personal choices. In the third part, I consider an initial response to Cohen's challenge, which questions whether his own position provides a plausible account of the scope of political justice. Finally, in the fourth part, I consider a second response, which asks whether Cohen overstated the difference between his own views and Rawls's and, in doing so, overstated the difference between socialist and liberal egalitarianism.

4.2 Rawls's Theory of Justice

Rawls characterized his theory of justice as "justice as fairness" (Rawls, 2001). The theory aims to describe the principles of justice for a society understood as a fair system of cooperation among free and equal persons. A distinct feature of Rawls's theory is that it takes "the basic structure of society" to be "the primary subject of political justice" (Rawls, 1971, p. 3; 2001, p. 10). The basic structure of society is its main social and political institutions, including its major legal and economic arrangements. Together, these institutions make up a social scheme which specifies fundamental rights and duties and distributes benefits and burdens arising from social cooperation. While Rawls did not provide an exhaustive list of such institutions, he mentions examples such as the constitution, the judiciary, the structure of the economy, the system of ownership and property, and the family. According to Rawls's theory, whether a society is just depends on whether its basic structure is regulated by the principles of justice.

Rawls gave two main reasons for prioritizing the basic structure (Rawls, 1971, p. 7; see also Scheffler, 2006, pp. 104-06; Hodgson, 2012). The first is that it has profound and pervasive effects on people's lives. Society's main institutions shape a person's life prospects, opportunities, aims, and expectations from the beginning of their life. They have a strong influence on a person's desires and aspirations, and even their sense of justice. These institutions can also create significant inequalities among people. Specifically, they can produce inequalities depending on how they interact with contingent features of a person's life, such as their good or bad luck. For Rawls, the first task of the principles of justice is therefore to regulate such institutions to eliminate unfair inequalities (Rawls, 1971, p. 7).

The second reason Rawls gave for why the basic structure is the primary subject of justice is that social and economic institutions function over time to maintain the conditions of background justice. If the basic structure is properly regulated by the principles of justice, then we can "regard distributive justice as a case of pure background procedural justice" (Rawls, 2001, p. 54). In other words, rather than looking to whether a specific transaction between persons is intrinsically fair, we can look instead to whether that transaction was created under just institutions and background conditions. This feature of the framework enables people to be free to advance their chosen ends within the limits set by the basic structure.

It follows that under Rawls's framework there is an "institutional division of labor" between the principles that govern the basic structure and those that apply directly to individuals and associations acting under that structure (Ibid.). Rawls explained that justice as fairness is a "special case of the problem of justice" and not a general or all-encompassing conception of justice (Rawls, 1971, p. 7; 2001, p. 11). Accordingly, we should not assume that the principles of justice appropriate to the institutional structure of society are the same principles that should directly govern the choices of individuals. While the principles of justice may shape and limit personal choices within the basic structure, they do not directly regulate such choices.

Getting to the heart of Rawls's theory, Rawls held that two principles of justice must govern the basic structure:

1. Each person has the same indefeasible claim to a fully adequate scheme of equal basic liberties, which scheme is compatible with the same scheme of liberties for all; and
2. Social and economic inequalities are to satisfy two conditions: first, they are to be attached to offices and positions open to all under conditions of fair equality of opportunity; and second, they are to be to the greatest benefit of the least-advantaged members of society.[1]

Rawls explained that these principles and sub-principles are ordered in terms of priority in the sense that the first must be fully met before the second applies. The first principle requires that institutions provide all members of society with full and equal rights and liberties. The first part of the second principle requires substantively fair equality of opportunity—not merely formal equality of opportunity. As Rawls put it, "those who have the same level of talent and abilities and the same willingness

[1] This is Rawls's revised statement of the principles. See Rawls (2001, pp. 42–43). For Rawls's earlier version of the principles, see Rawls (1971, p. 53).

to use these gifts should have the same prospects of success regardless of their social class of origin" (Rawls, 2001, p. 44). Finally, the second part of the second principle, known as "the difference principle," requires that any inequalities a society's basic institutions permit must be to the advantage of the least-advantaged members of society. The difference principle and its application are the main target of Cohen's challenge.

4.3 Cohen's Challenge to Rawls

Cohen's challenge focuses on the inequality-generating incentives permitted by Rawls's theory. At times, Cohen framed his argument as a direct objection.[2] Other times, he framed it as resolving an ambiguity in Rawls's theory or as providing a more consistent interpretation of the theory than Rawls provided himself.[3] In either case, Cohen argued that if the difference principle is limited to society's basic institutions and not also applied to personal economic decisions, then Rawls's framework will permit inequality-generating incentive payments that undermine justice.

To see how this argument works, we should start with how the difference principle permits inequality-generating incentives in the first place. Recall that the difference principle says that inequalities are justified only so far as they make the worst off as well off as possible. This means that an institution that distributes resources between persons unequally is presumptively unjust. For an unequal distribution to be justified, the inequality must be to be to the advantage of the least advantaged. Consider, for example, how unequal salaries might sometimes be to the benefit of those with the lowest salaries. Suppose it's necessary to pay certain socially useful professions, like doctors and engineers, higher salaries to incentivize people to invest in the long years of education and low-paid training these jobs require. If so, then these higher salaries might be to the benefit of everybody, including the least advantaged members of society, because it's better for them to live in a society with enough doctors and engineers than to live in a society

---

[2] See e.g., Cohen (2008, p. 19).

[3] See e.g. Cohen (2002, pp. 136–37; 2008, p. 68).

without doctors and engineers. The difference principle may be consistent with this inequality because the incentive of higher pay is to the advantage of those paid much less.

Cohen observed, however, that although Rawls suggested that such inequalities would be justified by the need to provide compensation for the long period of education and training, this inequality would also be justified under the difference principle if doctors and engineers were simply selfish and demanded to be paid more than others (Cohen, 2008, pp. 32–33). If the talented selfishly refuse to work unless they are paid more, the difference principle still seems to permit accommodating their demands so long as paying the higher salary is better for the worst off than not having those professions at all. Yet such incentives are clearly only "necessary" insofar as the talented selfishly demand them. In other words, the difference principle appears to allow talented individuals—i.e. those who are in positions to significantly benefit the worst off—to hold their talents "hostage" (Cohen, 1992, p. 305). Cohen concluded that this result is surely inconsistent with the ideal of just society.

Here's an example to illustrate Cohen's point. In the film *La grande séduction*, a rural fishing village in northern Quebec is badly in need of a resident doctor. The village is economically depressed, with nearly all its residents living off welfare payments. However, a manufacturing company is considering building a new factory near the village, promising job opportunities to many of the villagers. The difficulty is the company requires a resident doctor in the village before building the factory. The villagers concoct an elaborate and comedic scheme to seduce a doctor from Montreal to move to the village.

Suppose, though, that instead of seducing the doctor by deceiving him into believing the villagers shared his interest in cricket and jazz, the villagers had instead petitioned the government to pay him a much higher salary than he received in Montreal. Perhaps the villagers even agreed to raise their taxes to cover the doctor's higher salary. And suppose, too, that the doctor realized his fortunate bargaining position and decided to exploit the village's desperation. In this alternative plot, we can imagine that the doctor would be content to work in this village for a modest salary raise but nonetheless demands an exorbitant raise. This higher salary would, of course, further increase the economic inequality between the doctor and the other villagers than if he had accepted the lower salary. But the inequality may still be justified under the difference principle so long as paying the doctor the higher salary is still better for the villagers than not having a doctor at all.

This example is meant to show Cohen's point that some inequality-producing incentives are only required because the talented selfishly demand them. Since the talented might have agreed to do the work for a lower incentive, these demands create greater inequalities than are strictly necessary and leave the least advantaged worse off than had the talented not demanded the incentives. Cohen's point is that the unequal distribution of resources resulting from such market-maximizing behaviour seems plainly unjust. Yet if Rawls's principles of justice are confined to the institutions that make up the basic structure of society, then such inequalities are permitted. So, Cohen concluded that the principles of justice must apply not only at the level of institutional design but also at the level of personal choice. The choice to demand the extra incentive could not be justified under the difference principle, and therefore would be precluded by an account of justice that includes such behaviour within its scope.

Cohen supported this conclusion by asking whether the talented who leverage their position by demanding the extra incentive could justify their demand to the worst off in their community (Cohen, 2008, pp. 35–47). Cohen called this the "Interpersonal Test." The idea here is that a principle of justice should be able to serve as a justification when uttered from one member of society to another. The inequality-generating incentive described in the case above could not pass this test. That's because the doctor could not justify his demand for the extra-high salary to the poor villagers. The higher salary might be justified in an impersonal sense: given the fact of the demand, it may be all-things-considered better for the villagers to give more in taxes to pay the higher salary. But this argument is entirely unpersuasive if offered by the doctor himself. Like a kidnapper who demands a ransom in exchange for the release of a hostage, the talented person who selfishly withholds their labor for a greater payout has created the fact which makes the impersonal argument possible. And the creation of that fact—either the taking of the hostage or withholding one's labour for selfish reasons—cannot serve as a justification to those with whom one purports to share a normative community.

To remedy this shortcoming of Rawls's theory, Cohen argued that justice requires an egalitarian ethos of justice in society (Cohen, 2002, p. 128; Cohen, 2008, p. 123). Citizens must share an ethos under which the principles of equality and justice inform their personal decisions. With this, Cohen therefore rejected Rawls's division of labor between institutions and individuals.[4] This shared commitment to equality and justice is described as an "ethos" because it's not a matter of state legislated coercive rules. Nor is it a matter of people mechanically applying principles of justice in their decision-making process. Rather, it's the idea that in a just society people will be personally committed to justice and equality in such a way that they will naturally act with respect for such principles in everyday life (Cohen, 1992, p. 384). Members of a political community who share this ethos would not selfishly demand more when doing so is not strictly necessary and would further increase social and economic inequality. Accordingly, a society that exhibits Cohen's more expansive conception of justice would not have the kind of unjustified inequalities that Rawls's more narrow conception of justice permits.

In developing this challenge, Cohen took himself to be endorsing Marx's claim that emancipation requires the realization of political principles in everyday life:

> "Human emancipation will only be complete when the real, individual man has absorbed into himself the abstract citizen; when as an individual man, in his everyday life, in his work, and in his relationships, he has become a *species-being*; and when he has recognized and organized his own powers *(forces propres)* as *social powers* so that he no longer separates this social power from himself as *political* power" (Marx, 1843, p. 46).[5]

Marx wrote these words in the context of criticizing liberalism. The criticism is that by excluding certain spheres of life from political scrutiny, liberalism permits forms of egoistic behavior within those spheres that

[4] For a related but distinct argument that the same normative principles apply to both institutions and persons acting under those institutions, see Murphy (1998).

[5] See also Cohen (2008, p. 1).

undermine political emancipation.[6] Cohen's challenge to Rawlsian liberalism elaborated on this idea to argue that everyday decisions can affect distributive justice, and thus that the principles of distributive justice cannot be limited to institutions alone (Cohen, 2002, p. 131).

4.4 Cohen's Own Dilemma

There are two main lines of response to Cohen's challenge. The first, considered in this section, focuses on the seemingly implausible implications of Cohen's own position as to the scope of justice. The second, taken up in the next section, focuses on whether Cohen underestimates the resources within Rawls's theory to preclude the kinds of inequalities to which Cohen objects.

The first response effectively turns Cohen's challenge on its head: in criticizing Rawls for defining the scope of justice too narrowly, Cohen may have defined it too broadly (see Estlund, 1998; Williams, 1998; Daniels, 2002; Baynes, 2006; Smith, 2006; Thomas, 2011). To see the merits of this response, notice that Cohen's claim that the principles of justice must apply to personal choices must mean they apply to a person's motivation for their choice. It's not enough for the principles to apply to the consequences of their choice because we do not know whether the doctor who demands an extra incentive to work in a rural community creates an unjustified inequality unless we know why they demand the extra incentive. The unequal effects of the doctor's choice may satisfy the difference principle if the inequality is to the benefit of the worst off. But the motivation for the decision will not satisfy the difference principle if the demand is merely an attempt to leverage their position for self-interested reasons.

Before teasing out this response, it's worth noting two features of Cohen's challenge here. First, Cohen embraced not merely a normative but something of a moralist conception of social justice. As others have pointed out, there's a certain irony in the fact that Cohen, the analytic

6 See Estlund (1998, p. 99).

Marxist, criticized Rawls, the liberal, for focusing too much on the structure of society rather than the motivations behind individual choices (Thomas, 2011). While analytic Marxism famously diverges from traditional Marxism by explicitly engaging in normative theory, Cohen goes even further by locating justice partly in the intentions behind personal behavior. Second, Cohen's position stands in tension with Marx's famous statement that the point of philosophy is not merely to understand the world but to change it (Marx, 1845, p. 145). Ultimately, Cohen claimed that although personal choices are within the scope of justice they are beyond the reach of coercive state or social mechanisms. He thus seemed content to point out a problem without offering a solution. This is no accidental feature of Cohen's approach, given that he wrote that "the question for political philosophy is not what we should do but what we should think, even when what we should think makes no practical difference" (Cohen, 2008, p. 268).

Back to the response. If, in Cohen's view, the principles of justice must in some sense apply to the motivations of individual persons in everyday life, then the question arises as to whether his position is overly demanding. Taken on its face, one might worry that this view implies a draconian society in which every personal decision is subject to coercive oversight. But, as mentioned, Cohen resisted this conclusion. He did so, in part, by walking back the demands of justice on personal choices. From his early formulations of the challenge, Cohen emphasized that a just and egalitarian society does not require "extreme moral rigor" on the part of citizens, and he accepted that "every person has a right to pursue self-interest to some reasonable extent (even when that makes things worse than they need be for badly off people)" (Cohen, 1992, p. 302). Cohen granted that people have a "legitimate personal prerogative" and insisted that citizens should not to be "slaves to social justice" with respect to their "legally unconstrained choices" (Cohen, 2008, p. 10). He did not, however, explain the limits to the "personal prerogative" or what counts as a "reasonable extent" of self-interest. Nor did he specify exactly how the principles of justice apply to individual choices, beyond comments like that "the individual who affirms the difference principle must have some regard to it in his economic choices" (Ibid; Cohen, 2002, p. 122).

So how demanding is the egalitarian ethos? Cohen said that the egalitarian ethos must "guide" or "direct" or "inform" personal choices (Cohen, 2008, pp. 123–124). At other times, he said that in a society with an egalitarian ethos, citizens will "affirm" or be "committed" to the principles of justice in their everyday life (Ibid. p. 32). Perhaps Cohen's clearest statement on the matter:

> "It is not true that, in the society I have in mind, a person would have to worry about unfortunate people every time he made an economic decision. Liberals would regard that as oppressive, and, whether or not they are right, one function of the egalitarian ethos is to make conscious focus on the worst off unnecessary. What rather happens is that people internalize, and—in the normal case—they unreflectively live by, principles which restrain the pursuit of self-interest" (Cohen, 1992, p. 384).

This appeal to internalized norms of justice avoids the worry about external enforcement or mechanical application. Still, Cohen gave little guidance as to how exactly such principles would figure in personal decision-making or how they would interact with the personal prerogative. Indeed, he admitted that it would be impossible to determine if people were motivated by the rules of justice, and "it would severely compromise liberty if people were required forever to consult such rules" (Cohen, 2008, p. 123). All said, Cohen accepted a "modest right of self-interest" that permits individuals to give greater weight to their own interests to some degree, but insisted that this right would not result in serious inequalities (Cohen, 1992, pp. 302–303). Cohen did not take himself to have the burden of specifying how the principles apply at the personal level because if he has shown that the principles apply at all at the personal level, then he has shown that they apply beyond the basic structure (Cohen, 2008, p. 10). Yet, for his critics, the details of how the principles would apply to personal choices are critical to assessing whether they legitimately do. Cohen's position might only avoid the charge that it's overly demanding at the price of transparency.

Another difficulty for specifying Cohen's position arises from examples of inequality-generating choices that are not directly captured by his challenge against self-interested market maximizers.[7] Consider choices motivated by affection. People often act to benefit their loved ones in inequality-generating ways. Parents care for and materially support their own children but not other people's children. Or consider choices motivated by a sense of moral obligation. If I borrow and damage your expensive guitar, it's uncontroversial that I have a moral obligation to compensate you for the damage. But, if all my economic decisions are to be informed by the difference principle, should I instead give the money I owe you to a local welfare program? Similar questions arise for decisions that are virtuous but do not minimize inequality as much as possible. Must the corporate lawyer who spends one day a week volunteering at a soup kitchen instead spend that time working extra hours and donating the extra income to the least well off? It seems such choices should be permitted in a just society, yet it's not clear that they are consistent with Cohen's view that principles of distributive justice must guide personal choices.

One response to this objection might be to note that although some inequality-producing choices may be consistent with justice, others are not. Consider wealthy parents who evade inheritance taxes to gift their children millions of dollars. Such behavior may be motivated by affection, but Cohen can maintain it compromises distributive justice. Or consider wealthy alumni who make huge donations to the elite private universities they attended. Cohen could reasonably ask whether that's just given that donating that money to less wealthy schools could improve the position of the least well-off in society much more. In other words, Cohen can hold true to his conviction that society would be more just if these wealthy parents and donors had a stronger internal commitment to egalitarian justice.

Although Cohen did not offer a detailed account of how principles of justice should constrain personal decisions, he could perhaps have done so by appealing again to his idea of the Interpersonal Test. The Interpersonal Test is part of Cohen's broader idea of a "justificatory community," in which citizens can justify their behavior to each other in terms that

[7] See Estlund (1998, p. 101).

pass the test (Cohen, 2008, pp. 43–44). One could draw on this framework to say that while the principles of distributive justice do not dictate personal choices, individuals must be capable of justifying their inequality-producing choices to other citizens. This framework could rule out purely self-interested demands for incentives, while making room for moderate self-interest and other normative reasons to justify a decision. One could even go so far as draw on other ideas in Rawls's political philosophy, such as the idea of reasonable pluralism among citizens or the idea of public reason, to fill out what counts as a justifiable choice (Rawls, 2001, pp. 33–34, 89–93). Under this framework, one could show that in a just society citizens will be concerned with social justice in everyday life even if not controlled by its demands (Estlund, 1998, p. 112).

Interestingly, this line of thought reveals a relational dimension to Cohen's challenge, despite it being framed in distributive terms. Relational egalitarians say that the unjust form of inequality we should care about in society is not unequal distributions as such, but rather unequal relations among citizens (Anderson, 1999, 2010). The Interpersonal Test invokes the idea that justice concerns the terms on which citizens relate to one another. The focus on justification rather than bare distribution points toward thinking of equality and justice in relational terms. It focuses, that is, on whether citizens can look each other in the eye as equals when they are making inequality-generating personal decisions (see Pettit, 2012, p. 84). As Cohen writes, defending inequality on the basis of incentives (as Rawls does):

> "... presupposes a model of society as a noncommunity, in which relations among human beings are construed as strategic, with people taking one another into account as so many opportunities for, and obstacles to, gain, rather than as fellow citizens by whom they can be asked to justify the way they live" (Cohen, 2008, p. 15).

Whether or not Cohen has the resources to specify how the principles of justice apply to individual decisions, his position faces another objection. As Cohen acknowledged, the complexity of the ethical motivations and prerogatives that may underlie a demand for an incentive means it will be difficult if not impossible to know whether a given demand compromises justice.[8] Yet many political theorists argue that justice includes a "publicity" requirement: we should be able to evaluate whether a given decision or transaction is just or not (Williams, 1998). If the motivations informing personal decisions are not public information and cannot be subject to public scrutiny in the way public institutions are, then perhaps they do not fall within the scope of political justice. Cohen ultimately accepted that the egalitarian ethos is inconsistent with publicity but denied that publicity is a requirement of justice (Cohen, 2008, pp. 344–372). Cohen supported this view by appealing to other contexts, such as his favorite camping-trip example (Cohen, 2009), where he argued justice requires us each to do our part even if we cannot specify exactly what this means in the abstract. If that's right, then justice does not always require publicity in the precise sense this objection assumes.

We might question the extent to which the degree of publicity required for rules governing a camping trip provides an appropriate analogy for the requirements of publicity for social justice. This line of inquiry leads to broader questions about the extent to which camping trips and the like can supply the proper norms and organizational structure for society as a whole. Rather than following that line, I'd prefer to consider a different response to Cohen. This response looks not to Cohen's own commitments, but to the egalitarian and communitarian commitments inherent in Rawls's project.

4.5 Rethinking Rawls and the Liberal/Socialist Divide

The second response to Cohen's challenge is to argue that Rawls's theory of justice already contains the resources to accommodate Cohen's concerns. In other words, Rawls's theory, properly understood, does not permit the kind of inequality-generating choices that Cohen criticized. As noted earlier, Cohen himself occasionally framed his critique not as a rejection but as a clarification of Rawls's view. As one scholar of Cohen

[8] See Williams (1998).

puts it, "the bottom line of [Cohen's] critique is that an egalitarian ethos in citizens is a necessary condition for a just society *on Rawls' own terms*" (Vrousalis, 2015, p. 73). Another writes that "Cohen's critique identifies the most plausible version of Rawls's egalitarianism" (Thomas, 2011, p. 1099).

There are two main ways to motivate this response. The first is to highlight the importance of Rawls's first principle of justice for limiting inequality.[9] Recall that the first principle requires that all persons enjoy substantively equal access to the basic social, civic, and political liberties. Cohen arguably underappreciated the extent to which this requirement constraints serious distributive inequalities. The need for equal social and political power may prohibit incentives that generate substantial economic inequalities between citizens. Once again, we see how the objection to distributive inequalities can be framed as undermining relational equality between citizens.

The second way to motivate this response is to argue that something like an egalitarian ethos is already implicit in Rawls's theory of justice.[10] If this is correct, then a just basic structure of society would not be compatible with unrestrained egoistic behavior. Cohen's challenge would be answered. This reading is supported by Rawls's descriptions of the effects of just institutions. At one point, Rawls wrote that institutions must be designed "to foster the virtue of justice and discourage desires and aspirations incompatible with it" (Rawls, 1971, p. 231). In another place, he wrote that "the basic structure shapes the way the social system produces and reproduces over time a certain form of culture shared by persons with certain conceptions of their good" (Ibid, p. 269). If just institutions would shape people's internal sense of justice to the extent that they would "in everyday life … affirm and act from the first principles of justice," (Rawls, 1980, p. 521) then it seems an ethos of justice or equality is already part of the Rawlsian framework.

---

[9] For different versions of this argument, see Smith (2006), Estlund (1998), Van Parijs (2002), Tan (2004), Baynes (2006), Thomas (2011).

[10] For different versions of this argument, see Cohen (2001), Scheffler (2006), Thomas (2011, 2012).

This line of response invites a broader question: just how egalitarian was Rawls? Or, how far apart did Cohen's socialism and Rawls's liberalism really stand? Many writers have argued that Rawls's liberalism was more socialist than is often appreciated. Some have pointed to the radical implications of Rawls's recognition in his later works that his theory of justice cannot be realized under laissez-faire capitalism or welfare-state capitalism.[11] Rawls explained that only property-owning democracy or liberal socialism could satisfy the principles of justice.

Two recent works make this case in detail. Both focus on the egalitarian implications of Rawls's liberalism. The first is William Edmundson's *John Rawls: Reticent Socialist*, which makes the case that Rawls shifted to embrace a more socialist conception of liberalism in his later works (Edmundson, 2017). The second is Daniel Chandler's *Free and Equal: A Manifesto for a Just Society*, which provides a roadmap for putting Rawls's egalitarian ideas to work to help resolve some of the most significant social and economic issues of the twenty-first century (Chandler, 2024).

The growing recognition of Rawls's egalitarian commitments calls into question the depth of disagreement between him and Cohen over the scope of justice. Perhaps Cohen offers the most compelling interpretation of Rawls, rather than an alternative. This may help explain Cohen's telling remark that he would "neither disavow nor dislike" being described as a "left-Rawlsian" (Cohen, 2008, p. 12).

References

Anderson, E. (1999). What is the point of equality? *Ethics, 109*(2), 287–337.

Anderson, E. (2010). The fundamental disagreement between luck egalitarians and relational egalitarians. *Canadian Journal of Philosophy, 40*(sup1), 1–23.

Baynes, K. (2006). Ethos and institution: On the site of distributive justice. *Journal of Social Philosophy, 37*, 182–196.

Chandler, D. (2024). *Free and Equal: A manifesto for a just society*. Knopf Publishing.

[11] See also Thomas (2011).

Cohen, G. A. (1992). Incentives, inequality, and community. In G. B. Peterson (Ed.), *The Tanner lectures on human values.* (Vol. 13). University of Utah Press.

Cohen, G. A. (1995). The Pareto argument for inequality. *Social Philosophy and Policy, 12*(1), 160–185.

Cohen, G. A. (1997). Where the action is: On the site of distributive justice. *Philosophy & Public Affairs, 26*(1), 3–30.

Cohen, G. A. (2002). *If you're an egalitarian, How come you're so rich?* Harvard University Press.

Cohen, G. A. (2008). *Rescuing justice and equality*. Harvard University Press.

Cohen, G. A. (2009). *Why not socialism?* Princeton University Press.

Cohen, J. (2001). Taking people as they are? *Philosophy & Public Affairs, 30*(4), 363–386.

Daniels, N. (2002). Democratic equality: Rawls's complex egalitarianism. In S. Freeman (Ed.), *The Cambridge companion to Rawls* (pp. 241–276). Cambridge University Press.

Edmundson, W. A. (2017). *John Rawls: Reticent socialist*. Cambridge University Press.

Estlund, D. (1998). Liberalism, equality and fraternity in Cohen's critique of Rawls. *Journal of Political Philosophy, 6*.

Hodgson, L-P., "Why the basic structure?" *Canadian Journal of Philosophy* 42, no. 3/4 (2012): 303–34.

Marx, K. (1978). On the Jewish Question (1843). In R. C. Tucker (Ed.), *The Marx-Engels Reader* (2nd ed.). Norton.

Marx, K. (1845). Theses on Feuerbach. In *The Marx-Engels Reader*, 2nd ed.

Murphy, L. (1998). Institutions and the demands of justice. *Philosophy & Public Affairs, 27*(4), 251–291.

Nozick, R. (1974). *Anarchy, state, and Utopia*. Basic Books.

Pettit, P. (2012). *On the people's terms*. Cambridge University Press.

Rawls, J. (1980). Kantian constructivism in moral theory. *The Journal of Philosophy, 77*(9), 515–572.

Rawls, J. (1993). *Political liberalism.* Columbia University Press (expanded edition: 2005).

Rawls, J. (1971). *A theory of justice*. Belknap Press of Harvard University Press (revised edition: 1999).

Rawls, J. (2001). In E. Kelly (Ed.) *Justice as fairness: A restatement.* Harvard University Press.

Scheffler, S. (2006). Is the basic structure basic? In C. Sypnowich (Ed.), *The egalitarian conscience* (pp. 104–106). Oxford Univ. Press.

Smith, P. (2006). Incentives and justice: G.A. Cohen's egalitarian critique of Rawls. *Social Theory and Practice, 25*, 205–235.

Tan, K.-C. (2004). Justice and personal pursuits. *Journal of Philosophy, 101*, 331–362.

Thomas, A. (2011). Cohen's critique of Rawls: A double counting objection. *Mind, 120*(480), 1099–1141.

Thomas, A. (2012). Property-owning democracy, liberal republicanism, and the idea of an egalitarian ethos. In M. O'Neill & T. Williamson (Eds.), *Property-owning democracy*. Wiley-Blackwell.

Van Parijs, P. (2002). Difference principles. In S. Freeman (Ed.), *The Cambridge companion to Rawls* (pp. 200–240). Cambridge University Press.

Vrousalis, N. (2015). *The political philosophy of G.A. Cohen: Back to socialist basics*. Bloomsbury Academic.

Williams, A. (1998). Incentives, inequality, and publicity. *Philosophy & Public Affairs, 27*(3), 225–247.

5

Socialist Justice: Reflections on G.A. Cohen's Political Philosophy

Christine Sypnowich

'While Marx believed that capitalism was unjust, and that communism was just, he did not always realize that he had those beliefs.'
G.A. Cohen

5.1 Introduction

What is socialist justice? G.A. Cohen spent his philosophical career thinking about this question. Growing up in a working-class, Jewish communist community in Montreal, the radical beliefs about equality

I am grateful to Matt McManus and participants in the Centre for Studies in Social Justice seminar at Oxford University for helpful comments on an earlier version.

C. Sypnowich (✉)
Department of Philosophy, Queen's University, Kingston, Canada
e-mail: christine.sypnowich@queensu.ca

B. Burgis and M. McManus (eds.), *Analytical Marxism and Democratic Socialism in the 21st Century*, Palgrave Studies in Classical Liberalism,
https://doi.org/10.1007/978-3-032-02894-5_5

and freedom instilled in him at an early age shaped his outlook thereafter. Accordingly, as a political philosopher, it was the ideal of socialist justice that motivated his engagement with the canonical liberal writings that came to prominence during his career. This ideal motivated, for example, Cohen's argument that Robert Nozick's libertarianism was more interested in protecting property than liberty, or his position that John Rawls's liberal theory had too modest an understanding of equalizing wealth. In his writings on equality, Cohen provided trenchant analyses of mainstream liberal views, but he also ventured important arguments about the key constituents of an alternative, socialist conception of justice.

The path that Cohen took to thinking about socialist justice is an interesting one. Cohen's Marxist background informed his political philosophy, but at first, that background hampered it. Radical political convictions were central to who Cohen was and how he saw the world, but initially these convictions were kept separate from his professional life as a philosopher. For the young Jerry, the political was personal, not philosophical, to coin a phrase.[1] As far as he was concerned, the philosophical consisted in honing one's skills of rigorous argument—the tools of Oxford analytical philosophy—to address a range of non-socialist questions. The belief in a society where people enjoy full equality and relate to each other in a spirit of community never faltered, but therein lay the reason for the lack of appetite to study or interrogate them. Cohen often recalled how he came to undertake graduate studies in philosophy in Oxford 'already steeped in Marxism', and as a result, 'unlike most of my politically congenial contemporaries, I did not look to university philosophy to furnish me with ideas that matter' (Cohen, 1988a, p. xi). Thus, Cohen's early scholarship was outside of the realm of political theory and certainly didn't involve engaging with arguments for socialism.

Of course, Cohen came to change his mind on this, for a variety of reasons. The shift came first with Cohen's celebrated work on Marx (Cohen, 2000a), where he deployed the skills of analytical philosophy

[1] Indeed the original feminist slogan, 'the personal is political', as we will see, proved central to Cohen's critique of Rawls's theory justice. The status in Cohen's work of Rawls's famous claim, that 'justice is political not metaphysical', is more complex.

to make a plausible case for the 'scientific' doctrine of economic determinism and validate the historical materialist understanding of social change. This was not normative philosophy, but the project was clearly inflected by radical ideals, the urge to validate a progressive political view, and attracted like-minded scholars to form the 'Analytical Marxist' or as Cohen liked to call them, 'No-Bullshit Marxist' group who shared this outlook.

However, what truly made a radical engagement with normative philosophy possible for Cohen, paradoxically, was his disenchantment with historical materialism. By the 1980s, the era when rightwing politicians Thatcher and Reagan enjoyed significant popularity with the working class, Cohen concluded that the Marxist view of historical change was untenable. What he dubbed the 'obstetric' view of socialism, where the working class merely presided over the inevitable arrival of a new, emancipated society flew in the face of historical reality. Classical Marxist assumptions—such as that never-ending abundance would inevitably be produced by advanced economies, or that the working class had an unassailable role as an agent of social change—could no longer be sustained. Environmental crisis, and, with the rise of the New Right, right, the decline of working-class identification with radical politics, had made for a new sense of urgency about making a case for the path to socialist justice (Cohen, 2000b, pp. 75–77).

Cohen contended that in these new circumstances where one could not take for granted that 'history is on your side' (Rosen, 2010), it was the duty of radical philosophers to produce normative arguments for their ideals. What is liberty, or equality, and why should it be pursued? Note that not just any argument would do. It was crucial that the demanding standards of analytical philosophy, which Cohen had so thoroughly mastered in his Oxford studies, be brought to bear on this important task. Thus, Cohen's passion for socialist justice, at first a personal matter outside his professional career, prompted him to deploy his philosophical skills to questions of equality and freedom. The result was a corpus of exceptional insight, analytical acumen, and political significance.

Cohen was diffident about his contribution to political philosophy, saying that his work was largely interpretive, rather than original.[2] In print, he referred to himself as an 'interlocuteur valable' in the philosophical community catalysed by John Rawls's work (Cohen, 2008, p. 14). Some leftwing critics agreed with him, expressing impatience with Cohen's work on egalitarian justice, unkindly complaining that it amounted to 'mere footnotes to Rawls' (Sayers, 2000, p. 41). This assessment is certainly unfair. Nonetheless, although Cohen was a penetrating critic of liberal philosophies of justice, he did not develop a systematic account of socialist justice of his own. And thus, his understanding of socialist justice is best understood as a collection of ideas and arguments rather than a full-fledged doctrine or theory.

One explanation for this more piecemeal approach, perhaps, is that Cohen's political outlook inhibited him. After all, he had been confident that historical materialism provided the tools for a complete account of human society. By the time he came to doubt this, he was steeped in the tough-minded approach whereby political commitments are parsed into precise premises and conclusions and tested for their validity. Cohen noted how his approach—the product of his Oxford (rather than Harvard) education—involved interrogating normative judgements in particular cases, with the result that ethical commitments are defended in small steps (Cohen, 2008, pp. 3–4). They cannot be satisfied all the time, nor is there a systematic method to render them a complete theory. For Cohen, this was a virtue, but it was also, of course, a constraint. These methodological considerations, as well as his disenchantment with the grand theory of Marxism, probably convinced Cohen that a holistic theoretical system was unavailable and foolhardy to pursue (Sypnowich, 2024, pp. 170–1). But justice nonetheless cried out for philosophical, if piecemeal attention. We should not underestimate the originality and significance of the results.

The picture that emerges on Cohen conception of socialist justice is, on the one hand, inspiring and original, but also paradoxical and controversial. This essay draws on, and develops, the ideas in my recent book, G.A. Cohen: Liberty, Justice and Equality. In what follows, I consider

[2] Conversation with G.A. Cohen, March 2009.

the fascinating trajectories of Cohen's philosophical career, to focus on two dimensions of Cohen's ideal of socialist justice. First, I outline Cohen's nuanced and rich understanding of how justice, both substantive and procedural, is central to the socialist project. Second, I analyse the complex scope of Cohen's egalitarianism, which, I shall argue, transcends, but is also hampered by, the limitations of contemporary liberal egalitarianism.

5.2 Justice 'just is'

A prominent debate among left-wing philosophers in the 1970s and 1980s centred on whether the criteria of justice was even relevant for Marx's critique of capitalism. After all, as Cohen's canonical work on Marx made clear, the historical materialist view focused on the structures of capitalist society which carried within them the seeds of their own destruction. Marx understands capitalism in terms of a base and superstructure, where material phenomena, that is, economic forces and relations, are determining of non-material phenomena, that is politics, culture and law. Many interpreted this to mean that morality was a mere creature of the economic order it served and thus played no constitutive role in Marx's analysis. Allen Wood, for example, stressed the complex way in which Marx's condemnation of capitalism eschewed moral terms; for all the talk of workers' servitude, he argued, Marx's critique was not an ethical one, but rather rested on an account of the system's irrationality that would spell its own demise. According to the 'Tucker-Wood thesis', Marx's historical materialism ruled out assessing a social order with reference to normative criteria. In other words, one could not say that Marx thought capitalism unjust.[3]

Cohen was highly impatient with what he took to be the scholastic preoccupations on this matter. The question of whether Marx had any truck with rights, law, and indeed morality itself, was usefully dispatched with the statement, to quote the epitaph of this paper, 'while Marx

[3] Robert Tucker initiated this debate back in the 1960s; see Tucker (1964, p. 20) and Wood (2004, pp. 127–42); see also Lukes (1985).

believed that capitalism was unjust, and that communism was just, he did not always realize that he had those beliefs'.[4] Writing shortly after his celebrated canonical work on Marx, Cohen's response to the preoccupation with the socialist pedigree of justice-talk signaled an approach that would shape his work thereafter. Although critical of Marxism for its 'venerable, deep, and disastrously illuded self-conception', Cohen offered by way of explanation that Marxism deemed socialism inevitable, yes, but also morally right. For example, exploitation, where the worker is 'robbed' of his product, must be understood as a species of injustice for Marx, as well as a part of the historical materialist story that exploitation would inevitably be replaced by non-exploitative communist relations of production.[5] Indeed, what else could be at issue in the dispute between Marxists and defenders of capitalism, if not justice? Cohen's conclusion that the Marxist account of social change was no longer plausible rested on his fidelity to the idea of objective moral ideals, such as justice, which as he liked to put it rather whimsically, 'just is' (Sypnowich, 2024, p. 152).[6] This was a view he traced to Marx's critique of capitalism, even if Marx's historicism dissembled this.

When it came to spelling out what socialist justice consists in, however, Cohen took his lead from, not Marx, or not just Marx, but rather, liberal egalitarians like Rawls. Although Cohen's 'magnum opus', *Rescuing Justice and Equality*, centred on the failings of Rawls's theory of justice, the premise of the enterprise was the 'greatness' of Rawls's contribution in making a systematic, normative case for a more equal distribution of wealth (Cohen, 2008, pp. 11–13). Cohen's appreciation was in part methodological, since in the 1970s Rawls had broken new ground in making a case for rational argument about political principles in the context of a philosophical culture still mired in the scientism of postwar positivism. But Cohen also saluted Rawls's substantive contribution in defending the egalitarian ideal. Certainly, Rawls envisaged that

[4] Cohen (1995b, p. 139; 2000c, pp. 101–4). See also Cohen (1983) and Geras (1983). Raymond Geuss argues that the standard understanding of ethics in English-speaking philosophy as concerning what we ought to do has little purchase in German philosophy in general. See Geuss (2003).

[5] Although Cohen came to dispute the labour theory of value; see Cohen (1988b), p. 212.

[6] Sypnowich, p. 152.

his principles of justice would help constitute a society significantly more equal than the welfare state capitalism of his day (Rawls, 2001, p. 135).

Nonetheless, Cohen had profound disagreements with Rawls on the scope of justice. Indeed, that was the motivation for Cohen's book, which sought to 'rescue' justice from liberal egalitarianism, and in particular, Rawls's idea of incentives for the talented and productive. Rawls warns about the prospect where 'greater taxes interfere so much with economic efficiency that the prospects of the least advantaged in the present generation are no longer improved but begin to decline' (Rawls, 2005, p. 253). Thus, there are grounds, Rawls concluded, for allowing the well-off to keep a greater portion of their income. Society might legitimately permit those who Cohen called the 'high fliers' to retain some portion of their economic advantage if that would boost productivity from which the worst off would benefit. This qualification is made almost parenthetically by Rawls, as though there is no controversy at stake.[7] It was this position that prompted the 'socialist liberal' political theorist C.B. Macpherson to contend twenty years before Cohen's book, that Rawls's ethical distributive principles do not prevail over, but are overridden by, capitalist market relations of production (Macpherson, 1985, p. 13).

For his part, Cohen responded with an immanent critique, contending that such a concession to wealth inequality betrays Rawls's own ideals, as evoked by the 'natural lottery', that market success is morally arbitrary. Cohen reflected on the preposterous exchange that would ensue if the well-off person tried to explain to the badly off person the need for a policy which reduces the funds available to ameliorate disadvantage. How could one justify this to those who would bear the brunt of that reduction? The 'I-thou' character of such an exchange, Cohen argued, helps one appreciate the injustice of incentives (Cohen, 2008, pp. 35–48).

Cohen was prompted to target this aspect of Rawls's theory in light of the arguments at the time of Britain's Conservative government, which

[7] Cohen puzzles over a shift in Rawls's thinking on this, from his 1958 essay, 'Justice as Fairness' and *Theory of Justice*; see Cohen (2008), pp. 177–80. Philippe Van Parijs (2003, pp. 203-4) counters that the most cogent case for capitalist inequality is not that the expectation of reward induces productivity, but rather that those who are most innovative or efficient find market success, taking wealth and economic power from their less capable rivals.

called for lowering taxes on the rich with the rationale that benefits for the worse off would 'trickle down' if the rich were allowed to keep a greater portion of their wealth. Cohen complained: 'We were ceaselessly told that movement contrary to that policy, in a socialist egalitarian direction, would be bad for badly off people by advocates of a regime that seems itself to have brought about the very effect against which its apologists insistently warned' (Cohen, 2008, p. 29).[8] Indeed, once the idea of incentives is rejected, Rawls's very assumption that remedying the position of the worst off might necessitate inequality—the essence of the difference principle—looks suspect.[9]

The incentive issue inspired Cohen to elaborate further on the personal obligations of the better off. If true to their principles, egalitarians should abstain from seeking incentives, but also, Cohen concluded, be prepared to help remedy wealth inequality in their everyday behaviour. For Cohen, principles of justice should apply, not just to the 'basic structure' of society, as Rawls called political and economic institutions, but also to people's personal choices. Cohen asked, therefore, 'if you're an egalitarian, how come you're so rich?'—the much-quoted title of one of his most popular essays.[10] Cohen contended that a successful egalitarian society required more than conformity to institutional rules. People should also do what they can in their personal lives to further the aim of equality—be it donating to charity, accepting high taxes, or choosing occupations that would make a greater social contribution. The argument for charitable behaviour certainly went against the focus on institutions and structures typical of welfare liberal

[8] See also an earlier version of this argument in Cohen (2000d).

[9] Cohen's Analytical Marxist colleague, John Roemer, comments that the pervasiveness of 'selfish optimisation' is such that 'even the most influential left-wing political philosophy of the twentieth century, that of Rawls, is deeply infected by it'. See Roemer (2012, p. 292).

[10] Cohen published an article of that name which was then included as 'Political Philosophy and Personal Behaviour', ch. 10 in *If You're an Egalitarian, How Come You're So Rich?*. Others have replicated the title in papers, blogs, reviews, etc., for example: *'If you're an egalitarian how come* you're trying to sell an undergraduate arts degree that costs more than an MBA?' '...how come you're a philosopher?' '...how come you claimed so much in expenses?' '...how come you wanna be so poor?' '...how come you don't believe in genetic enhancement?' '...how come you read bedtime stories to your children?' '...how come you're so inegalitarian about your body?' '...how come you send your children to private school?' Colin Macleod (2012) contends that more intractable is the 'rich libertarian' problem'.

and socialist positions. Yet at the same time, the idea that we should all play our part in the egalitarian society hearkens to Marx's distributive principle of, not just 'to each according to their needs', but also 'from each according to their ability'.

Cohen admitted that to discharge this obligation individuals needed the support of a 'social ethos' that inculcates in us a commitment to the egalitarian ideal and a preparedness to do what we can to further socialist justice. Cohen also permitted exceptions—there should be room for 'personal prerogatives' in light of people's individual circumstances (Cohen, 2008, pp. 219–22). How they would be negotiated is left unspecified, but Cohen believes the social ethos can play its role to promote socialist justice without detailing our particular duties. Individuals would make reasonable judgements in their own cases about where their duties lie, without judging harshly the judgements of others, allowing for understandings such as 'Max has a bad back' or 'Sally has a difficult child' (Cohen, 2008, p. 353).

To illustrate what kind of social relations this would involve, Cohen often invoked the solidarity of the British during the Blitz of the Second World War, where citizens voluntarily made sacrifices for the common good (Cohen, 2008, pp. 142–3; 353). For Cohen, this required a sense of community, but community was also the payoff of such relations, a context of human connection and solidaristic meaning that was valuable in itself. Jonathan Wolff amplifies this idea, saying that, these values are not merely instrumental to just outcomes: there is 'more to a society of equals than a just scheme of distribution of material goods'; some goods are non-material and 'depend on the attitude people have toward each other' (Wolff, 1998, pp. 104–5; 111–119). The socialist ideal of a common humanity, where the pursuit of equality involves transcending the attitudes of greed and fear to find fellowship and connection with others, is a theme that recurs in Cohen's life and work.

5.3 Flourishing and Equality

For all his emphasis on how ideas of solidarity and fellowship are bound up with the pursuit of equality, Cohen showed little interest in how connections with others might be conceived as constituents of equality itself. Marx contended that, rid of the alienation of capitalist production, the communist community would not only meet people's material needs, but also enable people to flourish, in the widest sense of the word. People would enjoy 'all-round development', fraternity with others, the realization of their capacities and the fulfilment of their creative potential.[11] This is in sharp contrast to Rawls, who insisted that the political community, and indeed political philosophy, should avoid questions about how to live, a view that was affirmed by subsequent liberal political philosophers.[12] With his metric of primary goods, the 'all-purpose means' to whatever ends people might have, Rawls ruled out appeals to considerations of wellbeing, human fulfilment, or living well (Rawls, 2008, p. 153n27). For Rawls, considerations about the 'good life' were too controversial, too compromising of the liberal principle of personal freedom, to be incorporated into a theory of justice.[13]

Cohen mounted no direct objection to this narrow understanding of the metric of equality. In his critique of the difference principle, Cohen tended to assume primary goods as the 'equalisand', and Rawls's anti-perfectionism about the good life is not among the targets of Cohen's critique. Yet Cohen wasn't completely silent on such matters. In an unrelated discussion about the role of occupational choice, he complained that 'Rawlsian justice is blind to the distribution of everything but social primary goods' (Cohen, 2008, pp. 200–1). As a result, Cohen continued, considerations like 'quality of work experience' play no role. Moreover, in another passage Cohen retorts that what's at stake in the real world is not primary goods, but 'the facilitation of a fulfilling life' (Cohen, 2008, p. 293).

---

[11] These ideas about the central role played by a conception of human flourishing in the understanding of socialism are developed in my *Equality Renewed: Justice, Flourishing and the Egalitarian Ideal* (Sypnowich, 2017); see also Kandiyali (2018, 2024).

[12] For example, Kymlicka (2002, p. 216) and Quong (2010).

[13] For an effort to make a Rawlsian case for perfectionism, see Tahzib (2022).

Intimations of these more perfectionist themes can also be found in Cohen's earlier work on the idea of 'access to advantage', a metric he tentatively proffered in his critique of Ronald Dworkin's emphasis on resources. Access to advantage answers the 'equality of what' question with, not goods, income or resources, but something akin to the idea of functionings, as developed by Amartya Sen and Martha Nussbaum, which also suggests perfectionist ideas.[14] Advantage consists in 'a heterogeneous collection of desirable states of the person reducible neither to his resources bundle or his welfare bundle' (Cohen, 2011a, pp. 59–60). As for access, for Cohen, the idea captures both the opportunity and capacity to obtain a good. Access to advantage thus aims to capture a range of considerations, including that people enjoy wellbeing whatever their favoured disputes, that pain and disability be mitigated, and that account be taken of the shortfalls in flourishing caused by 'despondency' or 'gloominess'.[15] That a theory of justice should take account of wellbeing is put particularly forcefully by Cohen in his remark that it matters whether an occupation is fulfilling, in the sense of 'psychological satisfaction and extent of realization and exercise of creative powers' (Cohen, 2008, p. 368).

These remarks indicate a more wholesale critique of Rawls than one focussed on who gets how many primary goods. If wellbeing is a key consideration for a theory of justice, then the shortcomings of Rawls's approach lie not just in the limited extent of the redistribution of goods. Also problematic is Rawls's instrumentalist metric for equality and his insistence that principles of justice make no commitment on questions of how to live. Ideas about wellbeing, however, never came directly into play in Cohen's dissection of Rawls's egalitarian position (Sypnowich, 2024, pp. 88–9).

Yet the theme of wellbeing might have contributed, not just a trenchant critique of the exclusive focus on the quantifiable in Rawls's view

[14] See Sen (1992) and Nussbaum (2010); I argue for a perfectionist interpretation of their views in Sypnowich (2017, pp. 62–5, 139–141).

[15] Cohen (2011b, pp. 20, 18, 28). Although Cohen later conceded that his position amounted, not to a theory, but to a 'repository of considerations with which an acceptable theory must come to terms', he continued to believe that there is not a single thing which must be equalized, and that both resources and welfare should be taken into account when devising an egalitarian distribution, 'Afterword to ch. 1 and 2' in Cohen (2011b), pp. 61–4.

of distributive justice, but also a qualitatively different view of what it is to be equal. This would have added up to a powerful alternative view, one that builds on the inspiring and compelling insights of the socialist tradition, and which would have earned Cohen a place in political philosophy, not just as Rawls's most acute critic, but also the source of a powerful, indeed superior, alternative position. It's a pity, therefore, that Cohen's masterful critique of Rawls left to one side the matter of how people live and find meaning in the socialist community.

I have pondered that perhaps Cohen's parsimonious method, his insistence that an analytical approach proceed by small steps with rigour and precision, did not permit him to stray into controversial debates that involved a more holistic understanding of the aims of political philosophy (Sypnowich, 2024, p. 161). Moreover, Cohen offered a 'division of labour' rationale for why he didn't address certain questions, e.g., global justice, even though he had quite radical views about them (Tormey, 2009, p. 359). Given Cohen's meticulous approach in an already long (430 pages) book about Rawls, he may well have decided, even if tempted to pronounce on such questions, that they should be put off for another day, or more likely, for another philosopher (Sypnowich, 2024, p. 89). Whatever the reason, in the end, Cohen's thoughts on access to advantage, with its rich sense of the importance of the constituents of human wellbeing for distributive justice, remains an unfinished chapter in his thought.

5.4 Law and Socialism

It would seem plausible that the ideal of socialist justice should encapsulate, not just distributive or economic justice, but also law and legal institutions more broadly. However, the 1980s scepticism about the concept of justice and its place in Marxist theory had reverberations for a progressive understanding of law. Indeed, the Left tended to be association with a kind of 'legal nihilism', since the debate about Marx and justice was linked to the view that legal institutions—courts, individual rights, impartial legal processes—were in principle at odds with canonical views about the nature of socialism. Here too Cohen made his mark, rejecting such views in an incisive and invigorating way.[16]

At stake was the classical Marxist claim that law and state would disappear with the full flowering of communist society. For Marx and Engels, legal institutions are shaped by the more fundamental economic relations of any given society. Under capitalism, law's function is to mediate the self-regarding interests of bourgeois owners of private property, and to cement the class interests of the bourgeoisie. From this they concluded that in an ideal communist society without private property or class divisions, law would be unnecessary. Law would not even need to be abolished; it would simply 'wither away' when its preconditions disappeared.[17]

The Soviet legal theorist, Evgeny Pashukanis, elaborated a sophisticated form of this view. Pashukanis affirmed that law is necessary due to the relations of private property and class conflict that obtain under capitalism; remove those conditions and you remove the need for law. Pashukanis's 'commodity theory of law' postulates that the very form of legality embodies the relationship of economic exchange under capitalism. The legal subject is an abstract commodity owner 'elevated to the heavens' (Pashukanis, 1980, ch. 4). Indeed, the relationship between the parties in a contract constitutes the model for all other social relationships under capitalism, so that the values of the market permeate all dimensions of human society.

Pashukanis drew upon the arguments of Marx's 'On the Jewish Question', that law is required to mediate the relationships of self-interested property owners, and thus that bourgeois rights were those of 'man separated from the community, from himself and from other men', and as such, found their apogee in capitalist market relations (Marx, 1978, p. 35; Sypnowich, 1990, p. 3). Under communism, in contrast, Pashukanis proposed that the individual 'submerges his ego in the collective and finds the greatest satisfaction and meaning of life in this act'

[16] This discussion draws on my ideas in Sypnowich (2025).

[17] I elaborate this view in Sypnowich (1990, ch. 1 and ch. 5). For an opposing view, see Schoikhedbriod (2019).

such that individuals' concerns are supplanted with those of the community as a whole (Pashukanis, 1980, ch. 4; see also Campbell, 1983). This position turned out to be challenging to put into practice after the October Revolution, but also political suicide for the Bolshevik jurist by the 1930s, when Stalin's project of using the coercive apparatus of state and law to secure his authoritarian regime was in full vigour. In 1937, Pashukanis was named an enemy of the people and disappeared (Sypnowich, 1990, p. 18).[18]

Cohen's ambitious understanding of egalitarian distribution, so closely allied to his Marxist convictions about the imperative of meeting human needs, did not entail fidelity to orthodox Marxist (or what in another context Cohen jokingly referred to as 'palaeo-Marxist') (Tormey, 2009, p. 353) views when it came to law. Indeed, in a 1995 essay, Cohen was unequivocal in his dismissal of the idea that selflessness would be so abundant under communism that law would be superfluous. Pashukanis, he argued, showed 'an infantile unwillingness to countenance a measure of self-denial as a way of dealing with the inevitable difficulties of social existence' (Cohen, 1995b, pp. 134–5).

This position was in sharp contrast to Cohen's ideas in another, slightly earlier essay, where he was much more optimistic about the ease with which we would relate to each other under socialism. Under conditions of surplus, Cohen predicted, socialism would be akin to a jazz band of self-directing individual musicians who, with no social coordination or censure, nonetheless produce beautiful music together. Theirs would be 'a concert of mutually supporting self-fulfilments, in which no one takes the fulfilment of others as any kind of obligation' (Cohen, 1995b, pp. 122–3). Equality, he supposed, could be achieved in the same way. Key to this ideal was Marx's prediction that the productivity unleashed by capitalism would make for abundance under communism. After all, if we live under conditions of abundance, then we need not deny ourselves. However, Cohen came to conclude that in even the most ideal socialist society individuals would need to set some limits to the pursuit of their interests. The jazz band metaphor was accordingly abandoned in subsequent writings (Vrousalis, 2012).

[18] See Sypnowich (1990, p. 18).

5.5 Self-Interest and Community

Cohen's change in view was made in light of the declining fortunes of socialist politics in the 1980s and 1990s, where, as we noted above, Cohen came to see the need for normative arguments for socialism and a reckoning with the moral complexities of the socialist social order. Also noted above was the role of the environmental crisis, and arguably Cohen's changed outlook was principally due to his increasing disenchantment with the progressivist optimism that scarcity could be abolished. As Cohen argued, decades before governments proclaimed a climate emergency, the problem of scarcity is here to stay: the earth's stores are not 'lavish enough' to solve the problem of scarce resources since whatever our relations of production, 'the planet earth rebels' (Cohen, 1995a, p. 7).

The 'circumstances of justice' was an idea developed by David Hume to capture why we might need legal institutions and a political order to mediate disagreement. Human societies are typically characterized by moderate scarcity and self-interest, which is why justice is both necessary and possible. If there was abundance, or we were selfless angels, justice would be gratuitous; if there was extreme scarcity or we were fiends, justice would be impossible (Hume, 1751, p. 36). The assumption of a changed human nature, the new, 'communist man', is typically regarded as key to social transformation. However, Cohen astutely pointed out that the superfluity of resources is key; we needn't be angels if there's more than enough to go around. With that confidence in abundance gone, a normative theory of distributive justice was now needed, to persuade people of the merits of the socialist cause, but also to outline the constituents of socialist justice. And without the abundance premise, socialists would now need to countenance the persistence of disagreement and difference, for which legal institutions would be needed to perform a mediating role. Cohen therefore argued, not that individuals' egoism was insurmountable, but rather that socialist justice involves individuals overcoming their self-regarding interests to take account of the interests of others.

Indeed, the idea that we are either egoists or altruists is a crude way of understanding the nature of acting on behalf of others. Bernard Williams proposed that altruism be construed, not as 'a strenuous and unsolicited benevolent interference' but as a general disposition to consider the interests of others as making a claim on the person such that they may need to limit their projects (Williams, 1973, p. 250). Such an understanding looks like a pragmatic course, but it also makes for conceptual coherence. A successful altruist must demarcate the boundaries of individuals and their interests, which means admitting the validity of self-oriented interests. Altruistic behaviour would be neither possible nor effective if everyone defines their interests to be to further those of others; there would be no one who would admit to having self-regarding interests that others could try to fulfill as their own. Thomas Nagel makes the case in his essay on altruism when he notes that 'altruistic reasons are parasitic upon self-interested ones; the circumstances in the lives of others which altruism requires us to consider are circumstances which those others already have reason to consider from a self-interested point of view' (Nagel, 1970, p. 16).

In one of his last publications, Cohen submitted that socialism's biggest challenge was figuring out 'how to design the machinery to make it run'. Capitalist societies devised the brilliant though flawed idea of a market to coordinate production and distribution. Similarly, Cohen says, we need to devise 'clever ways of harnessing and organizing our capacity for generosity to others' (Cohen, 2009, pp. 57–8). Even if we are persuaded that individuals have a personal responsibility to engage in egalitarian behaviour, it remains challenging to consider how they are to understand and act on this responsibility, which by its very definition lies outside the scope of what is legally required. Socialism will consist in, not just egalitarian distributive justice, according to Cohen. A corollary of the meeting of human needs will be a change in attitudes and social relations: the elimination of 'greed and fear'. This requires, as we've seen, a social ethos to inculcate socialist attitudes.

5.6 Equality and the Rule of Law

However, for a social ethos to inspire what Cohen calls 'uncoerced equality-supporting choice' (Cohen, 2000d, p. 131), there must be institutional resources as well. These include the institutions of the basic structure, of course, such as the distributive mechanisms of a socialist or welfare state, and a range of progressive policies on everything from health care to pensions to public education. There is also the institution of the law itself: first, and most obvious, to organise and coordinate the egalitarian policies of the basic structure; and second, in law's role of providing the institutional rules that shape informal attitudes. The principles of the rule of law can inform how we understand our personal obligations to treat each other fairly, to respect people's freedom and agency. The rule of law ideal involves understanding how the authority of the state must be exercised by means of, not arbitrary decree, but law, a set of norms about governance that impose restrictions on the use of force and power (Sypnowich, 2025).

There are three important implications here. First, the concepts of the rule of law, due process or procedural justice, all involve the idea that law should be general, that it take the form of *rules*, directed to more than a particular situation or individual. The law rules us all: citizens, government, police and judges; rulers as well as the ruled, all must submit to the rule of law. Second, by requiring that the state govern by rules rather than arbitrary decrees, the rule of law provides a measure of consistency in the state's actions. Third, if law is to command obedience, we must know what it asks of us. Thus, another idea key to the rule of law is that law should meet certain procedural requirements so that it is capable of being obeyed. As Fuller notes, the rule of law requires that law be relatively certain, clearly expressed, open, prospective and adequately publicized (Fuller 1969, pp. 33–94). If law fails to meet these criteria, it is self-defeating.

We cannot obey the law if we do not know what it asks of us, if it is secret, or if it tells us that what we did yesterday is today now illegal. These procedural standards enable the individual to understand what the law requires, to be able to adjust plans and act accordingly. An unpredictable, arbitrary political order, whatever its purposes, undermines the ability of the individual to choose how to live. Thus, perhaps paradoxically, freedom to act involves knowing what actions are not permitted, since to be able conduct oneself without fear of violating the norms of the political community, one must have a clear understanding of the parameters set by those norms as they are encapsulated in law.

Contrary to the hostility to law of the socialist tradition, far from being 'beyond justice', the functioning socialist society might be the best context for the realisation of procedural justice. In earlier work (Sypnowich, 1990, ch. 3), I rejected the Hayekian bias that the market is the handmaiden of proceduralism, proposing instead that it is capitalist inequality that undermines the rule of law. Class divisions and the interests of private property can distort the law enforcement agenda, render legal representation patchy and unequal, and involve a judiciary recruited from the more advantaged classes in society whose decision-making betrays the biases of that privilege. Social equality, in contrast, would further procedural justice. If individuals are to engage in 'voluntarily just behaviour' that supplements the legal institutions of a fully egalitarian society, those institutions would need to provide guidance, in particular, procedural principles where citizens interact on the basis of open, transparent and universally applicable rules.

The normativity of proceduralism is not intuitive. It can be hard to accept that those with whom one disagrees, or worse, finds thoroughly reprehensible, are entitled to due process. It can seem an unwarranted encumbrance that our ends, however just, cannot be pursued by any means; indeed that just ends are deprived of their just character and should be sacrificed if there are no just means to pursue them. In their efforts to 'do justice' in their everyday lives socialist citizens would need the procedural principles that attend the substantive policies of egalitarian justice. The rule of law, therefore, provides a vital procedural framework within which individuals can articulate and mediate their differences, and pursue the ambitious ideals promulgated by a social ethos of egalitarianism. Here we must amend Hume: justice is not a 'cautious, jealous virtue' appropriate only for societies of self-interested owners of private property. Justice would not be 'useless' (Hume, 1751, p. 34) in the society beyond private property. Rather, in the socialist society of equals, which has transcended market relations, justice would find both its purpose and its full realisation.

5.7 No-sucker Socialism

This argument about the role of proceduralism in a socialist society points to a larger lesson about the inevitability of constrain in even the most ideal of circumstances. Cohen's conviction that socialism would involve a commitment on the part of individuals to live ethically, at some personal cost to their self-interest, is one such constraint, a sobering caveat, perhaps, to the utopian ideals typically associated with post-capitalism. However, these demanding ethical obligations play a critical role in promoting an ambitious egalitarian distribution. In his metaphor of the socialist camping trip, where fellow-feeling prevails and human needs are met, Cohen was able to give evocative expression to the Marxist principle of contribution according to ability and distribution according to need. Campers, of diverse abilities and resourcefulness, share knowledge and knowhow to ensure all enjoy their time together. Those who know of a good fishing hole, or where there might be some delicious apples to pick, relay their intelligence to the others with no regard for market-oriented ideas of profiting from one's advantaged position (Cohen, 2009).

Against this image of generosity and fellowship, however, Cohen also proposes a quite stringent test for the amelioration of disadvantage. Here is a constraint that has prompted considerable controversy. Cohen contended that 'socialist equality of opportunity' entails the remedy of disadvantage only if it is the result of unchosen circumstance, or bad brute luck. The influence of Ronald Dworkin is, I think, quite decisive here. Cohen parted company with Dworkin on many other issues, such as the 'expensive tastes' problem, which concerned whether an egalitarian distribution should compensate for diverse tastes and interests. Contra Dworkin, Cohen took the view that unchosen expensive tastes, e.g. for photography rather than fishing, should be satisfied, a nod to the Marxist principle of distribution according to need (Dworkin, 2002,

p. 51; Cohen, 2011b, pp. 12–13, 24–5).[19] Moreover, as we saw earlier, Cohen took a broader view of what is to be distributed, insisting that access to advantage better captured what was at stake than Dworkin's metric of resources.

However, when it came to the idea of equality of opportunity, Cohen sided with Dworkin. For Dworkin, disadvantage that is the result of circumstance or bad brute luck warrants amelioration, but disadvantage that is the result of choice or deliberate gambles does not (Dworkin, 2002, pp. 73–8). Cohen agreed: 'Brute luck is an enemy of just equality, and, since the effects of genuine choice contrast with brute luck, genuine choice excuses otherwise unacceptable inequalities' (Cohen, 2011b, 29). Indeed, Cohen understood his entire career to be guided by an 'animating conviction' about the unfairness of one's lot being determined by luck (Cohen, 2008, p. 7), going so far as to applaud the luck egalitarian doctrine as a response to the right-wing critiques of the 'Nanny State'. Cohen enthused: 'Dworkin has, in effect, performed for egalitarianism the considerable service of incorporation within it the most powerful idea in the arsenal of the anti-egalitarian right: the idea of choice and responsibility' (Cohen, 2011b, pp. 31–2).

What became known as 'luck egalitarianism' emerged as a highly influential doctrine, the merits of which sparked considerable debate. Space doesn't permit a full discussion here,[20] but it is important to note that Cohen's luck egalitarian position was intended to demonstrate that most instances of inequality result from unchosen circumstances and are thereby eligible for remedy.[21] Moreover, remedy that is not permitted at the bar of justice might nonetheless be warranted on humanitarian grounds—luck egalitarians insist they are not proposing that the improvident go hungry. Furthermore, since Cohen's contributions, exponents of luck egalitarianism introduced further refinements to ensure that there

[19] Dworkin, *Sovereign Virtue*, 51; Cohen (2011, pp. 12–13, 24–5).

[20] I discuss this debate in connection with Cohen in Sypnowich (2024, pp. 115–24). See the development of these ideas in (many of whom are Cohen's students) Lippert-Rasmussen (2001), Olsaretti (2009, 2015), Stemoplowska (2009), Otsuka and Williams (2004) and Parr and Williams (2021).

[21] Cohen's Analytical Marxist colleague John Roemer produced a radical version of the doctrine which sought to correct for different choice-making capacities according to demographic data to ensure reward truly tracks effort. See Roemer (1998).

is some mitigation of the impact of bad decisions on people's material conditions. It's pertinent that although critics of luck egalitarianism associate the creed with the Victorian idea of the 'deserving poor', luck egalitarians themselves tend to avoid such moralising terms. Nonetheless, from the point of view of socialist justice, as expounded thus far, luck egalitarianism suggests an incongruous, grudging attitude to the needy. The idea that some disadvantaged people, if feckless and imprudent, or to put it less controversially, suffering the consequences of ill-fated choices or gambles, might go without assistance, certainly seems in tension with the socialist ideal of community and fraternity, so manifest in Cohen's critique of Rawls's concession to incentives, as noted by thinkers as diverse as Nicholas Vrousalis (2015) and David Miller (2015). Indeed, it's worth recalling that Rawls's difference principle, for all its socialist failings, had no such strings attached, seeking to improve the position of the worst off, however they came by their disadvantage.

Recall, too, that Cohen's rich egalitarian argument doesn't deploy any criteria of deservingness. Egalitarians' personal obligation to contribute to equality doesn't involve scrutiny of the choices that reduce people to going to food banks or begging on street corners.[22] Andrew Williams has noted how the spirit of community that animates the socialist ideal is at odds with the 'divisive claims about prudence and virtue' that attend luck egalitarian principles (Williams, 2013, p. 82). For some socialists, luck egalitarianism seems to hearken more to Stalin's dictum that 'those who do not work do not eat' than it does to Marx's original ideal of distribution on the basis of need (Sypnowich, 2023).

It is puzzling why Cohen is particularly preoccupied with determining the merits of the disadvantaged. True, he remarked that 'there are more reasons for objecting strongly to the corporate welfare bum than the able-bodied plain welfare bum who gets as much as the working stiff does'. However, this point was an aside in another context, where the focus was on how unjust inequality is more objectionable than unjust

[22] I consider how luck egalitarian considerations might be brought to bear on the decision to give to beggars in Sypnowich (2006).

equality.[23] Why did Cohen take up luck egalitarianism, so in tension with the generous ideals eloquently expressed in so many of his writings, especially the evocative story of the socialist campers who share and share alike? Indeed, in his own life, Cohen displayed a spontaneous generosity, unfailingly giving to beggars, even jokingly advising them 'you must spend this on alcohol'. In so giving, and moreover, in so advising, Cohen in his actions flouted the idea that responsibility is a condition for distribution. And Cohen found philosophical insight in these encounters, writing how they enabled a human connection where 'our eyes meet with a certain mutual understanding' that permits people be 'open to each other' (Sypnowich, 2024, pp. 28–9).

In fact, Cohen admitted that the focus on responsibility, however much it might be demanded by his understanding of justice, risked undermining relations of mutual understanding and comradeship. In the camping trip context, Cohen proposes that inequalities that result from choice or deliberate gambles, though fully just, should be remedied 'in the name of community'. Cohen is uncomfortable with this upshot, and remarks, without resolving the matter, that 'it would be a great pity of if we had to conclude that community and justice were potentially incompatible moral ideals' (Cohen, 2009, pp. 34–8; See also Cohen, 2011b, p. 933). To return to the rich egalitarian argument, perhaps the call for personal contributions to remedy inequality was a way of making up for the shortfalls in compensation dictated by Cohen's tough line on responsibility. However, in that context, the personal obligation to contribute is presented as an element of justice, not community, with the odd upshot that voluntary giving is a demand of justice, whereas state distribution on the basis of need alone is not. One wonders how the justice/community divide operated in Cohen's mind when he gave to beggars, even making jokey entreaties to spend alms in an arguably irresponsible way. Was this a humanitarian gesture expressing community, or was it a personal effort to remedy injustice?

There are several potential reasons for Cohen's turn to a focus on responsibility as a criterion for egalitarian distribution. First there is

[23] Cohen, 'Luck and Equality', 121. The phrase 'corporate welfare bums' was coined by David Lewis, former leader of the New Democratic Party of Canada. See his *Louder Voices: Corporate Welfare Bums*, also Wolff (2010, p. 340).

Cohen's value pluralism, his idea that one's ethical commitments 'present themselves in competitive array' (Cohen, 2008, p. 7 and Sypnowich, 2024, pp. 170–1). Thus, however important, justice must jostle for position among rival considerations, giving Cohen an 'out' perhaps, when it comes to competing considerations in the formulationof his ideas on equality. Perhaps his methodological commitments, his espousal of an analytical, 'no-bullshit' philosophy also played a role. Thus, Cohen would be motivated to eschew vague radical ideals that 'wish away' difficult problems such as free riders who shirk their duty to contribute. For Cohen, the principle of reciprocity involves giving to those in need, but it also might mean, more stringently, being tough on those who fail to do their share. Cohen explains the socialist camping philosophy 'does not require me to be a sucker who serves you regardless of whether (if you are able to do so) you are going to serve me' (Cohen, 2009, 38–35). In short, perhaps no-bullshit Marxism entailed no-sucker socialism.[24]

Cohen might also have been influenced by what could be called the juridical culture of Anglo-American political philosophy. Dworkin rose to prominence first as a legal philosopher, with an impressive corpus on adjudication, rights, and the sources of law, and these preoccupations likely played some role in the development of his theory of luck egalitarianism. The idea of responsibility, so central to criminal law, would have been an attractive resource to address the increasing hostility to the idea of 'handouts' from the state. Consider the rising rhetoric of 'welfare bums' articulated by, not just the well-off, but also working-class people who resented their taxes going towards non-contributors. Cohen, intent on avoiding what he deemed Pollyanna legal theories such as that of Pashukanis, that imagined socialism to be devoid of conflict, doubtless had some affinity for Dworkin's strategy.

Indeed, that Cohen did not pursue further his more perfectionist understanding of egalitarianism might also be attributed to the 'juridicalisation' of political philosophy. By juridicalisation I mean the ways in which legalistic notions of neutrality prevent an engagement with questions of inequalities in human wellbeing. Here it is not just Dworkin, but also, as I noted above, Rawls, who prompted a pervasive unease among

[24] As I propose in Sypnowich (2024, pp. 133–4).

liberal egalitarians with more substantive understandings of equality. The model of an impartial legal process, which removes human connection and a concern for wellbeing, might also undergird the preoccupation with responsibility as a test for the allocation of goods. It is disappointing that a concern for impartiality and proceduralism should be allowed to have imperialistic designs on all political questions, so that the community backs away from seeking the wellbeing of its weakest members (Sypnowich, 2017, pp. 85–7).

Cohen's egalitarianism thus marshalled the idea of responsibility in a complex way. Concerns for personal responsibility generated a high bar for egalitarian distribution insofar as individuals are called upon to make efforts to remedy inequality outside of the requirements of coercive institutions. Yet considerations of responsibility lowered that bar insofar as needy persons whose choices contributed to their disadvantage were disqualified from amelioration, at least at the level of just institutions. In the former case, community is part and parcel of the understanding of justice, but in the latter, community is a contrasting, remedial principle that compensates for the limitations of justice. I have suggested that this paradoxical result can be resolved if the juridical is put in its place. Socialist justice should affirm the procedural ideals that check the dangers of arbitrary power, but not at the cost of reducing the ambit of egalitarian distribution, be it by disqualifying some disadvantaged persons from egalitarian remedy, or by excluding considerations of wellbeing from the constituents of equality.

5.8 Conclusion

Jerry Cohen made an enormous contribution to political philosophy. Incisive, radical, committed, and witty, his work was the fruit, not just of his immense talent, but many fascinating influences—his communist family background, his Oxford training, and the interesting times in which he lived. The power and significance of his work is hard to overstate. Cohen tested ambitious socialist convictions by means of sharp, rigorous, analytical argument, and those that withstood such scrutiny he defended with a robust, compelling analysis. Thus, he adeptly demonstrated the limitations of Rawls's egalitarianism and made a powerful case for a stirring, radical alternative: socialist justice.

The context in which Cohen penned his writings in political theory—characterized by the rise of the New Right, the decline of a socialist consciousness among the working class, the collapse of the Soviet Union, and the environmental crisis—were difficult times in which to hold fast to one's socialist creed. The overturning of so many progressive assumptions about the planet and the world cried out for a tough-minded assessment of the role, value and limits of socialist ideals. Accordingly, Cohen took on the task of defending what he took to be integral commitments and shedding those he deemed sentimental or woolly. In so doing, it must be stressed that he performed an invaluable service—for political philosophy and for the pursuit of social change.

One shibboleth which Cohen usefully dispatched was the idea that socialism would be a society beyond law and legal institutions. I have pointed out how Cohen's critique of Pashukanis's naiveté about post-capitalist altruism affirmed the need for a socialist approach to legality, stimulating a valuable corpus of arguments and ideas to which I, among others, was inspired to contribute. Moreover, the view that even under conditions of socialist justice, people's differences and disagreements would need the rule of law and individual rights had wider significance for a robust egalitarianism. Cohen's demanding social ethos whereby people are expected to further equality in their personal choices, I have argued, is well served by an understanding of proceduralism which can check the potential for unfair assertions of power in the context of ambitious egalitarian goals.

However, I have argued that in other cases, Cohen's parsimonious approach stayed his hand in ways that held him back. The limited discussion of a wellbeing approach to the metric for equality is one example. Cohen's idea of access to advantage creatively combined resources and welfare, noting the importance of not just physical capacity and the meeting of material needs, but also cheerfulness, fellowship and well-being. Cohen proffered this view in his exchanges with Dworkin, rejecting the focus on resources alone, and making a case for access rather than the narrower idea of opportunity. However, he did not deploy this promising alternative view in his critique of Rawls, and thus we are left with a set of ideas that are, though suggestive and exciting, not developed at much length. Thus, the deleterious effect of the Rawlsian insistence on neutrality about the good, so contrary to the spirit of socialist ideals of self-realisation, was left largely unchallenged.

Particularly disappointing, to my mind, is Cohen's turn to luck egalitarianism. The idea that the remedy of disadvantage depends on prudence seem quite at odds with Cohen's socialist ideals of community and personal obligation to one's fellows. True, luck egalitarians distinguish the demands of justice from humanitarian considerations, the latter permitting the remedy denied by the former. Moreover, socialists like Cohen take an expansive reading of what counts as brute luck that merits egalitarian redress. Nonetheless, the picture of justice versus community seems a far cry from the socialist ideal.

One of Cohen's last writings was, as discussed above, 'Why Not Socialism?', an engaging essay making the case for an alternative to capitalism. The title evinces the essay's character—making both a rational case and an emotional appeal. Central to the former is Cohen's case for luck egalitarianism, what he calls 'socialist equality of opportunity'. Yet, arguably the heart of the essay is the less closely argued, as[25] but thoroughly inspiring, ideal of socialist fellowship. This ideal certainly enjoyed a robust and persuasive defence in Cohen's groundbreaking work on the limitations of Rawls's difference principle. Cohen's critique of Rawls will likely prove one of his most significant philosophical contributions.

At a time when irrational thought in the service of inequality and division is rampant throughout the world, Cohen's example remains vital. Let us hope that thinkers on the Left will carry on Cohen's legacy of astute, analytical criticism without sacrificing the ideals of community and fellowship so crucial to the ideal of socialist justice.

[25] As John Roemer observed in his 'Address at G.A. Cohen Memorial Service'.

References

Campbell, T. (1983). *The left and rights*. Routledge and Kegan Paul.

Cohen, G. A. (1983). Review of *Karl Marx*, by Allen Wood. *Mind*, 92, 367, July.

Cohen, G. A. (1988a). Preface. In *History, labour, and freedom: themes from Marx*. Oxford University Press.

Cohen, G. A. (1988b). The labour theory of value and the concept of exploitation. In *History, labour, and freedom: Themes from Marx*. Oxford University Press.

Cohen, G. A. (1995a). Introduction: History, ethics, and Marxism. In *Self-ownership, freedom and equality*. Cambridge University Press.

Cohen, G. A. (1995b). Self-ownership, communism, and equality: Against the Marxist technological fix. In *Self-ownership, freedom and equality*. Cambridge University Press.

Cohen, G. A. (2000a). *Karl Marx's theory of history: A defence*. Oxford University Press.

Cohen, G. A. (2000b). Hegel in Marx: The obstetric motif in the Marxist conception of revolution. Ch. 4 in *If you're an egalitarian, how come you're so rich?* Harvard University Press.

Cohen, G. A. (2000c). Equality from fact to norm. Ch. 6 in*If You're an Egalitarian, How Come You're So Rich?* Harvard University Press.

Cohen, G. A. (2000d). Justice, incentives, and selfishness. Ch. 8 in *If you're an egalitarian, how come you're so rich?* Harvard University Press.

Cohen, G. A. (2000e). Political philosophy and personal behaviour. Ch. 5 in *If you're an egalitarian, how come you're so rich?* Harvard University Press.

Cohen, G. A. (2008). *Rescuing justice and equality*. Harvard University Press.

Cohen, G. A. (2009). *Why not socialism?* Princeton University Press.

Cohen, G. A. (2011a). Equality of what? On welfare, goods and capabilities. Ch. 2 in *On the currency of egalitarian justice, and other essays in political philosophy*. M. Otsuka (Ed.). Princeton University Press.

Cohen, G. A. (2011b). On the currency of egalitarian justice. Ch. 1 in *On the currency of egalitarian justice*, and other essays in political philosophy. M. Otsuka (Ed.). Princeton University Press.

Dworkin, R. (2002). *Sovereign virtue: The theory and practice of equality*. Harvard University Press.

Fuller, L. (1969). *The morality of law*. Yale University Press.

Geras, N. (1983). *Marx and human nature: Refutation of a legend*. Verso.

Geuss, R. (2003). Outside ethics. *European Journal of Philosophy, 11*, 1.
Hume, D. (1751) *An enquiry concerning the principles of morals, an enquiry concerning the principles of morals*, A. Millar.
Kandiyali, J. (Ed.). (2018). *Reassessing Marx's social and political philosophy: Freedom, recognition, and human flourishing*. Routledge.
Kandiyali, J. (2024). What makes communism possible? The self-realisation interpretation. *Philosophy, Politics and Economics, 23*, 3.
Kymlicka, W. (2002). *Contemporary political philosophy*. Oxford University Press.
Lippert-Rasmussen, K. (2001). Egalitarianism, luck and responsibility. *Ethics, 111*(3), 548–579.
Lukes, S. (1985). *Marxism and morality*. Oxford University Press.
Macleod, C. (2012). If you're a libertarian, how come you're so rich? *Socialist Studies, 8*(1).
Macpherson, C. B. (1985). *The rise and fall of economic justice and other essays.* Oxford University Press.
Marx, K. (1978) On the Jewish Question. In: *The Marx–Engels Reader.* R. Tucker (Ed.). Norton.
Miller, D. (2015). The incoherence of luck egalitarianism. In A. Kaufman (Ed.), *Distributive justice and access to advantage: G. A. Cohen's egalitarianism.* Cambridge University Press.
Nagel, T. (1970). *The possibility of altruism.* Princeton University Press.
Nussbaum, M. (2010). *Creating capabilities: The human development approach.* Harvard University Press.
Olsaretti, S. (2009). Responsibility and the consequences of choice. *Proceedings of the Aristotelian Society, 109*, 2.
Olsaretti, S. (2015) Rescuing justice and equality from libertarianism. In: A Kaufman (Ed.), *Distributive justice and access to advantage: G.A. Cohen's egalitarianism.* Cambridge University Press
Otsuka, M., & Williams, A. (2004). Equality, ambition and insurance. Aristotelian Society Supplementary Volume 78(1)
Parr, T. and Williams, A. (2021) Fair Insurance defended, amended, and extended. In D Sobel and S Wall (Eds.), *Oxford studies in political philosophy* (Vol. 8). Oxford University Press.
Pashukanis, E. (1980). The general theory of marxism and law. In P. Beirne & R. Sharlet (Eds. and introd.), *Selected writings on Marxism and law.* Academic Press.
Quong, J. (2010). *Liberalism without perfection.* Oxford University Press.
Rawls, J. (2001). *Justice as fairness: A restatement*. Harvard University Press.

Rawls, J. (2005). *A theory of justice*. Harvard University Press.
Rawls, J. (2008). *Lectures on the history of political philosophy*. Harvard University Press.
Roemer, J. (1998). *Equality of opportunity*. Harvard University Press.
Roemer, J. (2012). Ideology, social ethos and the financial crisis. *Journal of Ethics, 16*(3).
Rosen, M. (2010). *Jerry Cohen—An appreciation*. Unpublished talk given at Columbia University, 3 June.
Sayers, S. (2000). Whatever happened to analytical Marxism? *Radical Philosophy*, 104, November/December.
Schoikhedbriod, I. (2019). *Revisiting Marx's critique of liberalism: Rethinking justice, legality and rights*. Palgrave Macmillan.
Sen, A. (1992). *Inequality reexamined*. Oxford University Press.
Stemoplowska, Z. (2009). Making justice sensitive to responsibility. *Political Studies, 57*(2), 237–259.
Sypnowich, C. (1990). *The concept of socialist law*. Oxford University Press.
Sypnowich, C. (2006) Begging. In C Sypnowich (Ed.), *The egalitarian conscience*. Oxford University Press.
Sypnowich, C. (2017). *Equality renewed: Justice, flourishing and the egalitarian ideal*. Routledge.
Sypnowich, C. (2023). 'What's wrong with equality of opportunity' and 'why equality matters'. In D Chasman, J Cohen (eds), *Is equality of opportunity enough?* Boston Review.
Sypnowich, C. (2024). *G.A. Cohen: Liberty, justice and equality*. Polity Press.
Sypnowich, C. (2025), The rule of law and the social ethos. In M. Sevel (Ed.), *The Routledge handbook of the rule of law*. Routledge.
Tahzib, C. (2022). *A perfectionist theory of justice*. Oxford University Press.
Tormey, S. (2009). Simon Tormey interviews Gerald Cohen. *Contemporary Political Theory, 8*(3), 351–362.
Tucker, R. (1964). *Philosophy and myth in Karl Marx*. Cambridge University Press.
Van Parijs, P. (2003). Difference principles. In S. Freeman (Ed.), *The Cambridge Companion to Rawls*. Cambridge University Press.
Vrousalis, N. (2015). *The political philosophy of G. A. Cohen: Back to socialist basics*. Bloomsbury.
Vrousalis, N. (2012). Jazz Bands, Camping trips and decommodification: G. A. Cohen on community. *Socialist Studies, 8*(1).
Williams, A. (2013) How gifts and gambles preserve justice. *Economics and Philosophy, 29*.

Williams, B. (1973). Egoism and altruism. In *Problems of the self*. Cambridge University Press.

Wolff, J. (1998). Fairness, respect and the egalitarian ethos. *Philosophy & Public Affairs, 27*(2), 97–122.

Wolff, J. (2010). Fairness, respect, and the egalitarian "ethos" revisited. *The Journal of Ethics, 14*(3/4), 335–350.

Wood, A. (2004). *Karl Marx*. Routledge.

Part III

Normative Defenses and Critiques of Democratic Socialism

6

Is There a Conflict Between Justice and Non-exploitation?

Michael Kates

6.1 Introduction

Although socialists care deeply about achieving social justice *and* combating worker exploitation, there appears to be a conflict between the two. For, as G.A. Cohen recognized, non-exploitation[1] seems to require that workers receive a wage that reflects the value of their productive contribution, but almost half of the population doesn't work.[2] The question thus arises as to how socialists can ensure that non-workers receive a just distribution of economic resources while at the same time guaranteeing laborers fair compensation for their work.

[1] By "non-exploitation" I simply mean the value that is instantiated when workers are *not* exploited and so receive fair compensation for their work.
[2] See Bruenig (2018) for this empirical observation.

M. Kates (✉)
Saint Joseph's University, Philadelphia, USA
e-mail: mkates@sju.edu

B. Burgis and M. McManus (eds.), *Analytical Marxism and Democratic Socialism in the 21st Century*, Palgrave Studies in Classical Liberalism,
https://doi.org/10.1007/978-3-032-02894-5_6

This chapter explores various ways to resolve this conflict and considers which one of them is most fully consistent with Cohen's own view.

As I will explain in more detail below, what makes Cohen's discussion of this problem so instructive is that not only does he clearly explain *why* there's a conflict between justice and non-exploitation, but his own solution to this problem exposes just how *difficult* it is to strike the right balance between the two. Indeed, it's partly for this reason that Cohen's own writings on this issue seemed to waver between two distinct, and ultimately incompatible, positions. Accordingly, if socialists wish to make progress on this issue, then they must figure out whether Cohen's treatment of this problem can be improved.

My discussion proceeds in three stages. First, I begin by fleshing out Cohen's own understanding of why there is a conflict between justice and non-exploitation. This account highlights the surprising affinities between socialist concerns about exploitation and the libertarian principle of self-ownership, and shows why socialists are, in turn, more vulnerable to libertarian critiques of the welfare state than liberal egalitarians like John Rawls. Second, I sketch three possible ways of conceiving the relation between justice and non-exploitation, i.e., which value is more fundamental from a socialist point of view, and try to determine what exactly is Cohen's view on the issue. In contrast to Nicholas Vrousalis' interpretation, I show that Cohen's position on the relation between justice and non-exploitation is more consistent than it initially looks. Third, I defend a novel account of why it's a mistake for socialists to reject the independent moral significance of exploitation. In so doing, I provide strong grounds for believing that both justice and non-exploitation are *equally* fundamental from a socialist perspective.

Before moving on, one final note about how I will be using the terms "justice" and "exploitation." For the purposes of this chapter, I will follow Cohen in assuming that *justice* concerns the overall "distribution of benefits and burdens to individuals" (Cohen, 2008, 126) in society and that a worker is *exploited* "when unfair advantage is taken of [them]" (Cohen, 1995a, 151). This implies that although exploitation is *an* injustice, in the sense that it deprives workers of what they are rightfully entitled to, exploitation and injustice are *not* one and the same concern. An individual can, in other words, be treated unjustly without being exploited, since there is more than one way to deprive someone of a just distribution of benefits and burdens. To simplify matters, we might say that whereas exploitation is primarily concerned with how *workers* are (mis)treated, justice is concerned with how *citizens* are treated and thus with the distribution of benefits and burdens in society as a whole. The question that I will be exploring in this chapter is whether it's possible to jointly reconcile the demands of justice and non-exploitation, and, if not, which value is of primary moral significance.

6.2 Why There is a Conflict between Justice and Non-Exploitation

To see the full force of this problem, let's begin by exploring Cohen's most sustained discussion of why there's a conflict between justice and non-exploitation. In "Marxism and Contemporary Political Philosophy, or: Why Nozick Exercises Some Marxists More than he Does any Egalitarian Liberals" (Cohen, 1995a, 144–64), Cohen weaves together intellectual autobiography and philosophical analysis to explain why Analytical, or "Non-Bullshit," Marxists like Jon Elster, John Roemer, and himself largely abandoned traditional Marxist "questions about base and superstructure and forces and relations of production" for more traditional normative concerns in moral and political philosophy (Cohen, 1995a, 144). In Cohen's telling, the main of impetus for this transformation was a change in the class structure of capitalist societies—changes which, in Cohen's view, "raise[d] normative problems which did not exist before, or, rather, which previously had little political significance" (Cohen, 1995a, 144–45). But what exactly was the change that occasioned this transformation and how, in turn, did it trigger moral concerns for Cohen and other Analytical Marxists?

As Cohen traces his own intellectual journey and development, he came to political philosophy as an (until then) lifelong committed Marxist—one who harbored a "certain paradigm of injustice" (Cohen, 1995a, 145) first and foremost in his mind. That paradigm, he explains, is "the relationship between the propertied capitalist and the propertyless wage worker, which Marxists take to be a relationship of unjust exploitation" (ibid.) Or, as he put it more fully, "It is a moral datum for politically committed Marxists…that there is injustice whenever an owner of capital…extracts product from a worker who lacks capital of his own and who is therefore forced to yield part of his product to a capitalist in exchange for access to means of production" (ibid.)

But that, of course, simply raises the question as to why that extraction is "unjust"—as opposed to, say, just a piece of good luck on the part of the capitalist who happens to own a form of property that the worker lacks. Why, in other words, is it unjust for capitalists to extract part of the product that workers create and appropriate it for themselves? According to Cohen, Marxists believe that this extraction is unjust "largely" for the reason that the transfer of product from the worker who creates it to the capitalist who does not involves what Marx called "the theft of another person's labour time" (ibid.). More precisely, "the wage the worker receives matches only part of the time he spends at work, so that hours which should, as a matter of justice, belong to the worker are stolen by his capitalist superior" (ibid.).

Part of what makes this objection so powerful is that it mirrors, in several crucial respects, the central injustice of feudalism. As Cohen put it, "It is manifestly true, a matter not of theory but of observation, that the serf spends part of time working for himself and another part in unrecompensed work for the lord" (Cohen, 1995a, 146). But this, of course, is also true of workers under capitalism, although the truth is much harder to discern. Indeed, the truth of that proposition is obscured by at least two features of the relationship between capitalists and workers. First, workers under capitalism are free to enter and exit contractual relationships with any capitalist that they choose. And even though this freedom is largely formal—in the sense that they are ultimately forced to work for *a* capitalist if they want to buy food—this was nevertheless not a freedom that serfs enjoyed under feudalism, since they had no choice but to work for a particular lord. Second, since workers are paid an hourly wage for their work, it's much less obvious that, like the serf under feudalism, we can divide their labor time into paid and unpaid work. But even though it's less obvious, it's fairly easy to see why it's true. For if workers received a wage that reflected the value of their productive contribution, then capitalists would, by implication, receive no income for what they do. After all, as the Marxist economist Joan Robinson reminds us, merely "*owning* capital is not a productive activity" (Robinson, 1966, 18). But since capitalists obviously earn profits in virtue of their ownership of the means of production, there must be a portion of the working day during which workers are making a productive contribution but getting back nothing in return.

Notice, however, that if the main injustice of capitalism is that capitalists steal labor time from their workers, then that implies that the labor time in question properly belongs to the worker. For, as Cohen aptly notes, "you can steal from someone only that which properly belongs to him" (Cohen, 1995a, 146). Accordingly, "the Marxist contention that the capitalist exploits the worker depends on the proposition that people are the rightful owners of their own powers" (ibid.). But that proposition is nothing less than the "principle of self-ownership," one of the central principles underlying the libertarian political philosophy of right-wing thinkers like Robert Nozick. Or, as Cohen expresses the principle more fully, self-ownership is the idea that "a person should be sovereign with respect to what he will do with his energies. He should not deploy them under another person's orders in the manner of a slave *and* have part or all of his product taken from him for nothing in return" (Cohen, 1995a, 147; emphasis in original).

Now as Cohen is at pains to emphasize, if the Marxist contention that workers are exploited under capitalism rests on the principle of self-ownership, then it follows that there are two distinct "elements" in that criticism—a point that is underlined by Cohen's highlighting of the word "and" in the sentence quoted above. On the one hand, workers are "subject" to the "will" of capitalists (Cohen, 1995a, 147). The latter, in other words, must obey the former's "commands." Workers cannot, for example, labor under their own initiative, but must instead follow the orders of their "boss." On the other hand, workers under capitalism are "deprived" (ibid.) of the product of their labor—that which they, and they alone, produced. The worker, that is to say, is the only who made a productive contribution, but the capitalist is able to use his position of power and authority to extract a share of the benefits.

These two points are separate because someone's time can be stolen from them—in the sense that, during that time, they are forced to work under someone else's command—without being deprived of what they produced during it. To mark the distinction between these two independent injustices, call the first the "Subjection Thesis" and the second the "Deprivation Thesis:"

> *Subjection Thesis*: Exploitation is unjust because it makes workers subject to the will of capitalists, i.e., it forces them to obey the latter's commands.

> *Deprivation Thesis*: Exploitation is unjust because it deprives workers of what they are rightfully entitled to, i.e., what they, and they alone, produced.

Although both of these claims lie at the heart of the Marxist criticism that capitalism is unjust, it's arguably only the latter that is central to the concept of exploitation. After all, one person can be subject to another person's will without, at the same time, being exploited. For example, if a sexist husband dominates and controls his wife but does not deprive her of the product of her labor, then he surely treats her unjustly despite the fact that he does not, strictly speaking, exploit her. Or, as Cohen put it, "A proletarian is wronged even if he is not, in Marx's sense, exploited, because his inefficient employer never gets round to assigning him a task while he waits, idly, in the factory" (ibid.) Deprivation is, therefore, fundamental to exploitation in a way that subjection is not. For that reason, it will be the main focus of our discussion.

In any event, the important point to emphasize is that the Deprivation Thesis is central not only to the Marxist charge of exploitation, but to the libertarian principle of self-ownership as well. But if that's right, then Marxists seem to be forced to accept a political conclusion that they would normally spurn. For it's a further implication of the principle of self-ownership that "the welfare state does to tax-paying workers exactly what, in the Marxist complaint, capitalists do to workers: it forcibly extracts product from them, and, libertarians would add, without benefit of the contract that workers sign with capitalists" (Cohen, 1995a, 151). It follows that "libertarians lay siege to, and embarrass, Marxists in political philosophy" (Cohen, 1995a, 152). For, as Cohen goes on to remark, "it is hard to see how welfare state extraction from a worker could be justified if the...capitalist's extraction is not." Indeed, Cohen believes that it's precisely because liberals like Rawls outright reject the principle of self-ownership that they have no trouble defending the welfare state from libertarian critics like Nozick. Of course, they also display a corresponding lack of moral concern with worker exploitation. Rawls' Difference Principle, for example, is only concerned with the just distribution of benefits and burdens between citizens and is thus completely silent on the question of whether it's wrong for employers to take unfair advantage of their employees. But that simply reinforces the surprising affinities between Marxist critiques of worker exploitation and the libertarian principle of self-ownership.

Cohen, therefore, conjectures that it's the "difficulty" that Marxists have had with the analogy between capitalists and the welfare state that "explains why so much energy has been...devoted to political philosophy" by himself and other members of the "Non-Bullshit Marxism Group." In particular, this has forced them to "rethink the theory of exploitation in a fundamental way, in order to condemn neither the redistribution of the welfare state, nor, *a fortiori*, the still more egalitarian redistributive dispensations which, as Marxists, or semi-Marxists, we endorse" (Cohen, 1995a, 152).

At this point, however, a critic might object that there cannot be a genuine tension between the Marxist theory of exploitation and the aims of the welfare state, because Marx himself, in his sketch of what a future communist society would look like, endorsed a principle that seemed to require a significant amount of redistribution. As Marx famously put it, a future communist society would be governed by the principle, "From each according to his ability, to each according to his needs," and the latter part of that principle clearly welcomes a form of redistribution that is similar in character to the redistribution that is carried out by the welfare state. How, then, can we square this communist principle with Cohen's claim that, at the heart of Marxism, is another principle—the principle of self-ownership—that conflicts with those very same redistributive aims? Indeed, as Cohen himself acknowledges, communists have also been at the forefront of the political movement to defend the welfare state from right-wing attempts to destroy it. But if that's the case, then how can a core Marxist theoretical commitment stand in tension with one of their central political aims?

Cohen's response to these objections is that they do not present a genuine problem to his claim. For, as Cohen argues, "communists saw the struggle for the welfare state as a struggle for basic minima for *working* people in particular: public provision was regarded as a modest rectification of the wrongs done to labour with respect to the product of its activity (Cohen, 1995a, 153; emphasis in original). In other words, Cohen believes that Marxist concerns about exploitation were fully compatible with the redistributive aims of the welfare state, because the welfare state, in the Marxist self-understanding, ultimately sought to correct for the maldistribution of economic resources brought about by the injustice of worker exploitation. And so, on this view, "two claims to recompense, *need* and *entitlement through labor*, are fused" (ibid.; emphasis in original). Or, put differently, "revolutionaries and progressives saw the set of exploited producers as roughly coterminous with the set of those who needed the welfare state's benefit" (ibid.).

But whatever communists believed, there is in fact a tenson between the claim that "I made this and I should therefore have it" and the claim that "I need this" (Cohen, 1995a, 154). The tension lies in the fact that, as Cohen clearly notes, "Starving people are not necessarily people who have produced what starving people need, and, if what people produce belongs as of right them, the people who have produced it, then starving people who have not produced it have no claim on it" (ibid.) Indeed, it's because these two groups—the exploited and the needy—are different that we face the problem with which this chapter began. For if the injustice of exploitation rests on the principle of self-ownership, and the principle of self-ownership blocks the redistributive aims of the welfare state, then it's not clear how a socialist who cares about achieving social justice *and* combating worker exploitation can reconcile these two claims.

6.3 How the Conflict Between Justice and Non-Exploitation Should be Resolved

Following Cohen, let's suppose that there is indeed a conflict between a just distribution of benefits and burdens between citizens and the "producer entitlement doctrine" (Cohen, 1995a, 154) that, as Cohen put it, lies at the foundation of the critique of worker exploitation. The question we now turn to is: How should socialists respond? Should they give priority to the value of justice or to the value of non-exploitation? Or is there a way for them to recognize the fundamental moral importance of both values at the same time? To answer these questions, I sketch three different accounts of the relation between justice and non-exploitation and show which one of them Cohen endorsed. For reasons of space, my discussion of these accounts will necessarily be brief. But I nevertheless hope to show not only what their strengths and weaknesses are, but why Cohen's embrace of one of them provides the basis for future work on this issue.

6.3.1 Non-exploitation has Priority over Justice

According to the first view under consideration, if there's a conflict between the demands of justice, on the one hand, and the demands of non-exploitation, on the other, then it's the latter that must receive priority from a socialist perspective. In slogan form, we can say that this view puts *non-exploitation first.*

Now as a historical matter, aspects of this view have been defended by a long line of pre-Marxist socialist thinkers. Prominent figures worth mentioning in this regard include William Godwin, Charles Hall, Pierre-Joseph Proudhon, and Ferdinand Lassalle.[3] However, on a more substantive level, it's instructive to note that there are certain natural affinities between this view and some of the central themes in the socialist tradition. For example, this view closely mirrors the idea alluded to earlier that

[3] For a discussion of these thinkers, see Menger (1899).

exploitation is the "paradigm" of injustice under capitalism. But if that's the case, then it seems to follow quite straightforwardly that we should prioritize the interests of workers. By the same token, the claim that we should put non-exploitation first seems to accord with socialist views about the revolutionary potential of the working class and the related idea that class struggle is the motor force of human history.

More importantly for our present purposes, this view seems to be entailed by the truth of the Deprivation Thesis. For if exploitation if unjust because it deprives workers of what they are rightfully entitled to, i.e., what they, and they alone, produced, then it seems to follow that no one else is entitled to it *but* workers. In other words, a natural corollary to the principle that A is entitled X is that A and *only* A is entitled to it. Implicit in the content of the Deprivation Thesis, therefore, is the notion of *absolute* entitlement—the idea that workers have an absolute right to the proceeds of their labor. This, of course, has the fortunate consequence for socialists that if workers, and only workers, are entitled to the fruits of their labor, then capitalist have no right to extract a share from it in the form of profits.

The unfortunate flipside of this claim, however, is that if workers, and only workers, are entitled to the fruits of their labor, then not only are capitalists not entitled to anything, but neither are any other non-workers. Indeed, the realization that putting the interests of workers first negates the claims not only of capitalists but also of other non-workers, forms the basis for an objection that is over one hundred years old. In the words of the Austrian social and legal theorist Anton Menger: "Any attempt to carry to a logical conclusion the idea of the labourer's right to the whole produce of his labour is immediately confronted with the numerous persons who are incapable of work (children, the aged and invalids, etc.), and who must depend for the satisfaction of their wants on unearned income" (Menger, 1899, 5). Interestingly, Cohen himself was aware of this objection and quoted it approvingly on at least two separate occasions. The first time was in the essay we already discussed, whereas the second time was in a far more obscure piece published in *Socialist Renewal*.

In a short essay in that journal entitled, "Is Socialism Inseparable from Common Ownership?" (Cohen, 1995b), Cohen examines the relation between socialism and equality in the context of a debate over Clause IV of the British Labour Party Constitution. That clause's aim was "To secure for the workers by hand or by brain the *full fruits* of their industry and the most equitable distribution thereof that may be possible upon the basis of the common ownership of the means of production, distribution and exchange, and the best obtainable system of popular administration and control of each industry or service." In Cohen's view, although there's a necessary connection between equality and socialism, in the sense that "equality of fundamental circumstance" is only compatible with "*common* ownership of the means of production" (Cohen, 1995b, 1; emphasis in original), there's a fundamental tension between that very same value and the other part of Clause IV which "assigns to workers the full fruits of their industry" (Cohen, 1995b, 2). As Cohen puts it, "Equality itself requires revision of the 'full fruits' phrase, on behalf of those who, because of their social or personal circumstances, are not able to contribute labor" (ibid.) In other words, if giving workers the full fruits of their industry implies that non-workers have "no claim to sustenance," then that's a sufficient reason to reject that part of the clause.

I fully agree. It's completely implausible to suppose that children, students, caregivers, the unemployed, the elderly, and people with disabilities have *no* right to a fair share of economic resources, or that they are *only* entitled to what workers are willing to give them out of their own generosity.[4] To the contrary, each one of these groups has an independent *claim* to a fair share of economic resources, not as a matter of charity, but as a matter of justice. They are, in Rawls' memorable phrase, "self-originating sources of valid claims" (Rawls, 2001, 23). It follows that we should we reject the view that puts exploitation first for the same reason that we should reject libertarianism: both leave the fate of non-workers to the mercy of workers and those who happen to have an independent source of wealth. Indeed, this conclusion also shows us

[4] Strictly speaking, caregivers do in fact engage in productive labor, but, as feminists have correctly reminded us, they do not receive any wages for their work.

why the welfare state is necessary not only to overcome the defects of capitalism, but to supplement even the most ideal forms of socialism. For even if all workers received a fair wage for their labor, there would still need to be a way to transfer economic resources to those who are unable to work.[5]

More broadly, it's worth pointing out that the reason why we reached this result is that there appears to be a tension among the following three propositions:

(1) Workers are entitled to an income that reflects the value of their productive contribution.
(2) Capitalists (*qua* capitalists) are not entitled to an income.
(3) (Non-capitalist) non-workers are entitled to an income that, at the very least, meets their basic needs.

Socialists can affirm (2) and (3), or (1) and (2), but they cannot simultaneously affirm (1), (2), and (3), because, as we've seen, all three propositions seem to be jointly inconsistent. They thus appear to be caught on the horns of a trilemma. And so, the question becomes: Which propositions should socialists reject and which ones should they affirm? This is not an easy question to answer, because each one of these propositions seems to reflect a basic socialist commitment.

6.3.2 Justice has Priority over Non-exploitation

If it's not possible for socialists to simultaneously affirm all three of the above propositions, and it's implausible to reject proposition (3), then perhaps the most promising response to this trilemma is to reject proposition (1), i.e., the claim that workers are entitled to an income that reflects the value of their productive contribution. This strategy—which puts *justice* first and so denies the fundamental moral significance of exploitation—is the one defended by Analytical Marxists like John Roemer and, according to Vrousalis, by Cohen himself.

[5] Conceiving of the welfare state as a system for transferring income from workers to non-workers is one of the central themes of Matt Bruenig's writing. See, e.g., Bruenig (2019).

Broadly speaking, the motivation for this view stems from the difficulties we already encountered. If taking exploitation seriously means that socialists must disregard the basic needs of non-workers, then perhaps that should force them to reevaluate the centrality of this concern. Indeed, this is the idea explored in Roemer's work. For example, Roemer answers the question posed in the title of his paper, "Should Marxists be Interested in Exploitation?" (Roemer, 1986) with a resounding "no." In his view, although Marxists have traditionally been concerned with worker exploitation, and, in particular, the forced transfer of surplus product from workers to capitalists, he believes that should no longer be true. More precisely, the mistake lies in focusing on the unequal exchange between workers and capitalists, as opposed to the underlying distributive background within which that exchange occurs. As Roemer puts it, "… for the sake of clarity and consistency, I think exploitation conceived of as the unequal exchange of labour should be replaced with exploitation conceived of as the distributional consequences of an unjust inequality in the distribution of productive assets and resources" (Roemer, 1986, 65). In other words, what matters, according to Roemer, is not the unequal flow of resources from workers to capitalists, but the unjust distribution of the stock of economic resources in society as a whole.

What's more, there are at least two reasons to believe that Cohen broadly agreed with Roemer's view. On the one hand, despite the similarities it shares with Marx's account of worker exploitation, Cohen ultimately came to reject the principle of self-ownership. For example, in an essay entitled, "Self-Ownership: Assessing the Thesis," Cohen argued that Nozick's principle fails to capture what socialists actually care about. As Cohen puts it, "Libertarians think that, if you reject the thesis of self-ownership, then you license slavery, you restrict human autonomy, and you endorse the treatment of people as mere means" (Cohen, 1995a, 1995b, 230). But, in Cohen's view, that's not true. One can condemn slavery, support autonomy, and oppose treating people as a mere means to one's ends without endorsing the principle of self-ownership. Indeed, it's precisely because the principle of self-ownership is sometimes "confuse[d]" (ibid.) with those values that helps to explain why so many socialists have been attracted to in the first place. Once these are distinguished, however, then there also seem to be grounds for rejecting the

Deprivation Thesis. For if workers are not the "rightful owners of their own powers," as the principle of self-ownership suggests, then it's not necessarily unjust to deprive them of the fruits of their labor. And if it's not unjust to deprive them of the fruits of their labor, then it seems to follow that socialists should ultimately be concerned about the justice of the distribution of benefits and burdens among citizens and not the unfair treatment of workers in and of themselves.

On the other hand, Vrousalis has also presented fairly convincing textual evidence to suggest that Cohen endorsed this view. For example, in a celebrated essay in support of the thesis that the relationship between the labor theory of value and the concept of exploitation is one of "mutual irrelevance" (Cohen, 1988, 209), Cohen also addressed the question of why it's unjust for capitalists to extract surplus product from workers. According to Vrousalis, Cohen's answer turns on the justice of the "distributive background" against which their transaction occurs. In Cohen's words: "…the crucial question for exploitation concerns the justice of the distribution of the means of production" (Cohen, 1988, 234). Vrousalis calls this the "distributive paradigm" and claims that Cohen's endorsement of it commits him to the following view: "The labourer is exploited, and the capitalist exploits, if and only if exchange in which they are engaged occurs against the background of an unjust distribution" (Vrousalis, 2015, 91). In other words, Cohen allegedly believes that the value of non-exploitation derives entirely from its connection to distributive justice and so is not fundamentally morally significant.

Let's provisionally assume that Vrousalis' interpretation is correct and that Cohen does indeed subscribe to the distributive paradigm. The question nevertheless arises as to whether this is the right way to understand the relation between justice and non-exploitation. I submit that it's not. There are at least two reasons why socialists should not deny the fundamental moral significance of exploitation. One is based on a counterexample provided by Vrousalis himself, whereas the other builds on Vrousalis' insight and attacks this view on a more fundamental level.

Begin with Vrousalis' counterexample first. Suppose, he says, that, "A finds B in a pit. A can get B out at little cost or difficulty. A offers to get B out, but only if B agrees to sign a sweatshop contract with A" (Vrousalis, 2015, 92). In Vrousalis' view, "This exchange is paradigmatic of exploitation: if this is not an instance of exploitation, then nothing is" (ibid.). Indeed, it's hard to see how anyone—let alone socialists—could disagree with this verdict. The problem, however, is that it "is inconsistent with the distributive paradigm" (ibid.). That is to say, A's offer would be exploitative even if it were made against the backdrop of a *just* distribution of economic resources: "B may, for example, have chosen not to purchase cheap insurance against falling in pits or against being rescued afterward" (ibid.). But, as Vrousalis points out, "It does not follow, and it is false, that the offer is not exploitative: A can rescue B without asking for anything but instead uses B's vulnerability in order to improve her own lot" (ibid.). And so, the upshot is that, "asset injustice furnishes no necessary condition for exploitation and therefore no proper basis for a charge of exploitation" (Vrousalis, 2015, 93).

Although I see the force of Vrousalis' counterexample, I think his criticism of the distributive paradigm can go deeper. The important point is not simply that there can be exploitation without injustice, but that since the former cannot be reduced to the latter, the wrong of exploitation is independently morally significant. It is, in other words, morally wrong to exploit someone, even if that doesn't affect the overall distribution of benefits and burdens in society. And although space prevents me from fully defending this claim here, allow me to sketch the main line of argument.

The basic idea is that exploitation is an *interpersonal* wrong, that is, a wrong that one party perpetrates against another. According to the Marxist picture, the wrong of exploitation involves capitalists extracting surplus labor from workers, but it can also be cashed out in terms of the more generic wrong of one person taking unfair advantage of another person's vulnerability or desperate situation. What matters for the purposes of my argument is that exploiters do not simply act wrongly, but that they wrong *someone*. And although this might seem like a fairly trivial point, it actually has important consequences for how we understand the moral significance of exploitation. Specifically, I would like to briefly mention the following three implications.

First, if exploitation is an interpersonal wrong, then the duty not to exploit someone shares the shares the same characteristics and features of other so-called "directed duties."[6] As the name implies, directed duties are duties that are *directed*, or *owed*, to a particular person—someone who would be wronged if the duty were violated. By way of example, consider the duty to fulfill a promise. If A promises B to meet her for lunch on Tuesday, then A has a duty *to* B to do exactly what he promised. Accordingly, if A fails to meet B for lunch on Tuesday, then not only has A acted wrongly, but he has *wronged* B. Contrast this with a more *impersonal*, or *nondirected*, duty like the duty to appreciate the value of nature. Although someone who fails to appreciate the value of nature plausibly acts wrongly, they have not wronged anyone in particular, since there is no one to whom that duty is owed. Directed duties thus specify a three-place relation between (1) an agent, (2) a required action, i.e., what the agent is morally obligated to do, and (3) a patient to whom the duty is directed.[7] Notice, however, that exploitation claims exhibit the exact same structure. If A, an employer, has a duty not to exploit B, his employee, then that is a duty that A specifically owes to B. A would thus wrong B in particular if he took unfair advantage of her vulnerability or desperate situation.

Second, and related to the above point, if A has a directed duty to B, then this generates a corresponding *claim* that B has against A for the performance of that duty. B may, in other words, demand that A do X, and so may be said to be entitled to the fulfillment of whatever X requires of him. For example, if A has a duty not to exploit B, then B is entitled to a fair wage from A. This is something that B is owed as a matter of right, and thus does not depend on A's discretion or generosity. For that reason, if A violates his duty to B, then not only does B have a justified *complaint* against A for her wrongful treatment, but she is entitled to hold him *accountable* for his failure to comply with the duty not to exploit her. And that means that A's violation of his directed duty to B triggers a residual set of duties on his part to remedy or repair the wrong in question. Most importantly for our present purposes, A now has a duty to compensate B for *his* wrongdoing.

[6] For seminal discussions of directed duties, see Thompson (2004) Sreenivasan (2010), and Wallace (2019).

[7] See May (2015) for this way of understanding directed duties.

It follows—and this is the third, and final, implication—that the wrong of exploitation must, in the first instance, be repaired by the exploiter himself, i.e., the direct perpetrator of the wrongdoing. Since A exploited B, and thus wronged her, A, and A alone, owes B compensation so as to ensure that B is no longer treated unfairly. Consequently, if A fails to compensate B for his unfair treatment, then an equivalent amount of money from C, a third party, to make up the difference, might make B equally well off from a financial perspective, but it does not fully remedy A's initial wrongdoing (since only A can do that). We can put this point another way by saying that if the amount of money that B is owed came from elsewhere, i.e., from the state, then this would not fully repair B's wrongful treatment, since not only would A still have his ill-gotten gains, but it would not change the fact that A *took unfair advantage of* B's vulnerability or desperate situation. In other words, even though state redistribution can partly remedy the wrong in question, it cannot wholly eliminate it. The wrong still remains because it centrally involves one party *using* another for their own self-enrichment. Notice, therefore, that if the above account of exploitation as an interpersonal or directed wrong is correct, then this supports the view that the value of non-exploitation is not derivative of the justice of the broader pattern of economic distribution. For if exploitation is primarily a wrong that one party perpetrates against another, then the victim of exploitation suffers not only from a distributional loss, i.e., the loss of a certain amount of income, but a relational harm that is separate and distinct (cf. Malmqvist & Szigeti, 2021). Contra the distributive paradigm, therefore, the wrong of exploitation is independently morally significant.

6.3.3 Neither Justice nor Non-exploitation has Priority Over the Other

In one of the last interviews published before his untimely death, Cohen discussed how the project of Analytical Marxism had changed over the years. One of those changes was the group's perspective on the moral significance of exploitation. As Cohen put it, "…in the normative domain it came to be thought by many of us that exploitation, while a very important concept, was essentially secondary, normatively speaking, to the concept of equality" (Tormey, 2009, 351). Indeed, that outlook forms the basis for the view that we examined in the previous section—one that, as I explained, puts justice first and holds that non-exploitation has only derivative normative significance. We also saw the textual evidence adduced by Vrousalis to suggest that Cohen subscribed to this view himself. However, in what follows, I want to cast doubt on that attribution and argue that, quite apart from its substantive problems, Cohen did not actually hold the view in question. To the contrary, there are strong reasons to believe that not only did Cohen think that the values of justice and non-exploitation were both equally fundamental, but that neither should have priority over the other from a socialist perspective.

Begin with some pieces of countervailing textual evidence. Notice, first, that Cohen's remark in the above quoted interview is ambiguous. In saying that "many of us" came to believe that exploitation is only of secondary normative significance, Cohen might either be saying that he *himself* now believes that, or he might instead be referring to the beliefs of *other* Analytical Marxists like Roemer. Interestingly, moments later in that same interview, Cohen states that, in light of this re-assessment of the value of exploitation, "*We* therefore had to articulate an appropriate egalitarianism and to determine what it implies…That's why so many of us began to discuss equality, rather than exploitation. It turned out that exploitation was downstream, normatively, from the injustice of inequality. And that realization loosened *our* tie to Marxism" (Tormey, 2009, 351–52; emphasis added). This seems to be further evidence for the former, more inclusive, interpretation, but Cohen still stops short of *explicitly* endorsing the claim that justice has priority over non-exploitation. What's more, it's not clear how to square that view with other, equally central, aspects of Cohen's thinking.

For example, one of the enduring and, in my view, highly attractive, features of Cohen's outlook was his value *pluralism*—the belief that there is a multiplicity of distinct, yet equally important, values that cannot be realized simultaneously. This is a belief that Cohen shared with Isaiah Berlin, one of his mentors, and that helped to distinguish him from thinkers like Rawls who argued for a more systematic value *unity*. In

Rescuing Justice and Equality, Cohen labelled this outlook "radical pluralism" (Cohen, 2008, 4) and noted that one of its implications is that "the normative requirements that we recognize present themselves in competitive array: they cannot all be satisfied all the time, nor do we have a method for systematically combining them. Discursively indefensible trade-offs are our fate" (ibid.). One of the hallmarks of Cohen's value pluralism, in other words, is the insistence that it's a mistake to think that we can establish definite priority relations among values, or rank-order them from least to most important. Yet that's precisely the ambition of the previous view. Given Cohen's endorsement of value pluralism, therefore, it seems more likely that he would have subscribed to a view that put neither justice nor non-exploitation first, and instead tried to balance them in a more intuitive or piecemeal fashion.

In fact, Cohen seems to have explicitly endorsed such a view in one of his most influential papers. In "On the Currency of Egalitarian Justice," Cohen flatly states that, "I believe that the primary egalitarian impulse is to extinguish the influence on distribution of *both* exploitation and brute luck" (Cohen, 1989, 908; emphasis added). And although his discussion in the paper is devoted almost exclusively to the latter consideration, it seems hard to resist the conclusion that, in seeking to eliminate the influence of both exploitation *and* brute luck on a person's economic circumstances, Cohen is highlighting the fact that he regards both of them as equally morally significant. Curiously, Vrousalis interprets this claim to mean that Cohen was developing a "luck egalitarian definition of exploitation" (Vrousalis, 2014, 91)—one that fits squarely within the distributive paradigm and asserts the primacy of (luck egalitarian) justice over non-exploitation. But this interpretation is contradicted by both the plain meaning of the word "and" in Cohen's description of the primary egalitarian impulse, as well as the fact that, later on in that very same paper, Cohen writes that the "grounding idea [is] that disadvantage is to be redressed when it reflects *either* exploitation or bad luck" (Cohen, 1989, 937; emphasis added).

Further evidence for attributing to Cohen the view that neither justice nor non-exploitation has priority over the other comes from the fact that he himself strongly criticized Roemer' defense of the distributive paradigm. Recall that according to the distributive paradigm, exploitation is unjust only if and because it reflects an injustice in the background distribution of economic resources. But in response to that claim, Cohen posed a very simple question: Is the background distribution unjust because there is something intrinsically wrong with one group of people owning more resources than another, or is it unjust because of what that inequality causes to obtain, namely, the fact that one group in society can exploit the other? Although Cohen believed that defenders of the distributive paradigm were committed to the former answer, he did not find it convincing. To the contrary, he believed that "an unjust distribution of means of production owes its injustice to the injustice of the surplus extraction that such a distribution facilitates" (Cohen, 1995a, 1995b, 201), i.e., to the fact that it enables capitalists to exploit workers. Cohen, therefore, "part[ed] company with Roemer" (Cohen, 1995a, 1995b, 206) on this issue.

Interestingly, Vrousalis eventually came around to this conclusion himself, arguing that Cohen "disavowed the distributive paradigm towards the end of his life" (Vrousalis, 2014, 96). His evidence for Cohen's "change of mind," as Vrousalis puts it, stems from one of the final essays he published in a *Festschrift* for Hillel Steiner. In that essay, Cohen defended the view that, "exploitation [is] a distinct form of injustice, and not particularly a matter for egalitarianism" (quoted in Vrousalis, 2014, 97). For that reason, Vrousalis thinks that Cohen ultimately came to the realization that not only is the distributive paradigm false, but that it's a mistake "to subsume claims of exploitation under distributive injustice, where they do not belong" (Vrousalis, 2014, 98). And whether one agrees with Vrousalis that there is a decisive break between an "early" and "late" Cohen on this matter, or one instead subscribes to my view that Cohen was fairly consistent all along, the crucial point is that Cohen believed that both justice and non-exploitation were equally fundamental from a socialist perspective.

Quite apart from this exegetical question, however, the real difficulty lies in figuring out how to combine the values of justice and non-exploitation in a single social system. As we've seen, this difficulty can be expressed in the form of a trilemma. Socialists believe that (1) workers are entitled to an income that reflects the value of their productive contribution; (2) capitalists are not entitled to an income solely in virtue of their ownership of the means of production; and (3) non-workers are entitled to a level of income that, at the very least, satisfies their basic needs. But it does not seem possible to simultaneously satisfy all three propositions. Of course, the fundamental problem, from a socialist point of view, is how to combine (1) and (3), since the more the former is satisfied, the less that seems to be true of the latter. It's thus not clear that justice and non-exploitation can both be regarded as equally fundamental, even if that was Cohen's actual position.

Perhaps the only way to escape the horns of this trilemma is to modify or revise these two propositions. Indeed, I think this is the most promising approach for socialists who take both values seriously. More precisely, the revision would take the form of weakening the sense of "entitlement" at issue. Broadly speaking, the idea would be that workers are entitled to an income that reflects the value of their productive contribution, but that entitlement would be a *pro tanto*, rather than an *absolute*, one. In this way, one can argue that workers have a right to receive fair compensation for their labor, but that right could be overridden or outweighed by other, equally important, considerations, e.g., the fact that non-workers also have a *pro tanto* entitlement to a level of economic resources that meets their basic needs. One advantage of this view is that most philosophers already agree that few, if any, rights or entitlements are absolute to begin with; it's thus not obvious why these would be any different. But it also raises the question of how to properly balance the values of justice and non-exploitation. Cohen may have believed that "discursively indefensible trade-offs are our fate" (Cohen, 2008, 4), but it would surely be helpful if socialists had more than that to say. Even worse, if the demands of justice and non-exploitation pull in two different directions, then an acceptable compromise between them might not even be possible.

6.4 Conclusion

This chapter examined the relation between justice and non-exploitation from a socialist perspective. In particular, I explored G.A. Cohen's own writings on the issue. As I argued, Cohen believed that neither justice nor non-exploitation should have priority over the other in cases of conflict, but are instead both equally fundamental. The question nevertheless remains as to how these values should be combined in a single social system. Although Cohen believed that there's no reliable method for weighing different values against each other, it's an entirely separate question whether that's the correct way to approach the issue. Socialists thus need to devote more attention to this problem. The viability of Analytical Marxism and democratic socialism in the twenty-first century may depend on it.

References

Bruenig, M. (2019). Family fun pack. *People's Policy Project*. Retrieved November 1, 2024, from https://www.peoplespolicyproject.org/projects/family-fun-pack/

Bruenig, M. (2018). The best way to eradicate poverty: Welfare not jobs. *People's Policy Project*. Retrieved November 1, 2024, from https://www.peoplespolicyproject.org/2018/09/18/the-best-way-to-eradicate-poverty-welfare-not-jobs/

Cohen, G. A. (1988). *History, labour, and freedom: Themes from Marx*. Oxford University Press.

Cohen, G. A. (1989). On the currency of egalitarian justice. *Ethics, 99*(4), 906–944.

Cohen, G. A. (1995a). *Self-ownership, freedom, and equality*. Cambridge University Press.

Cohen, G. A. (1995b). Is socialism inseparable from common ownership. *Socialist Renewal, 1*, 1–8.

Cohen, G. A. (2008). *Rescuing justice and equality*. Harvard University Press.

Malmqvist, E., & Szigeti, A. (2021). Exploitation and remedial duties. *Journal of Applied Philosophy, 38*(1), 55–72.

May, S. C. (2015). Directed duties. *Philosophy Compass, 10*(8), 532–532.
Menger, A. (1899). *The right to the whole produce of labour: The origin and development of the theory of labour's claim to the whole product of industry.* MacMillan and Co.
Rawls, J. (2001). *Justice as fairness: A restatement*. Harvard University Press.
Roemer, J. (1986). Should Marxists be interested in exploitation? *Philosophy and Public Affairs, 14*(1), 30–65.
Sreenivasan, G. (2010). Duties and their direction. *Ethics, 120*(3), 465–494.
Thompson, M. (2004). What is it to wrong someone? A puzzle about justice. In R. J. Wallace, P. Pettit, S. Scheffler, & M. Smith (Eds.), *Reasons and value: Themes from the moral philosophy of Joseph Raz* (pp. 333–384). Clarendon Press.
Tormey, S. (2009). Simon Tormey interviews G.A. Cohen. *Contemporary Political Theory, 8*(3), 351–362.
Wallace, R. J. (2019). *The moral nexus*. Princeton University Press.

7

G.A. Cohen, the Neglect of Democratic Self-Management, and the Future of Democratic Socialism

Igor Shoikhedbrod

7.1 Introduction

This chapter examines G.A. Cohen's legacy as the twenty-first century's pre-eminent socialist philosopher in the Anglo-American analytical tradition. More specifically, the chapter tracks the evolution of Cohen's rigorous defense of socialist egalitarian norms and the influence that it continues to exert on contemporary political philosophers. Of particular importance to my discussion will be Cohen's neglected essay, "The Future of a Disillusion." There Cohen considers the future of socialism by reassessing classical socialist arguments against capitalism while defending socialist commitments to equality and community. Cohen also criticizes leading proposals for market socialism because they exhibited, in his view, instances of "Adaptive Preference Formation" (APF) and undermined key socialist norms. I will show that Cohen's

I. Shoikhedbrod (✉)
St. Francis Xavier University, Antigonish, Canada
e-mail: ishoikhe@stfx.ca

B. Burgis and M. McManus (eds.), *Analytical Marxism and Democratic Socialism in the 21st Century*, Palgrave Studies in Classical Liberalism,
https://doi.org/10.1007/978-3-032-02894-5_7

dissatisfaction with classical socialist arguments against capitalist markets led him to neglect democratic self-management (DSM)—an important institutional principle that can further freedom, equality, and community. Furthermore, I identify the extent to which the political philosophers most influenced by Cohen's defense of socialist equality continue to share his disregard for DSM. I argue that such disregard for DSM cannot be sustained without undermining values that remain central to the socialist project. More concretely, disregard for DSM represents a failure to extend the purview of justice to the workplace, which has a profound bearing on people's daily lives. If the purview of justice ought to extend to individual choices in the market, then neglecting the normative relevance of people's conditions of work, which are usually organized undemocratically and often yield profoundly unequal outcomes, will violate socialist commitments to freedom, equality, and community. Socialism, I maintain, cannot be defended consistently without honoring the institutional principle of DSM.

My argument will proceed in four steps. First, I situate Cohen's neglected 1991 essay in the broader context of his work and show how it led him to neglect DSM. I then take up the only proposal for market-based socialism that Cohen considered, which he took to be a pioneering model. This was the model theorized by Joseph Carens, which combines the coordinating function of the market with the use of moral incentives to generate an egalitarian distribution. After providing a brief overview, I subject the Carensian model to critique on two fronts. First, the Carensian model risks producing a psychologically conflicted self (i.e., a pre-tax individual motivated by profit maximization and a post-tax individual committed to full equality), which has the potential of undermining community in Cohen's specific sense of "communal reciprocity," as well as the stability of egalitarian commitments. Second, Carens' continued disregard for DSM represents a failure to extend the ambit of justice to the workplace, which *ceteris paribus*, would remain organized in an undemocratic and paternalistic manner. I show that this move is inconsistent with the spirit of Cohen's response to the Rawlsian basic structure objection. Moreover, when Cohen seeks to reconcile freedom, equality, and Pareto optimality with recourse to the Carensian model, he follows Carens in limiting the scope of freedom to occupational choice, which while important, overlooks the equality, autonomy, and welfare-enhancing features associated with DSM. After illustrating the drawbacks of disregarding DSM, I extend my critique to John Roemer's recently revised account of socialism. Finally, drawing on the work of Carol Gould, Erik Olin Wright and others, I argue for the inclusion of DSM as a consideration of justice in the sphere of production and show its instrumental role in furthering freedom, equality, and community—values that should remain vital to any defensible version of democratic socialism.

7.2 The Future of a Disillusion

G.A. Cohen is considered the leading Anglo-American socialist philosopher of the twenty-first century, and for good reason. His work has been praised for its analytical rigor and principled commitment to rescuing justice, equality, and community from their inconsistent application by prominent left-liberal and libertarian political philosophers.[1] This chapter reaffirms Cohen's place as the foremost socialist philosopher of our time by examining his enduring influence on contemporary political philosophers, especially Joseph Carens and John Roemer. One of Cohen's lasting contributions was to offer robust philosophic arguments for socialism on explicitly normative grounds, that is, by clearly articulating and defending underlying socialist values. The need for such a defense became even more necessary as the Soviet Union was on the brink of collapse and global capitalism reigned supreme, leading Cohen to pose anew the question of socialism and its future. In what follows, I reconsider the Cohen-inspired question of what socialism's future ought to be by revisiting his earliest response in "The Future of a Disillusion."

[1] Given his background, it would be more appropriate to call Cohen the most influential Anglo-Canadian socialist political philosopher. For a sense of Cohen's wide-ranging influence and contributions to contemporary political philosophy, which includes a well researched account of the interplay between the 'personal' and 'political' dimensions of Cohen's thought, including occasional tensions between them, see Sypnowich (2024). See also Sypnowich (2006). For an accessible introduction to Cohen's political philosophy, see Vrousalis (2015). Most of Cohen's later essays have been published posthumously in edited anthologies. See Cohen (2011a, 2013), and most recently Cohen (2014).

Revisiting Cohen's arguments in that essay will allow me to identify those features of the socialist project he sought to retain throughout his work (justice, equality, and community), and those he left behind (central planning, market socialism, and DSM).

A retrospective look at G.A. Cohen's essay, "The Future of a Disillusion," may strike some readers as a fruitless exercise in intellectual history rather than a serious engagement with Cohen's philosophical legacy. However, there is far more value to Cohen's essay than first meets the eye, especially if one reflects on the social, political, and economic challenges confronting the countries that previously made up the Soviet Union. Anyone who has read Cohen's essay with sufficient care will recall the vivid metaphor he used to encapsulate his complex relationship with the Soviet Union—likening it to that of a discontented son, who pummels his father's chest only to realize, melancholically, that his father is no more. In Cohen's rendition: "It is true that I was heavily critical of the Soviet Union, but the angry little boy who pummels his father's chest will not be glad if the old man collapses. As long as the Soviet Union seemed safe, it felt safe for me to be anti-Soviet. Now that it begins, disobligingly, to crumble, I feel impotently protective toward it." (Cohen, 1991, pp. 9–10)[2] As with many socialist intellectuals in the 1990s, the looming collapse of the Soviet Union was a major turning point for Cohen's political philosophy.[3] One can readily discern in Cohen's essay a profound dissatisfaction with some of the key arguments that had been put forward by the theoreticians of classical socialism, particularly Karl Marx and Frederick Engels. One of these arguments centered on criticizing the characteristically anarchic and inefficient tendencies of the capitalist market system, which runs roughshod over human beings and reduces them to "plaything[s] of alien powers."[4] Cohen now considers this classical socialist argument to be

[2] The same essay was later republished in Cohen (1995, pp. 245–265).

[3] In the second edition to his *Karl Marx's Theory of History*, Cohen concludes that "if the Soviet Union had succeeded in building an attractive socialism, then that would have been wonderful for socialism, but bad for the credibility of historical materialism." According to Cohen, this conclusion follows from the classical Marxist premise that an exhaustive development of a society's productive forces is a precondition for its revolutionary transformation. See Cohen (2000b, p. 394).

[4] See Marx (1978, p. 34).

misguided, originating in a problematic Hegelian-inspired view, which sees "the ascent of man from the kingdom of necessity to the kingdom of freedom" (Cohen, 1991, p. 17). Citing the work of David Miller approvingly in this context, Cohen suggests a wholescale abandonment of the socialist urge to replace impersonal market relations with concerted collective action, purpose, and planning. He insists that democracy and collective purpose are not one and the same, and that there is no good reason to insist upon collective purpose as an end-in-itself. It is ironic that Cohen traces Marx's desire for collective self-determination and democratic planning back to Hegel, who famously championed the market as a quintessentially modern and reciprocal system of needs in the *Philosophy of Right*.[5] Marx, too, was more nuanced in his attitude towards markets, at one point favoring worker-owned and managed cooperatives as a transitionary phase towards "associated production."[6] As we will see, Cohen's hasty conflation of collective action with central planning had the regrettable consequence of neglecting the principle of DSM and its role in furthering freedom, equality, and community, more about which in the subsequent sections.

After conceding that the classical socialist critiques of the capitalist market as anarchic and inefficient are unconvincing in the face of the Hayekian critique, as well as the disappointing realities of "actually-existing socialism" (Cohen, 1991, p. 17), Cohen turns his attention to those aspects of the socialist critique he thinks are worth retrieving and defending. The first of these critiques has to do with the claim that the inequalities resulting from market arrangements, including market socialist arrangements, are unjust. The second critique concerns the inference that the motivational presuppositions of market systems (ranging in mixed proportions of fear and greed) are destructive to

[5] See Hegel (2008), particularly pp. 182–210.

[6] Marx wrote that worker cooperatives represent "within the old form [of production] the first sprouts of the new," and that "the capitalist stock companies, as much as the co-operative factories, should be considered as transitional forms from the capitalist mode of production to the associated one, with the only distinction that the antagonism is resolved negatively in the one and positively in the other." Marx (1967, p. 440). After providing a textual overview concerning the ambivalent attitudes of classical Marxists towards cooperatives, Radoslav Selucky concludes that only a self-managed socialist economy would be consistent with Marx's commitment to the freedom of associated producers. See Selucky (1975, p. 61).

community. While identifying these enduring features of the socialist critique, Cohen takes issue with proposals for market socialism, which he sees as succumbing to APF. According to Cohen's formulation of APF—a concept he borrowed and reformulated from Jon Elster—a socialist prefers market socialism not because it is normatively appealing or just but because it appears readily available, institutionally feasible, and is broadly in vogue (Ibid, p. 14). In Elster's original rendition, the fox that once desired the sweet grapes convinces itself (subconsciously) that the grapes are actually sour, that is, after discovering that they are beyond its reach (Elster, 1983, p. 23). At this point in his essay, Cohen interprets David Miller's account of market socialism as succumbing to APF.[7] This is because market socialists like Miller regard the inequalities resulting from superior labor contribution as distributively just (i.e., an argument from desert) and inescapable, whereas Cohen continued to hold the opposite view.[8]

As far as Cohen was concerned, the only market-based model that could fulfill the demands of justice is the one pioneered by Joseph Carens in his 1981 book, *Equality, Moral Incentives, and the Market* (Cohen, 1991, pp. 18–19). Despite some reservations, Cohen continued to regard the Carensian model as the most promising one, referring to it in *Rescuing Justice and Equality* as an instance of the "ethical solution," and again, in "Why Not Socialism?," where Cohen drops reference to APF but retains his earlier views verbatim, while also incorporating a critical discussion of more recent proposals for market socialism. Since Carens' work is a reoccurring point of reference for Cohen, it helps to briefly unpack the Carensian model of moral incentives and to show why it remains at best neutral and at worst indifferent towards the institutional principle of DSM, which will carry undesirable normative consequences for Cohen's defense of socialism. I will define DSM throughout the chapter as the power of workers to jointly determine their conditions

[7] I will not assess the veracity of Cohen's charges against market socialists for succumbing to APF. It suffices to say that Cohen drops the concept in his final work on socialism. More importantly, my argument for DSM does not hinge on affirming or refuting Cohen's account of APF.

[8] For a recent restatement of this debate, see Miller (2014).

of work (and production more generally) at the level of the cooperative firm in accordance with such values as freedom (as autonomy or self-determination), equality, and community.

7.3 Toward a Critique of the Carensian Model: Community and the Ambit of Justice

In *Rescuing Justice and Equality*, Cohen praises the Carensian model of moral incentives as "an attempt at describing the nuts and bolts, the institutional realization, of such an ethical solution [one which has the potential for reconciling freedom of occupational choice, equality, and Pareto optimality]." (Cohen, 2009, p. 190) Elsewhere, Cohen remarks that although he does not endorse the Carensian model full stop, he thinks it "merits contemplation as a pioneering example of the ethical solution." (Ibid. n.11, p. 190)[9] Cohen's main reservations about the Carensian model are its emphasis on social duty, which has the potential for oppressing the talented because it does not set clear limits on the obligation to contribute one's labor, and its overlooking of comparative welfare (Cohen, 2009, pp. 369–370). My concern with the Carensian model is not its supposed oppression of the talented because this line of criticism has already been addressed charitably and persuasively in Carens' later work.[10] The more problematic feature of the Carensian model is the potential tension between pre-tax market relations and the egalitarian ethos, which can subvert community in Cohen's sense of "communal reciprocity." For the purposes of clarity, it is important to recall that Cohen uses two distinct but mutually affirming conceptions of community in *Rescuing Justice and Equality*. The first is justificatory community, which demands that inequalities be justified interpersonally. The second is communal reciprocity, which implies a shared sense

[9] Cohen reminds readers about the utopian character of Carens' book and its revealing subtitle, "An Essay in Utopian Politico-Economic Theory," in Cohen (2005, p. 70). Despite his residual reservations about the Carensian model, Cohen continued to think that it was sufficiently feasible in reconciling freedom, equality, and Pareto optimality. See Cohen (2009, p. 191).

[10] See, for instance Carens (1986), and more recently Carens (2003).

of egalitarian purpose and cooperative social relations in both production and distribution.[11] I am concerned with the latter conception, which I define here as democratic practices of cooperation in the spheres of production and distribution that can help reinforce just social relations in daily life. Since Cohen does not provide an alternative institutionalized framework for conceiving the "ethical solution," I take the Carensian model to be the closest institutional approximation of the ethical solution as he understood it.

It is regrettable that Carens' model of moral incentives has not received sufficient scholarly attention in recent years.[12] Cohen, for his part, provides a concise summary of the Carensian model in *Rescuing Justice and Equality*:

> There are pre-tax-profit-maximizing capitalists and workers who own no capital, but people acknowledge an obligation to serve others, and they therefore submit to the taxation that effects a fully egalitarian posttax [sic] distribution of income. Producers aim in an immediate sense at cash results, but they do not keep the money that accrues, and they seek it out of a desire to contribute to society. (Cohen, 2009, p. 190)

At its core, Carens' articulation of the "ethical solution" is an attempt at defending the socialist principle of distribution "from each according to abilities, to each according to needs," which he insists is "a compelling moral ideal, superior to the resigned, complacent, or enthusiastic acceptance of economic inequality that is offered by defenders of conventional capitalism and by many versions of liberalism" (Carens, 2003, p. 145). Carens interprets the first part of this principle ("from each according to abilities") as a moral duty to contribute one's labor to the production of goods and services that are then distributed to full equality (Ibid. p 149). Elsewhere, Carens explains that this moral duty is not legally coercive and that individuals are not expected to contribute everything they possibly can; the only expectation is working a full-time job. If someone chooses

[11] See Cohen (2009, p. 43), and Cohen (2005, p. 66), for his dual usage of community.

[12] One notable exception is the work of Pablo Gilabert (2015). However, Gilabert focuses mostly on the socialist principle of distribution and does not explicitly fault Carens, as I do, for disregarding DSM (and justice in production more broadly).

to work more hours, this is morally praiseworthy but is not required by justice (Carens, 2003, p. 145). The Carensian model is structured on a moral commitment to equality, where market mechanisms are used to allocate labor supply and resources for the purposes of achieving post-tax equality and productive efficiency (Ibid. p 33). Carens argues that the market can be used for efficiently allocating resources without the inequalities that pervade capitalist societies and standard market socialist schemes (Carens, 1981, p. 11). Apart from the logical and empirical requirements cited by Carens, his model is distinguished foremost by its emphasis on moral rather than monetary incentives.

Although Carens argues that his model would require a more intense socialization process than that of capitalist societies, including a more heightened recognition of productive contribution and greater knowledge of relative prices (Ibid. p. 97), he underestimates the disparities between pre-tax relations of production and post-tax redistributive outcomes. To put the matter another way, Carens advocates a market society in which individuals are initially encouraged to maximize productive output and cash results, except that unlike in a typical capitalist market society, individuals are driven by moral incentives to contribute their labor and do not get to keep their pre-tax incomes. These individuals would willfully endorse post-tax redistribution to full equality because they are committed to the value of equality. Much like Cohen, Carens submits that the practical implementation of the socialist principle of distribution requires a shared ethos that would inspire egalitarian choice and voluntary compliance with post-tax (redistributive) egalitarian outcomes. Carens maintains that "for distribution based on socialist principles to be possible, most people in a society must accept these principles as being morally required. This is what I mean when I say that socialism requires a shared public ethos." (Carens, 2003, p. 165).

In recent years, Carens has characterized the egalitarian ethos as a social device that performs functions analogous to price signals in a market economy. Carens submits:

> The egalitarian ethos is the mechanism that gives people a motivation to act on the information provided by the prices offered for labor, even though those prices no longer translate into personal income, or at least

> not fully so. The duty to contribute performs the function that the desire for income performs in a conventional market, that is, it gives people a reason to respond to price signals about the relative scarcity and relative value of their labor in different sorts of productive activities. (Carens, 2015, p. 71)

In all cases, the heavy conceptual lifting is accomplished by a powerful sense of moral duty or an egalitarian ethos in the Carensian model, both of which are presumed to exist from the outset and remain in effect between pre-tax market relations of production and post-tax egalitarian outcomes. However, one of the problems with the Carensian model is a possible tension between the pre-tax individual, whose daily life is governed by profit-maximization and competitive market relations, and the post-tax individual, who is expected to endorse post-tax equality because of a prior moral commitment to equality. This double existence is reminiscent of the Rawlsian state that seeks to apply the difference principle by taxing away the consequences of profit-maximizing behavior in the market. The obvious difference here is that Rawls does not redistribute to full equality (or, for that matter, according to differentially incurred basic needs) and does not emphasize a moral duty to contribute one's labor for the purposes of achieving an equal distribution.[13] In contradistinction, the Carensian model of moral incentives presupposes that individuals internalize a moral duty to contribute their talents and skills for the betterment of their fellow citizens. However, in both cases, the initial maximization of cash gains is then taxed to achieve a just distribution among individuals who are supposedly committed to justice.

The notion of a moral duty to contribute one's labor to the productive output of society is problematic when the society in question is still informed by pre-tax market principles of production, even if no one in this society owns capital assets or gets to keep their pre-tax incomes. The moral duty articulated by Carens demands that individuals contribute their talents and skills for the purposes of achieving post-tax equality,

[13] See Rawls' later work, *Justice as Fairness: A Restatement*, which is concerned with securing the necessary background conditions for justice as fairness in the preferred institutional form of property-owning democracy, although Rawls also remained open to liberal socialism. Rawls (2001).

but it demands this in the broader context of pre-tax market relations, which have the power of subverting community in Cohen's sense of communal reciprocity. In keeping with Cohen's understanding, community here implies possessing a shared egalitarian purpose and ethos that is expressed by cooperative solidarity in the sphere of production, as well as in distribution. While the moral agent in the Carensian scheme is expected to endorse post-tax equality, it is conceivable that this agent will not want to relinquish the relevant set of cash gains as a result of pre-tax market conditioning in the productive sphere that then becomes detrimental to community.[14] To be sure, Carens could retort that this individual was not genuinely committed to equality in the first place, which is a prerequisite of his model, but such a response begs the question since it assumes away what should be explained, or at the very least considered as a possibility. While one could assume away the possibility of a psychologically conflicted self, doing so will not persuade readers who are otherwise sympathetic to the Carensian solution.[15] To be clear, I am not opposed to using the coordinating function of the market for

[14] To be clear, I am not suggesting that the problem of egalitarian motivation can be addressed simply or exclusively with the implementation of DSM. Even if DSM is honored as an institutional principle, there remains an important redistributive role for the democratic socialist state, whose goal will be to implement taxation policies ("rules of regulation" in Cohen's terminology) that accord with socialist commitments to freedom, equality, and community. DSM can help further the realization of these values.

[15] Nicholas Vrousalis goes further in his critique of the Carensian solution, referring to this problem of the psychologically conflicted self in the Carensian scheme as an instance of "bourgeois schizophrenia." Vrousalis writes: "Market socialism, even Carensian market socialism, is a generalized, self-reproducing kidnapping, in the sense that both the victims of kidnapping and the victims of the market (in the non-innocuous sense of 'market') are dominated: only a handful of workers are ever given a reasonable exist option from the sort of institutionalized relationship that breeds fear and/or greed, in which their lives are embedded and reproduced." See Vrousalis (2015, pp. 122–123). While I agree with Vrousalis' point regarding the possible psychological instability associated with the Carensian model, Vrousalis makes the mistake of conflating Cohen's commitment to the decommodification of labor with decommodification in toto (i.e., the decommodification of labor, as well as goods and services). On this view, nothing short of wholescale decommodification and comprehensive planning will meet the demands of Cohen-style communal reciprocity. While it is true that the Carensian model does not decommodify labor, the models proposed by Carol Gould and David Schweickart do just that while also honoring the institutional principle of DSM. DSM is a concrete instance of democratic planning at the local level that meets the demands of communal reciprocity in ways that are feasible and consistent with socialist values. See Gould (1988, p. 145) and Schweickart (2013, p. 13).

the purposes of achieving robust levels of post-tax equality and productive efficiency; the practical realization of these goals will be integral in any decent version of democratic socialism. My critique of the Carensian model is a sympathetic one; it is intended to bring out the normative tensions and problems that arise when one takes this model seriously.

The first issue with the Carensian model, then, is that it overlooks the extent to which the tension between pre-tax market relations and post-tax equality can undermine community and the stability of egalitarian commitments, which Cohen actively sought to defend.[16] For this scheme to work, Carens also assumes that individuals will be concerned primarily with maximizing pre-tax incomes and productive outputs rather than desiring greater leisure time, expending their energies on care work, which continues to be undervalued (and often at the expense of racialized women), or participating more actively in their communities through volunteer work. It is doubtful that this assumption can be sustained given existing ecological realities, as well the combined precariousness, burnout, and job polarization confronting many working people in advanced capitalist countries.[17] In other words, there may be additional conflicts between the Carensian expectation of maximizing productive outputs and incomes, and commitments to safeguarding the environment by decreasing the carbon footprint, preferring greater leisure time relative to paid work, or volunteering in community affairs. Moreover, insofar as labor power continues to be regarded as a commodity in the Carensian scheme (i.e., there will be a market for labor), workers will be exposed to market exigencies and relations of domination analogous

[16] Rawlsians like Michael Titelbaum have conceded Cohen's point that the absence of an egalitarian ethos in daily life would compromise the stability of Rawlsian justice by rendering it psychologically implausible. Titelbaum criticizes the demanding character of Cohen's egalitarian ethos and proposes a Rawlsian ethos that would allow for greater "productive latitude" in the market. See Titelbaum (2008, pp. 295–296). Although Carens clearly presupposes an egalitarian ethos, his continued bracketing of workplace considerations leaves him vulnerable to similar charges of psychological implausibility, which can compromise community (Cohen-style communal reciprocity) and the stability of the egalitarian commitments that his model requires.

[17] See Standing (2011). Chi Kwok identifies a troubling polarization between high-skilled and low-skilled workers vis-à-vis access to the "goods of work." In Kwok's Rawlsian-inspired view, such polarization, which is particularly disadvantageous to low-skilled workers, "provides a pro tanto justification for workplace democracy." See Kwok (2020, p. 351).

to those experienced in conventional capitalist firms, issues about which Carens has remained surprisingly silent.

Cohen, for his part, derived the idea of communal reciprocity from the value of community in "Why Not Socialism?," where he defines communal reciprocity as

> the non-market principle according to which I serve you not because of what I can get in return but because you need my service, and you, for the same reason, serve me. Communal reciprocity is not the same thing as market reciprocity, since the market motivates productive contribution not on the basis of commitment to one's fellow human beings and a desire to serve them while being served by them, but on the basis of cash reward. The immediate motive of productive activity in a market society is typically some mixture of greed and fear, in proportions that vary with the details of a person's market position and personal character. (Cohen, 2005, p. 66)

Communal reciprocity is distinguished from market reciprocity both in the form and in the content of social relations. Market social relations are based on a combination of fear and greed according to Cohen, which bestows greater rewards and benefits upon winners while depriving losers of these same benefits and rewards. Communal reciprocity, on the other hand, depends on the recognition of the individual's desire to serve and be served by other individuals, where there is a more consistent relationship between the private individual and the egalitarian member of the public sphere. The failure of central planning and the inequalities produced by all market schemes led Cohen to conclude that while the socialist ideal to extend community to the economic sphere is desirable, it is not yet feasible (Ibid. p. 74). In the same context, Cohen considers the Carensian model in a favorable light. However, as I have tried to demonstrate in the foregoing section, Carens has failed to address the possible psychological tension between pre-tax market relations and post-tax egalitarian outcomes, a tension that can undermine community (as communal reciprocity) and compromise the stability of egalitarian commitments.

The foregoing claim that Carens overlooks a possible psychological tension between pre-tax and post-tax conditions should not be misunderstood as an a priori argument about the Carensian model. Instead, I follow the model's internal strictures and affirm the significance that Carens attaches to the practice of thinking through the institutional implications of one's principles. As Carens has himself acknowledged, adherence to this approach represents a significant methodological departure from Cohen's insistence on elaborating principles independent of factual considerations.[18] Carens writes: "In at least one respect, however, I agree with Rawls more than with Cohen. It is important for philosophers to think through the institutional implications of the principles that they defend." (Carens, 2015, p. 50) Consequently, the attribution of a psychological tension to the Carensian model is not the result of an a priori exercise; rather, it is an inference that arises from the practice of thinking through the institutional implications of the Carensian model, which disregards workplace organization and its profound effects in everyday life. Carens' disregard for workplace organization points to a second and more pervasive shortcoming, namely that his model limits the purview of justice to post-tax distribution, and thereby remains indifferent to the question of how production should be organized and by whom it ought to be controlled. Carens has maintained this position from the time of his earliest work to his most recent elaboration of the egalitarian ethos. Carens' overriding emphasis on post-tax distribution and his neglect of DSM in the sphere of production can be explained by his continued reliance on the Rawlsian index of primary goods, which includes basic rights, liberties, opportunities, income, and wealth, as well as self-respect, but not considerations of workplace organization and DSM in sphere of production.[19]

[18] Cohen criticizes Rawlsian constructivism for failing to properly distinguish between "normative principles" and "rules of regulation." See Cohen (2009, p. 276). The need to insulate normative principles from factual considerations (including institutional ones) remained a central feature of Cohen's approach to political philosophy. See Cohen (2011b, pp. 227–228). For an engaging socialist critique of Cohen's adherence to fact-insensitivity, see Nielsen (2012).

[19] Carens sees Rawls' theory of justice as offering a justificatory basis for his model of moral incentives. The index of primary goods is a central feature of Rawls' theory of distributive justice. See Carens (1981, pp. 108–11).

In his most recent work, Carens writes: "I leave aside questions about the ownership and control of non-human capital, except to assume that capital, too, is largely allocated through markets, regardless of whether we are imagining some form of market capitalism or market socialism or something in between like a property-owning democracy." (Carens, 2015, n.4, p. 52) In other words, Carens continues to think that his model of moral incentives accords with many of the basic premises of contemporary capitalist societies, including prevailing assumptions about how the workplace should be organized. The problem is that the institutional plausibility and normative appeal of the Carensian model are actively undermined by his indifference to the organization of production at the local level (i.e., at the level of the firm or cooperative enterprise). I submit that Carens cannot persuasively leave aside questions of ownership and control over production if his model is to deliver on its egalitarian promises.[20] The ownership and control of capital in the sphere of production should fall within the ambit of justice, especially for a thinker like Carens, who rightly gives more attention than does Cohen to the importance of thinking through the institutional implications of the principles that he defends (Carens, 2015, p. 50). Indeed, when one carefully considers the institutional implications of Carens' model of moral incentives, it becomes evident that his model has the potential of undermining community in Cohen's sense of communal reciprocity and arbitrarily restricting the purview of social justice to post-tax redistribution.

Earlier in the chapter, I noted that the tension between the pre-tax and post-tax individuals in the Carensian scheme is reminiscent of the Rawlsian state seeking to tax the profit-maximizing behaviors of citizens who are principally committed to justice. I will now demonstrate that, in setting aside the normative relevance of workplace organization, Carens restricts the application of justice in ways that are detrimental to the realization of socialist values. The irony here is that the same problems extend to Cohen, who followed Carens in disregarding DSM and its instrumental role in furthering freedom, equality, and community.

---

[20] For a recent perspective that links workplace democracy and economic democracy, see Vrousalis (2019).

Before moving forward, it helps to recapitulate the relevant features of Cohen's response to the Rawlsian basic structure objection. In *Rescuing Justice and Equality*, Cohen asks whether the purview of justice should extend beyond formal institutions to include individual choices in the market. In responding to the basic structure objection, Cohen acknowledges the influence of the feminist-inspired slogan that the personal (or private) is political. Not surprisingly, Cohen brings up the nuanced example of the family, which John Rawls at times includes and at other times excludes from the basic structure. The organization of the family depends to a greater extent on the informal outlooks and choices of its members. However, if coercive regulation is largely absent in the family, and the family is included in the basic structure of society (if not, it is still an important informal institution), then it becomes difficult for Rawls to overlook the relevance of individual choices for social justice. After all, a just society endorsing principles of gender equality in its formal institutions while ignoring the potentially sexist character of individual choices in the family or elsewhere cannot genuinely live up to the demands of justice. Similarly, a just society cannot consistently be called just when it restricts the ambit of justice to its formal structure while overlooking the profit-maximizing behavior of individuals in the private sphere (Cohen, 2009, p. 134). Cohen maintains that Rawls' uncertainty over the coercive character of the basic structure is rooted in his liberal outlook:

> as a liberal, Rawls is inclined to make coercion criterial for the bounds of justice, so that, once the state has done its work, and people comply with its laws, individuals in civil society are free of the demands of justice, but he also wants to claim that he sites justice as he does because of the 'profound effect' of what occurs there: that's what's supposed to justify the restriction of the ambit of justice to the basic structure. I argued that the two propositions are not co-tenable: matters that lie beyond the coercive domain also have a profound effect, and are therefore of interest from the point of view of justice. (Ibid. p. 146)

Now, if one follows Cohen's critique to the end, the force of his argument will apply just as well against the Carensian model, specifically in terms of the latter's disregard for the thoroughgoing application of justice in the sphere of production (i.e., at the level of the firm). Such a restriction of justice is not only inconsistent; it proves detrimental to the realization of socialist values, those being freedom, equality, and community. Cohen's response to the basic structure objection extends to the Carensian model because the workplace has a profound impact on people's daily lives and is therefore of interest from the point of view of justice. If the purview of justice extends to the family and to individual choices in the market (as indeed it must for Cohen), then it should also extend to the organization of the workplace. The failure to extend the purview of justice to the workplace would mean, *ceteris paribus*, that the workplace can remain organized in an undemocratic and paternalistic manner, which even liberal egalitarians increasingly regard as morally arbitrary.[21] A closely related problem with such a restriction of justice is that it rests on a circumscribed understanding of freedom that is limited to occupational choice. In his attempt to reconcile freedom, equality, and Pareto optimality, Cohen similarly follows Carens in limiting the scope of freedom to occupational choice, which while important, overlooks the equality, autonomy, and welfare-enhancing dimensions of DSM that are central to the realization of socialist values.[22] Consequently, aside from its role in realizing greater autonomy for individual workers who would otherwise remain subject to the arbitrary coercion or domination of owners and managers, DSM can also further the socialist values of equality and community.

Empirical studies on worker-owned and managed cooperatives, such as Mondragon, have consistently shown that the ratio of income disparity between elected managers and rank and file workers is 5:1, which is

---

[21] Although Elizabeth Anderson does not ultimately endorse DSM (regarding it as infeasible), she nonetheless provides a sustained critique of the arbitrary coercion that is exercised over workers by managers and owners in contemporary capitalist firms. See Anderson (2017). It is therefore all the more surprising that Carens continues to disregard the relevance of such arbitrary forms of coercion in the workplace and their implications for the thoroughgoing application of justice.

[22] It is puzzling that when Cohen does address the topic of "freedom in work" (Cohen 2009, pp. 205–214), he says nothing about the organization of the workplace. Cohen's circumscribed understanding of freedom is doubly puzzling because he was acutely aware that individual freedom of occupational choice can coexist with deep levels of collective unfreedom. See Cohen (1983). To be clear, Cohen's account of collective unfreedom in the above article does not rest on an affirmation of the labor theory of value.

significantly lower than the average ratio in capitalist firms.[23] In 2018, the average ratio of income disparity between managers and workers in the largest US firms was 278:1.[24] The upshot of these findings is that worker-owned and managed cooperatives are far more conducive to realizing socialist equality than are conventional capitalist firms. The autonomy-enhancing features of worker-owned and managed cooperatives have also been shown to improve the job satisfaction and psychological well-being of workers,[25] including helping motivate workers with the kinds of non-monetary and cooperative incentives endorsed by Carens and Cohen.[26] Two points follow from the preceding discussion. First, the application of justice cannot be limited to the distribution of post-tax equality because the workplace remains a fundamental site of justice (or injustice, as in the case of conventional capitalist firms). Second, it is not the case, as Carens would have it, that one can leave aside the question of how production is organized and by whom it is controlled at the local level. Democratically self-managed cooperatives are better equipped at realizing the values of freedom (as autonomy or self-determination), equality, and community that animate the socialist project. In this sense, the normative appeal and plausibility of the Carensian model demand that the purview of justice be extended to the workplace and that the institutional principle of DSM is honored. These inferences also extend to Cohen insofar as he follows Carens in disregarding the role of DSM in furthering freedom, equality, and community.

Although Cohen was unambiguously in favor of democracy, he did not extend his normative concern for democracy to the sphere of production. In acknowledging the veracity of the Hayekian critique of central planning, DSM receded in his political philosophy and became, at most, subsidiary to considerations of equality and community. On this reading, DSM did not seem institutionally viable for Cohen on a large scale; it seemed bound up with the unsuccessful Yugoslav experiment of self-managed socialism; and it allowed for unjustified inequalities between

23 See Arando et al. (2015), Barlett et al. (1992), Bogle (2008) and Malleson (2014).

24 See Mishel and Wolfe (2019).

25 See Boxall and Macky (2014).

26 See Lopes et al. (2017). For an earlier view, see Blumberg (1968).

fellow workers.[27] The most plausible explanation for the neglect of DSM in Cohen's work stems from at least two sources. First, already in Cohen's early work, one can observe a sustained critique of Marx for emphasizing production at the expense of a more capacious account of distribution.[28] Cohen's prioritization of distributive justice may have contributed to his subsequent neglect of DSM and justice in production more generally. Second, the collapse of the Soviet Union led Cohen to increasingly turn away from classical Marxist theory and its emphasis on realizing "associated production" and move towards the terrain of normative political philosophy and its quest for rigorous analytical justification.[29] Cohen describes his changing philosophic trajectory in a revealing chapter on equality (fittingly subtitled "from fact to norm"):

> It is partly because there is now patently no group [the working class] which has those features [constituting a majority, whose values coincide with freedom, democracy, equality, and even human happiness], and therefore, the will to and capacity for revolution, that Marxists, or what were Marxists, are increasingly impelled into normative political philosophy. The disintegration of the characteristics produces an intellectual need to philosophize, which is related to a political need to be clear as never before about values and principles, for the sake of socialist advocacy. Normative socialist advocacy is less necessary when the features coincide. *You do not have to justify a socialist transformation as a matter of principle when people are driven to make it by the urgencies of their situation, and in a good position to succeed* [my emphasis].[30]

---

27 For a restatement of this criticism, see Cohen (1992, p. 6).

28 More specifically, Cohen takes issue with Marx's critique of J.S. Mill for separating relations of production from those of distribution and assigning to the "laws of production" the unchangeable character of "physical truths." It is telling that Cohen sides with Mill against Marx because of Mill's more capacious treatment of distribution. See Cohen (2000b, pp. 108–111). I leave aside the question of whether Marx's critique of Mill was justified.

29 For a more elaborate discussion of Cohen's move from Marxism to normative philosophy and its broader implications for his account of socialism, see Sypnowich (2012).

30 See Cohen (2000a, p. 109). Elsewhere, Cohen notes that he "reluctantly settled for a socialist market" for a brief period after reading David Schweickart's book, *Capitalism or Worker Control?* See Cohen (2005, n.27, pp. 77–78).

A transformation in facts led Cohen to pursue a rigorous defense of socialist egalitarian norms. Although Cohen was convinced that norms should ultimately be insensitive to facts, it is worth noting that the impetus for his rigorous analytical defense of socialist norms was motivated, at least in part, by a profound change in the social, political, and economic facts on the ground.[31] Furthermore, with Marxism seemingly in disrepute intellectually and politically, normative socialist egalitarian advocacy appeared readily available for Cohen's taking; it was rigorous analytically and was also forward-looking in its aspirations in ways that classical Marxism was not. However, the path that Cohen ultimately chose also came with its normative drawbacks, one of which was to rescue justice, equality, and community while disregarding DSM, which remains integral to the furtherance of socialist values.

7.4 Roemer's Revised Version of Socialism and the Continued Neglect of DSM

John Roemer has recently revisited the topic of socialism with the aim of revising it philosophically. The motivating force of Roemer's contribution is to demonstrate "why the ethics of socialism should be reformulated, from being characterized as the elimination of exploitation, to being characterized as the elimination of distributive injustice." (Roemer, 2017, p. 263) In a manner that is strikingly similar to Cohen and Carens, Roemer emphasizes securing justice in distribution while neglecting the equally salient matter of achieving justice in production. Roemer is best known for his advocacy of a coupon-based model of market socialism.[32] What is most relevant for our purposes is that Roemer's recent article

[31] In a sympathetic critique and extension of Cohen's arguments concerning socialism and issues of feasibility, Pablo Gilabert has argued in favor of adopting a more dynamic and "transitional standpoint" of analysis. In Gilabert's view, it is not sufficient for socialists to ask whether a proposed political-economic system or model meets evaluative standards; it is also important to consider the extent to which it is feasible and contributes to further inroads in the realization of socialist ideals. See Gilabert (2011, pp. 61–62). I agree with Gilabert's point about the need for a "transitional standpoint" and think that the institutionalization of DSM would go a long way in contributing to the further realization of socialist ideals.

[32] See Roemer (1994).

is more deeply influenced by Cohen's defense of socialist equality. In rejecting Marx's theory of exploitation, Roemer places the overriding emphasis in his revised version of socialism on addressing distributive injustices rather than abolishing exploitative relations of production.[33] Roemer's disagreement with Cohen is over relevant nuances rather than substance. More specifically, he objects primarily to Cohen's claim that relations of communal reciprocity under socialism would depend on some measure of generalized altruism, as well as his view that the market cannot generate relations of cooperation. Roemer, for his part, prefers a principle of interaction that depends on a less demanding "ethos of solidarity." (Roemer, 2017, p. 263) What distinguishes Roemer's revised treatment of socialism more favorably from those offered by Cohen and Carens is that he ponders the question of how relations of cooperation and solidarity should be harnessed institutionally in a revised account of socialism. More specifically, Roemer submits:

> I believe a design for socialism must include, as well as a template for property relations (in particular, how firms will be owned), a template for how people will cooperate in the economic sphere... that design, I am saying, cannot be limited to new property relations in firms, but must also include institutionalizing, one could say formalizing, how people will cooperate. (Ibid.)

Although Roemer refers more favorably to worker-owned firms in this context, he shies away from endorsing DSM or acknowledging its role in furthering socialist equality of opportunity, which is consistent with his earlier rejection of workplace democracy.[34] Roemer ultimately follows Cohen and Carens in prioritizing the normative defense of socialist equality at the expense of DSM, and thus remains vulnerable to the

[33] I criticize Roemer's revised version of socialism primarily for neglecting DSM. Nicholas Vrousalis has recently criticized Roemer's revised version of socialism for failing to address unjust exploitation, which Vrousalis recasts as the "Non-Servitude Proviso." See Vrousalis (2021).

[34] Lest there be any doubt about this point, readers are advised to revisit Roemer (1996, pp. 32–36). Roemer's rejection of DSM is further confirmed by Harry Brighouse's interpretation of Roemer's "coupon socialism," as well as the sympathetic critique of Roemer's circumscribed conception of democracy by Erik Olin Wright. See Brighouse (1996, pp. 199–207), and Wright (1996, pp. 122–134).

criticisms that were outlined in the preceding section.[35] Like Cohen and Carens, Roemer ultimately emphasizes the importance of justice in distribution while simultaneously neglecting the centrality of justice in production.

7.5 A Future for Democratic Socialism: Honoring DSM and Realizing Freedom, Equality, and Community

The foregoing discussion was mostly negative in character, illustrating the ways that Cohen, Carens and Roemer have problematically neglected DSM and the normative problems to which this necessarily gives rise, both with respect to the application of justice and the realization of socialist values. I now wish to briefly recast the Cohen-inspired question concerning the future of socialism by providing a positive argument for DSM as a consideration of justice in production and as an institutional principle that can further socialist values. I will draw mostly on the work of Carol Gould, Erik Olin Wright, and others, who interpret DSM as an institutional principle that has the potential for furthering freedom, equality, and community in daily life.

Carol Gould's important point of departure in Rethinking Democracy is that the focus of discussions about justice in Anglo-American political philosophy have mostly been confined to considerations of distribution, thereby leaving unexamined matters pertaining to the organization of production (Gould 1988, p. 133).[36] As we have seen, Gould's critical assessment is evidenced by the work of Cohen, Carens, and Roemer,

---

[35] Considerations of the interplay between DSM and market socialism have not fared significantly better among contemporary critical theorists. While Nancy Fraser has argued persuasively in favor of an expanded account of socialism that overcomes the tradition's historical oversights and pitfalls, Fraser's account does not offer a normative argument for DSM. See Fraser (2020, p. 56). Similarly, while generally receptive to new forms of institutional experimentation and an expanded conception of democratic citizenship, Axel Honneth says next to nothing about the significance of DSM. See Honneth (2017).

[36] See more recently, Gould (2019). Gould does not develop a fully fledged argument for worker-owned and managed cooperatives in the above article, but it is consistent with her broader views and work to date.

specifically in their concern with distribution at the expense of production. With some notable exceptions, this troubling pattern has continued well into the twenty-first century.[37] Against the tendency of neglecting justice in production, Gould proposes that the institutional principle of self-management be considered through a more robust framework of justice, which she understands in terms of the development of "equal positive freedom" (Gould 1988, p. 133). Once the principle of self-management is deemed a matter of justice, workers at the level of the cooperative firm would have rights to jointly determine the planning and organization of production, including matters touching on workplace decisions, service delivery, the distribution of shares within the firm, as well as other relevant concerns (Ibid. pp. 144–145). Gould is careful not to conflate DSM with political democracy; both are differentiated and deemed integral to the realization of justice. Gould's model also has the virtue of reconciling freedom, equality and community (or what she occasionally refers to as "mutual reciprocity") without disregarding the workplace as a central site of justice in the manner of Cohen, Carens, and Roemer. Moreover, by retaining the coordinating function of the market, Gould's account of self-management does not succumb to the inefficiencies of central planning, nor does it grant undue discretionary powers to the state, since democratic control rests in a decentralized fashion with the firm's membership. This decentralized approach is important because it also overcomes the normative defects of Soviet-style central planning, which proved grossly inefficient and detrimental to freedom. In considering DSM a matter of justice, Gould's work lends itself constructively to broader philosophic proposals for economic democracy, such as those theorized by David Schweickart,[38] Tom Malleson,[39] and Paul Adler,[40] which show the compatibility between DSM and economic democracy.[41]

---

37 See Hsieh (2008).

38 See Schweickart (2011).

39 See Malleson (2014).

40 See Adler (2019).

41 To be clear, I am not claiming that worker-owned and democratically managed cooperatives are an all-encompassing panacea, especially under the existing constraints of global financial capitalism. I am arguing that worker-owned and democratically managed cooperatives are better

More recently, Erik Olin Wright has provided a compelling case for expanding and consolidating the democratic potential of worker cooperatives with the aim of realizing such socialist values as justice, freedom, equality, and community (solidarity). Wright's argument is in keeping with his broader challenge for socialists and anti-capitalists to envision "real utopias." Wright submits:

> Worker cooperatives are particularly salient for the possibility of economic democracy, for in a worker cooperative, workers own the firm and production is governed through democratic processes. While worker cooperatives produce for the market, they are organized around values very different from capitalist firms: solidarity, equality, democratic governance, dignity of work, community development [my emphasis]. (Wright, 2019, p. 77)

For Wright, worker-owned and democratically managed cooperatives count among a range of institutions and social practices that reinforce a "democracy-conforming market." On Wright's definition, a democracy-conforming market is one that is "effectively subordinate to the exercise of democratic power." (Ibid. p. 70) Although Wright's analysis needs further elaboration and defense, which falls beyond the scope of the present chapter, it captures an integral dimension of the socialist project that has largely been neglected by Cohen, Carens, and Roemer. This is the insight that the institutional practice of DSM within worker cooperatives is structured according to values that are very different from those of capitalist firms. These are values that honor freedom, equality, and community, whose realization is thwarted when DSM is disregarded as a concern of justice and deemed irrelevant to the realization of socialist values. As I have tried to demonstrate throughout the chapter, such a position cannot be sustained without compromising the application of justice and the defense of socialist values.

---

equipped at realizing socialist values than are conventional capitalist firms. For this reason, the organization of the workplace matters and cannot be ignored or bracketed.

7.6 Conclusion

It is telling that Cohen commences his introduction to *Rescuing Justice and Equality* by acknowledging the force of Marx's claim, in "On the Jewish Question," that human emancipation can only be realized when the private individual takes hold of their individual powers and interpersonal relations, thereby transforming these powers and relations into genuine social powers and relations, rather than projecting them onto the alienating power of the liberal state. Cohen maintains that "the Marx-inspired question is whether a society without an ethos in daily life that is inspired by a broadly egalitarian principle for that reason fails to provide distributive justice. To that question, Rawls, being a liberal, says no: here is the deep dividing line between us" (Cohen, 2009, p. 2). Cohen should have added in that context that, only a socialist society that is guided by the institutional principle of DSM and the values of freedom, equality, and community it seeks to further, is consistent with the thoroughgoing application of justice in daily life. As we have seen, the workplace has a profound bearing on people's daily lives and should therefore be of interest from the standpoint of justice and the consistent defense of socialist values.

It has been more than 30 years since the collapse of the Soviet Union. Upon revisiting Cohen's question about what the future of socialism should be, my answer is that socialists should honor the institutional principle of DSM as a basis for furthering freedom, equality, and community. Cohen's legacy is best captured by his commitment to the rigorous defense of socialist values. The trouble is that Cohen and the contemporary political philosophers most influenced by his account of socialist equality have continually disregarded DSM, which comes with serious normative consequences for justice and the realization of socialist values. The idea that workers ought to exercise joint control over their conditions of work (and production more generally) has deep roots in the socialist tradition and should remain central to the socialist project. Following in Cohen's footsteps, these roots and values require rigorous and consistent defense in any normatively appealing version of democratic socialism.

Acknowledgements I am grateful to the *Journal of Social Philosophy* for granting me permission to republish a slightly revised version of this essay, which previously appeared as Shoikhedbrod, I. (2023). "G.A. Cohen, the neglect of democratic self-management, and the future of democratic socialism." *Journal of Social Philosophy*, 54, 6–22. https://doi.org/https://doi.org/10.1111/josp.12439. Drafts of this essay were presented as part of the Political Philosophy Reading Group series in the Department of Philosophy at Queen's University. For their helpful comments on earlier drafts, both written and verbal, I am grateful to Joseph Carens, Frank Cunningham, Dan Goldstick, Samuel Hollander, Chi Kwok, Ori Lev, Alistair Macleod, Colin Macleod, Tom Malleson, Esteve Morera, Shlomi Segall, Hillel Steiner, Christine Sypnowich, Nicholas Vrousalis, Daniel Weinstock, Allen Wood, as well as various anonymous reviewers for the *Journal of Social Philosophy*.

References

Adler, P. S. (2019). *The 99 percent economy: How democratic socialism can overcome the crises of capitalism*. Oxford University Press.

Anderson, E. (2017). *Private government*. Princeton University Press.

Arando, S., Gago, M., Jones, D. C., & Kato, T. (2015). Efficiency in employee-owned enterprises: An econometric case study of Mondragon. *IRL Review, 68*(2), 398–425.

Barlett, W., Cable, J., Estrin, S., & Jones, D. C. (1992). Labour-managed cooperatives and private firms in North Central Italy: An empirical comparison. *IRL Review, 46*(1), 103–118.

Blumberg, P. (1968). *Industrial democracy: The sociology of participation*. Shocken Books.

Bogle, J. (2008). Reflections on CEO compensation. *Academy of Management Perspectives, 22*(2), 21–25.

Boxall, P., & Macky, K. (2014). High-involvement work process, work intensification and employee well-being. *Work, Employment and Society, 28*(6), 963–984.

Brighouse, H. (1996). Transitional and utopian market socialism". In E. O. Wright (Ed.), *Equal shares: Making market socialism work*. Verso.

Carens, J. (1981). *Equality, moral incentives, and the market: An essay in utopian politico-economic theory*. University of Chicago Press.

Carens, J. (1986). Rights and duties in an egalitarian society. *Political Theory, 14*(1), 31–49.

Carens, J. (2003). An interpretation and defense of the socialist principle of distribution. *Social Philosophy and Policy, 24*(1), 145–177.

Carens, J. (2015). The egalitarian ethos as a social mechanism. In A. Kaufman (Ed.), *Distributive justice and access to advantage.* Cambridge University Press.

Cohen, G. A. (1983). The structure of proletarian unfreedom. *Philosophy & Public Affairs, 12*(1), 3–33.

Cohen, G. A. (1991). The future of a disillusion. *New Left Review, 1*(90), 5–20.

Cohen, G. A. (1992). Is there still a case for socialism? *Social Scientist 20*(12), 3–18.

Cohen, G. A. (1995). *Self-ownership, freedom, and equality*. Cambridge: Cambridge University Press.

Cohen, G. A. (2000a). *If you're an egalitarian, how come you're so rich?* (p. 109). Harvard University Press.

Cohen, G. A. (2000b). *Karl Marx's theory of history: A defence*. Princeton.

Cohen, G. A. (2005). Why not socialism? In E. Broadbent (Ed.), *Democratic equality: What went wrong?* University of Toronto Press.

Cohen, G. A. (2009). *Rescuing justice and equality*. Harvard University Press.

Cohen, G. A. (2011a). In M. Otsuka (Ed.), *On the currency of egalitarian justice and other essays*. Princeton University Press.

Cohen, G. A. (2011b). How to do political philosophy. In M. Otsuka (Ed.), *On the currency of egalitarian justice, and other essays in political philosophy* (pp. 227–228). Princeton University Press.

Cohen, G. A. (2013). In M. Otsuka (Ed.),*Finding oneself in the other.* Princeton University Press.

Cohen, G. A. (2014). In J. Wolff (Ed.),*Lectures on the history of moral and political philosophy*. Princeton University Press.

Elster, J. (1983). *Sour grapes: Studies in the subversion of rationality*. Cambridge University Press.

Fraser, N. (2020). What should socialism mean in the twenty-first century? *Socialist Register, 56*.

Gilabert, P. (2011). Debate: Feasibility and socialism. *Journal of Political Philosophy, 19*(1), 52–63.

Gilabert, P. (2015). The socialist principle from each according to their abilities, to each according to their needs. *Journal of Social Philosophy, 46*(2), 197–225.

Gould, C. (1988). *Rethinking democracy: Freedom and social cooperation in politics, economy, and society*. Cambridge University Press.
Gould, C. (2019). Protecting democracy by extending it: Democratic management reconsidered. *Journal of Social Philosophy, 50*, 513–535.
Hegel, G.W. F. (2008). In S. Houlgate (Ed.), *Outlines of the philosophy of right*. Oxford University Press.
Honneth, A. (2017). *The idea of socialism: Towards a renewal*. Polity.
Hsieh, N.-h. (2008). Justice in production. *Journal of Political Philosophy, 16*(1), 72–100.
Kwok, C. (2020). Workplace autonomy and workplace democracy: The polarization of the goods of work autonomy in the two worlds of work. *Review of Social Economy, 78*(3), 351–372.
Lopes, H., Calapez, T., & Lopes, D. (2017). The determinants of workplace autonomy and employee involvement: A multilevel analysis. *Economic and Industrial Democracy, 38*(3), 343–345.
Malleson, T. (2014). *After occupy: Economic democracy for the 21st century*. Oxford University Press.
Marx, K. (1967). In F. Engels (Ed.), *Capital*: Vol. III. International Publishers.
Marx, K. (1978). On the Jewish question. In R. Tucker (Ed.), *Marx-Engels Reader*. Norton.
Miller, D. (2014). Our unfinished debate about market socialism. *Politics, Philosophy & Economics, 13*(2), 119–139.
Mishel, L., & Wolfe, J. (2019). CEO compensation has grown 940% since 1978. Report by the *Economic Policy Institute*, 4. Accessed: 6 February 2026. https://files.epi.org/pdf/171191.pdf
Nielsen, K. (2012). Rescuing political theory from fact-insensitivity. *Socialist Studies, 8*, 216–245.
Rawls, J. (2001). *Justice as fairness: A restatement*. Harvard University Press.
Roemer, J. (1994). *A future for socialism*. Harvard University Press.
Roemer, J. (1996). A future for socialism. In E. O. Wright (Ed.), *Equal shares: Making market socialism work* (pp. 32–36). Verso.
Roemer, J. (2017). Socialism revised. *Philosophy & Public Affairs, 45*(3), 261–315.
Schweickart, D. (2011). *After capitalism*. Rowman and Littlefield.
Schweickart, D. (2013). Tired of capitalism? How about something better? *Philosophic Exchange, 43*(1), 1–16.
Selucky, R. (1975). Marxism and self-management. In J. Vanek (Ed.), *Self-management: Economic liberation of man*. Penguin.
Standing, G. (2011). *The precariat: The new dangerous class*. Bloomsbury.

Sypnowich, C. (Ed.). (2006). *The egalitarian conscience: Essays in honour of G.A. Cohen.* Oxford University Press.
Sypnowich, C. (2012). G.A. Cohen's socialism: Scientific but also Utopian. *Socialist Studies, 8*, 20–34.
Sypnowich, C. (2024). *G.A. Cohen: Liberty, justice, and equality*. Cambridge: Polity.
Titelbaum, M. (2008). What would a Rawlsian ethos look like? *Philosophy and Public Affairs, 36*(3), 289–322.
Vrousalis, N. (2015). *The political philosophy of G.A. Cohen.* Bloomsbury.
Vrousalis, N. (2019). Workplace democracy implies economy democracy. *Journal of Social Philosophy, 50*, 259–279.
Vrousalis, N. (2021). Socialism unrevised: A reply to Roemer on Marx, exploitation, solidarity, worker control. *Philosophy & Public Affairs, 49*(1), 78–109.
Wright, E. O. (1996). Political power, democracy and coupon socialism. In E. O. Wright (Ed.), *Equal shares: Making market socialism work.* Verso.
Wright, E. O. (2019). *How to be an anti-capitalist in the twenty-first century.* Verso.

8

How Capitalism Preserves Liberty

Christopher Freiman

People living under capitalism have more wealth than those living under socialism.[1] But do they have more *freedom*?

Most libertarians and classical liberals seem to think so. (After all, Milton Friedman went with *Capitalism and Freedom*, not *Capitalism and Efficiency*.) But G.A. Cohen disagrees. He claims that private property

I owe thanks to the audience at a workshop hosted by the Georgetown Institute for the Study of Markets and Ethics for their helpful feedback on an earlier version of this draft.

[1] As I explain below, capitalist economies are characterized by private ownership of productive property whereas socialist economies are characterized by collective ownership of productive property. So on this view, social democratic economies with significant income redistribution but primarily private ownership of productive property count as capitalist.

C. Freiman (✉)
John Chambers College of Business and Economics, West Virginia University, Morgantown, USA
e-mail: christopher.freiman@mail.wvu.edu

B. Burgis and M. McManus (eds.), *Analytical Marxism and Democratic Socialism in the 21st Century*, Palgrave Studies in Classical Liberalism,
https://doi.org/10.1007/978-3-032-02894-5_8

ownership—the defining feature of capitalism—involves coercive interference with non-owners' freedom to use that property. If you stroll into Yankee Stadium without buying a ticket, you'll be forced to leave. Maybe this sort of interference is justified, but that doesn't make it any less of a restriction of individuals' freedom. Whatever else we might say about the relative merits of capitalism and socialism, we can't claim that people enjoy greater freedom under the former than the latter.

I'll argue that Cohen is wrong. I begin by clarifying the nature of Cohen's "internal" critique of capitalism—namely, that private property ownership violates negative liberty (1). I reply that socialism is a greater threat than capitalism to negative liberty in virtue of coercively interfering with privatization, whereas capitalism permits collectivization (2). In response to a socialist objection, I argue that the freedom to own or work for a privately owned business is indeed meaningful and ought to be protected (3). Finally, I show that workers are no more forced to work under capitalism than socialism (4).

8.1 Positive and Negative Liberty

To start, let's clarify what I mean by *socialism* and *capitalism*. A socialist regime will permit an individual to own personal property—say, a phone—but not productive property—say, the factory that produces phones. Under socialism, productive property is collectively owned in one way or another (more on this below). A capitalist economy, by contrast, is characterized by private ownership of productive property.

Defenders of capitalism typically understand capitalist freedom as freedom from certain kinds of interference—that is, as negative liberty.[2] If you want to start your own business, work for a privately owned business, and so on, the state won't stop you.

Some critics object that the capitalist conception of freedom neglects the significance of positive liberty—that is, the liberty to do what you want or to fulfill your plans. The freedom to start your own business

[2] But see Schmidtz (2010) and Tomasi (2012).

selling novelty nu metal merchandise isn't particularly meaningful if you lack the material resources to actually start that business.

I'll set aside the objection that the standard capitalist conception of freedom neglects positive liberty. Instead, I'll look at Cohen's claim that a capitalist regime that enforces private property rights violates *negative* liberty, in which case it cannot be said that those living under capitalism enjoy more freedom than those living under socialism—according to the account of freedom favored by defenders of capitalism themselves. Cohen's critique is especially intriguing because it meets moral defenses of capitalism on their own turf.

As Cohen puts it, in a capitalist economy, "lack of money *is* (a form of) lack of freedom, in the favoured sense of freedom, where it is taken to be absence of interference" (Cohen, 1995, p. 58, emphasis in the original). He analogizes money to state-issued tickets that permit holders to freely perform certain sorts of actions such as

> visiting one's sister in Bristol, or taking home, and wearing, the sweater on the counter at Selfridge's. Suppose that someone is too poor to visit her sister in Bristol. She cannot save, from week to week, enough to buy her way there. Then, as far as her freedom is concerned, this is equivalent to 'trip to Bristol' not being written on someone's ticket in the imagined non-monetary economy. The woman I have described has the capacity to go to Bristol. She can board the underground and approach the barrier which she must cross to reach the train. But she will be physically prevented from passing through it, or physically ejected from the train, or, in the other example, she will be physically stopped outside Selfridge's and the sweater will be removed. The only way that she will not be prevented from getting and using such things is by offering money for them. (Ibid.)

When the state prohibits this person from boarding the train or leaving Selfridge's without paying, it is not failing to help her or failing to give her something; it's coercively interfering with her.

Now, there are plenty of solid consequentialist reasons to restrict the freedom of non-owners to use private property without the permission of its owners. If you can't fence off land and enforce a prohibition against trespassing, you probably won't spend the time and burn the calories needed to plant a garden on it. So, you'll produce less food to consume and exchange for the goods and services produced by others than you would under a system that permits privatization. Indeed, Robert Nozick appeals to this kind of consideration to show that privatization can satisfy the Lockean proviso, roughly, that privatization must leave "enough and as good" for others (Nozick, 1974, p. 175). On the Nozickian view, the restrictions on freedom involved in the enforcement of private property rights are justified because the system of private property makes those whose freedom is restricted better off, or at least no worse off than they would otherwise be.

But Cohen objects that Nozick can't make this style of argument while remaining consistent with his broader theoretical framework. More specifically, this defense of privatization appeals to a broadly paternalistic-welfarist justification, which clashes with the deontological account of justice as non-interference he uses in other contexts (Cohen, 1995, p. 89). This spells trouble for Nozick. If the state may coercively interfere with a trespasser on the grounds that a system that restricts trespassing improves the material welfare of the trespasser herself, then the door opens to other kinds of paternalistic interference that Nozick would reject. For instance, it would be hard to resist the conclusion that the state may coercively interfere with a gambler's attempt to enter a casino on the grounds that a system that restricts gambling improves of the material welfare of the gambler herself.

For what it's worth, I agree with Cohen about Nozick's shifting standards here. So even if Nozick is right that a system of private property tends to work to the material benefit of everyone, he hasn't shown that private property enforcement is not a violation of negative liberty. But we shouldn't therefore conclude, as Cohen does, that capitalism and socialism are on a par when it comes to respecting negative liberty.

8.2 Collectivization and Privatization

As I mentioned earlier, socialist regimes collectivize productive property, although this can take different forms. Cohen seems to shy away from Soviet-style state ownership in favor of something like democratically run worker cooperatives.[3] I'll focus on cooperatives, but my criticism generalizes to any form of socialism.

First, notice that Cohen's analysis of property and coercion isn't restricted to private property—rather, it applies to collective property as well. Take a modified version of the train case. This time the train is collectively owned by the train workers. You attempt to ride the train without the permission of the worker-owners, and so they block your access. In doing so, the worker-owners restrict your negative liberty. The takeaway is that collective property rights, just like private property rights, are enforced via coercive interference.

Cohen wouldn't deny this point. He makes the more modest claim that people under capitalism do not enjoy *greater* freedom than people under socialism. Maybe the modified train case just shows that their freedom is roughly equal. But this move is too quick. As Nozick himself notes, capitalist regimes don't permit coercive interference with the collectivization of productive property, whereas socialist regimes permit coercive interference with the privatization of productive property.[4] So people in capitalist regimes are free to privatize *and* collectivize, whereas people in socialist regimes are not free to privatize.

To illustrate, first imagine a group of bakers under capitalism, each of whom owns some flour, butter, eggs, an oven, a blender, and so on. They decide that they'd like to go into business together, with the rights to the aforementioned property shared equally among them. A capitalist regime has no grounds for interfering with this arrangement—the bakers' property rights entitle them to pool their property together with others. In short, individuals are free to unilaterally collectivize their private property under capitalism.

By contrast, individuals are *not* free to unliterally privatize collective property under socialism. Imagine a cooperative bakery where ten workers collectively control the bakery's facilities and equipment. Mayfield, one of the worker-owners, objects to the working conditions but gets outvoted by his fellow worker-owners when he proposes a

[3] See, for instance Cohen (1983).

[4] On this point, see Nozick (1974, p. 163, 250–253).

reform. So Mayfield wants to go private and take 1/10th of the equipment with him. The other worker-owners once again veto him. When Mayfield attempts to enter the facility and seize some of the equipment for himself, the worker-owners forcibly prevent him from doing so. The upshot is that socialism permits interference with privatization, but capitalism does not permit interference with collectivization.[5]

One might reply that while the state does not coercively restrict workers' freedom to collectivize under capitalism, it is nevertheless the case that workers will generally be unable to do so. For instance, Cohen suggests that workers inclined toward cooperatives may struggle to connect with like-minded individuals, which in turn makes it difficult to get cooperatives off the ground (Cohen, 1983, p. 24). (I'll note in passing that Cohen's concern probably no longer applies given the ubiquity of social media.) But even if Cohen is right that socialist workers typically can't realize their plans for democratic cooperatives under capitalism, at most this shows that workers lack the relevant *positive* liberty. While this is an issue worth taking seriously, it fails to support the claim that capitalism is no more respectful of negative liberty than socialism.

Socialist regimes will also interfere with the exercise of people's rights of personal property and occupational choice in cases where capitalism does not. Suppose that Mayfield owns cooking equipment and ingredients as personal property at his home.[6] That is, he uses this property to bake bread for himself. Mayfield's neighbor Waylon is an aspiring baker who wants to learn the trade. Mayfield agrees to hire Waylon at a steady wage in exchange for Waylon's help baking bread with the use of Mayfield's personal property. Mayfield in turn sells this bread for a profit. Mayfield's property has now transformed from mere personal property to productive property and Mayfield himself is now a capitalist employer with Waylon as his employee. Capitalism has emerged from Mayfield's exercise of his personal property rights and Waylon's exercise of his right of occupational choice. But a socialist regime must interfere with their agreement if it's to retain its status as a socialist regime. As

---

[5] Cohen (1995, p. 30) suggests he wouldn't prohibit acts of privatization if they are few and far between, but he would if privatization becomes sufficiently widespread and could be suppressed without "tyranny."

[6] For more about this style of argument, see Freiman (2019).

Nozick says, "The socialist society would have to forbid capitalist acts between consenting adults." (Nozick, 1974, p. 163).

Are Capitalist FreedomsWorth Protecting?

Capitalism protects the liberty to work in a capitalist firm *or* a cooperative. Socialism only protects the latter. A socialist might object that the freedom to own a business or work as a wage laborer for a capitalist employer is simply not a meaningful freedom and thus not one that ought to be secured by the state. But this view is mistaken.

First, consider the freedom to become a capitalist employer. For many people, an important part of their life involves owning a business.[7] Think of it this way: private property rights give an individual creative control. You could easily imagine an entrepreneur who has a vision to, say, deliver affordable high-quality streaming music that people can enjoy in the comfort of their own homes, but doesn't want to convert this vision into a group project where each team member has equal input. Under socialism, she doesn't have this option.

The freedom to choose to earn a wage as an employee in a capitalist firm is also significant. As Don Lavoie notes, workers "may not want to take on the risk, expense, and responsibility involved in managing a firm." (Lavoie, 2016, p. 128) He continues,

> After all, there are potentially several advantages to workers who choose to specialize in earning wage income in order to be insulated from the vicissitudes of market competition. There is often an advantage in allowing someone else to be the boss and thereby reducing one's concerns to the fulfillment of a wage contract, letting the management fret about the firm's profit and loss statements. While there is nothing inherently wrong with workers' control, or ownership, or participation (for many small firms in particular, those organizational forms may prove more efficient), there is also nothing inherently wrong with a voluntary separation of the ownership, management, and employee functions. (Ibid.)

[7] See Tomasi (2012).

In brief, not all workers want to be, in Lavoie's words "risk-bearing entrepreneurs"—many prefer to work for a capitalist and earn a steady wage. (Ibid.)[8]

Lastly, I doubt socialists would demand that the state coercively restrict someone's freedom to make *leisure* choices in accordance with their own risk tolerance. Some people might like risky leisure—gambling in Vegas or BASE jumping. Others might like lounging on the beach while listening to Jimmy Buffett. The state should permit people to make both kinds of leisure choices. Similarly, the state should permit people to make labor choices in accordance with their own risk tolerance, including the choice to work as an employee for a capitalist employer.

Are Workers Forced to Sell Their Labor Under Capitalism?

I'll now turn to another socialist objection to capitalism, namely that it *forces* workers to sell their labor to a capitalist. Cohen runs with Nozick's case of Z—unless Z works for a capitalist employer, he'll starve. The question, then, is whether Z is "*forced* to work for some capitalist or other." (Cohen, 1995, p. 35, emphasis in the original).

Cohen answers in the affirmative. He attributes the following claim to Nozick: "If Z is forced to do A or B, and A is the only thing it would be reasonable for him to do, and Z does A for this reason, then Z is forced to do A." (Ibid.) Since, on Cohen's view, Z *is* forced to work for a member of the capitalist class or starve, and working for a member of the capitalist class is the only thing that would be reasonable for Z to do, and Z works for a member of the capitalist class for this reason, then Z is forced to work for a member of the capitalist class.

For argument's sake, I'll grant Cohen that Z is forced to work for a member of the capitalist class. But moving from the case of Z to a moral critique of capitalism is going to take some more work. First, as Cohen would no doubt agree, he is appealing to a general account of forcing that doesn't apply exclusively to capitalist work arrangements. Consider the following case (used in a different context) from Harrison Frye:

> Suppose you are suffering from a terminal but treatable illness. You must receive treatment from a doctor, or else you will die. In this situation, you

[8] Nozick (1974, pp. 255–256) makes a similar point.

> are forced to see a doctor in the same sense that a worker is forced to work for a capitalist (neither you nor the worker has an acceptable alternative). Further, you are not forced to see any particular doctor, much like the worker is not forced to work for any particular capitalist. (Frye, 2024, p. 376)

I'll add that, on Cohen's view, you're forced to receive treatment from a doctor even if all of the doctors are willing to treat you for free. Yet it doesn't seem like these doctors are doing anything wrong when they offer to treat your illness. It also doesn't seem as though there is something morally objectionable about a system that allows doctors to offer to treat your illness.

Indeed, Cohen's account of forcing implies that someone can be forced to do something even in the absence of a relationship to any another person. If Robinson Crusoe has no choice but to gather berries or starve, and gathering berries is the only thing it would be reasonable for him to do, and Crusoe gathers berries for this reason, then Crusoe is forced to gather berries.[9] At a minimum, then, we have reason to believe that this account of forcing is importantly morally different than the sort of forcing involved in, for instance, the socialist state's prohibition of capitalist wage labor.

More importantly, people can be forced—according to this account of forcing—to work for a cooperative under socialism. Suppose we have a socialist regime with no capitalist firms—only worker cooperatives. Lois is entering the workforce for the first time. Lois is forced to work for a cooperative or starve, and working for a cooperative is the only thing that would be reasonable for Lois to do, and Lois works for a cooperative for this reason; thus, Lois is forced to work for a cooperative. All else equal, then, workers are no more free under socialism than capitalism. (Maybe you're thinking that socialists can solve this problem by supplementing collectivization with income redistribution—hold that thought.)

But it actually gets worse for socialists. As noted earlier, individuals are free to work for a capitalist firm *or* a worker cooperative under capitalism (or to support themselves by owning a business). However, under

[9] See Nozick (1974, p. 263).

socialism, individuals are *not* free to work for a capitalist firm. Thus, individuals under capitalism are in fact *not* forced to work for a member of the capitalist class, but individuals under socialism *are* forced to work for a cooperative. So here again, we see that workers enjoy less freedom under socialism than capitalism.

It's also worth emphasizing that Z likely has a higher chance of simply *starving* (rather than working) in a socialist economy. Nozick explains:

> If each new worker acquires a right to an equal percentage of the annual net profit (or an equal ownership share), this will affect the group's decisions to bring in new workers. Current workers, and therefore the factory, will have a strong incentive to maximize *average* profits (profits per worker) rather than *total* profits, thereby employing fewer persons than a factory that employed everyone who could be profitably employed. (Nozick, 1974, p. 251, emphasis in the original)

So long as Z can be "profitably employed," he'll fare better under capitalism than (egalitarian) socialism.

Moreover, Cohen suggests that it's possible for a worker to freely sell their labor to a capitalist, although such cases are rare in his view. As he puts it, under capitalism, "everyone is entitled to work for no one. But the power matching this right is differentially enjoyed. Some *can* live without subordinating themselves, but most cannot. The latter face a structure generated by a history of market transactions in which, it is reasonable to say, they are *forced* to work for some or other person or group." (Cohen, 1995, p. 34, emphasis in the original) Presumably when Tom Brady came out of retirement to play another season for the Tampa Bay Buccaneers, he was not subordinating himself to the capitalist class. Why not? His net worth was somewhere in the ballpark of $200 million, so he wasn't forced to work for anyone.

Here's the lesson: wealth is a key safeguard against being forced to work under capitalism *or* socialism. And to understand why capitalism makes us rich, let's return to Cohen's case of the person who is prevented from taking a sweater and leaving the department store without paying. As Cohen puts it, money is freedom under capitalism. But if we replace capitalism, the freedom to acquire sweaters (for instance) will simply be determined by something else. We have to allocate sweaters *somehow*.[10] Maybe people wait in line until the supply of sweaters dries up. Or maybe the state runs a lottery and only those with winning tickets get sweaters.

These alternative distribution methods are worse than distributing sweaters by willingness to pay. First, notice that these alternative methods would also need to be backstopped with the threat of coercive interference—presumably the state will forcibly prevent you from skipping to the head of the line or grabbing a sweater without a winning lottery ticket. Second, requiring people to hand over money if they want a sweater incentivizes the production of sweaters. Allocating sweaters by queue or lottery doesn't have this effect. Plus, the prospect of getting money in exchange for sweaters incentivizes competitors to underprice Selfridge's to scoop up their customers. The result is that the real price of a sweater gets driven down, meaning that people can spend less on sweaters and more on other things.

Critically, the sweater case illustrates what actually happens in capitalist economies. In 1900, the average American household spent 14% of its income on clothing; in 1972, it dropped to 7.8%, and in 2018, it stood at 3% (Tupy, 2023). More generally, Americans are spending smaller percentages of their income on necessities (Ibid.). This means that they can allocate more resources to, e.g., saving an emergency fund as a cushion if they lose or quit their job or investing so they can retire early if they grow unhappy at work. These examples illustrate how wealth functions as a safeguard against subordination by enabling workers to be selective about when and where they work.

Even if I'm wrong and capitalism alone doesn't make us rich, the state could always address poverty without resorting to socialism by implementing a universal basic income that enables workers to exit bad jobs, build their own business, start a cooperative, or save for early retirement. Granted, this option isn't available to Nozick, but it is available to defenders of capitalism more generally. Although occasionally writers

---

[10] For an illuminating discussion of this general point, see Munger (2018, chapter 4).

on the left and the right say otherwise, redistribution is not socialism—indeed, Cohen himself seems to agree with this point[11] Progressive redistribution involves taxing relatively rich individuals to fund transfers to relatively poor individuals—it does not collectivize productive property. Indeed, many defenders of capitalism endorse redistribution.[12]

Another straightforward way to protect workers from bad jobs is by making more job options available to them. While socialists often defend the value of giving workers a voice in their working conditions, the power of exit is plausibly a more powerful instrument for securing better treatment for workers.[13] By analogy, we tend to rely on exit rather than voice in our role as consumers. If you dislike a store, you could complete the survey linked on the receipt, but you'll probably just shop somewhere else. Of course, it's harder to switch jobs than to switch stores, but the point is that having many job options will typically do more good for a worker than having a vote over their working conditions.

Crucially, workers are often deprived of job options precisely because the state fails to respect private property rights. For instance, the over-regulation of the housing market prevents commercial developers from building new housing in areas with booming labor markets (Hsieh, 2019). State and local regulations hinder the creation of new businesses and thus new job opportunities (Edwards, 2021). Immigration restrictions that interfere with the free exercise of private property rights reduce job creation.[14] High corporate income taxes can discourage entrepreneurial activity (Watson, 2019).

In closing, Cohen's criticism does indeed damage Nozickian libertarianism. But he wins the battle at the cost of the war. Cohen is unable to resist the conclusion that socialism is a greater threat to negative liberty than capitalism.

---

[11] See Cohen (1995, p. 35).

[12] See, for instance, Friedman (1962).

[13] For more on the importance of exit, see Taylor (2017).

[14] On the impact of immigrants on job creation, see Azoulay et al. (2022). On the claim that immigration restrictions violate private property rights, see Freiman (2022).

References

Azoulay, P., Jones, B., Daniel Kim, J., & Miranda, J. (2022). Immigration and Entrepreneurship in the United States. *American Economic Review: Insights, 4*, 71–88.

Cohen, G. A. (1983). The structure of proletarian unfreedom. *Philosophy and Public Affairs, 12*(1), 3–33.

Cohen, G. A. (1995). *Self-ownership, freedom, and equality*. Cambridge University Press.

Edwards, C. (2021). Entrepreneurs and regulations: Removing state and local barriers to new businesses. *Policy Analysis, Cato Institute* 916 (May 5, 2021). https://www.cato.org/policy-analysis/entrepreneurs-regulations-removing-state-local-barriers-new-businesses. Accessed February 10, 2026.

Freiman, C., & Thrasher, J. (2019). The right to own the means of production. In B. van der Vossen & J. Queralt (Eds.), *Economic liberties and human rights* (p. 2019). Routledge.

Freiman, C., & Hidalgo, J. (2022). Only libertarianism can provide a robust justification for open borders. *Politics, Philosophy & Economics, 21*, 269–290.

Friedman, M. (1962). *Capitalism and freedom.* University of Chicago Press.

Frye, H. (2024). Domination at work: Resisting the radical diagnosis. *British Journal of Political Science, 54*, 373–388.

Hsieh, C.-T., & Moretti, E. (2019). Housing constraints and spatial misallocation. *American Economic Journal: Macroeconomics, 11*, 1–39.

Lavoie, D. (2016). *National economic planning: What is left?* Mercatus Center.

Munger, M. (2018). *Tomorrow 3.0: Transaction costs and the sharing economy.* Cambridge University Press.

Nozick, R. (1974). *Anarchy, state, and utopia*. Basic Books.

Schmidtz, D., & Brennan, J. (2010). *A brief history of liberty*. Wiley-Blackwell.

Taylor, R. (2017). *Exit left*. Oxford University Press.

Tomasi, J. (2012). *Free market fairness*. Princeton University Press.

Tupy, M., & Bailey, R. (2023). Share of spending on household basics declines. *HumanProgress.org* (March 1, 2023). https://humanprogress.org/trends/share-of-spending-on-household-basics-declines/. Accessed February 10, 2026.

Watson, G., & Kaeding, N. (2019). Tax policy and entrepreneurship: A framework for analysis. *Tax Foundation* (April 3, 2019). https://taxfoundation.org/research/all/federal/tax-policy-entrepreneurship/. Accessed February 10, 2026.

9

Cohen's Equality of Opportunity Folly: Does Luck Egalitarianism Imply Atomism?

Lesley A. Jacobs

Most Anglo-American democratic socialists commit to a form of value pluralism, combining an embrace of equality, human rights, freedoms, and community. Influenced by the insights of George Orwell and other leftist critiques of Russian communism, human rights for democratic socialists are widely embraced because they place inherent limitations on how individuals are treated by political and social institutions, independent of the values of equality, freedom, and community.

G. A. Cohen's vision of socialism is distinctive among contemporary egalitarian democratic socialists because over his career he had little to say about the importance or primacy of human rights. His neglect of human rights has received surprisingly little scholarly attention, but has been on my radar my entire academic career. Cohen was my doctoral supervisor at the University of Oxford where I wrote a thesis that

L. A. Jacobs (✉)
Ontario Tech University, Oshawa, ON, Canada
e-mail: Les.Jacobs@ontariotechu.ca

B. Burgis and M. McManus (eds.), *Analytical Marxism and Democratic Socialism in the 21st Century*, Palgrave Studies in Classical Liberalism,
https://doi.org/10.1007/978-3-032-02894-5_9

advanced the independent value of human rights, which was subsequently published as a book by Oxford University Press titled *Rights and Deprivation* (Jacobs, 1993). Cohen's doubts about the concept of human rights made that book much better than it probably would have been because he constantly challenged my own thinking (and tacitly the ideas of Amartya Sen, Ronald Dworkin, Charles Taylor, and C.B. Macpherson who helped shape my beliefs about the importance of human rights). Although Cohen and I discussed the primacy of human rights many times, I never saw any evidence that our exchanges shifted his views.

For Cohen, it is community, not human rights, that set constraints on inequality and individual freedom in democratic socialism. Cohen explains:

> "Community" can mean many things, but the requirement of community that is central here is that people care about, and where necessary and possible, care for, on another, and, too, care that they care about one another. There are two modes of communal caring…The first is the mode that curb some…inequalities…We cannot enjoy full community, you and I, if you make, and keep, say ten times as much money as I do, because my life will then labor under challenges that you will never face, challenges that you could help me to cope with, but do not, because you keep your money. (Cohen, 2009, pp. 34–35)

This type of appeal to community by Cohen is certainly not unique. Indeed, it echoes in many respects the assertion of Alasdair MacIntyre that "Individualism is and always was the doctrine of successful thieves from the community" (MacIntyre, 1976, p. 181). The alignment on community between MacIntyre and Cohen I note here is done with some irony, but it is not a coincidence, in my view, that MacIntyre is a well-known sceptic of human rights, stating famously in his book *After Virtue* that, "there are no such rights and belief in them is one with belief in witches and in unicorns" (MacIntyre, 1981, p. 69).

The appeal to community is a consistent theme in his powerful critique of the liberal egalitarianism of John Rawls with regard to economic incentives and the difference principle (Cohen, 2008). And his rescue of self-ownership for socialism from Robert Nozick and other right-wing libertarians (Cohen, 1995). But the focus here in this paper is on its positioning in Cohen's short book *Why Not Socialism?*, which was published shortly after his death in 2009.

Socialist Equality of Opportunity and Luck Egalitarianism

Over the last twenty years of his life, Cohen was focused on refining what him and others called luck egalitarianism. In its simplest terms, luck egalitarianism holds that distributive equality should aim to counteract the impact of luck on people's life prospects and that individuals should not be held responsible for disadvantages resulting from bad luck, such as being born into poverty or suffering from illness.[1]

In his case for socialism, Cohen sketches out three different progressively more egalitarian forms of equality of opportunity, with the intention of advancing that socialism is committed to what he calls *socialist equality of opportunity*. The prevalent form in capitalist societies is *bourgeois equality of opportunity*, which,

> Removes socially constructed status restrictions, both formal and informal, on life chances...This form of equality of opportunity widens people's opportunities by removing constraints on opportunity caused by rights assignments and by bigoted and other prejudicial social perceptions. (Cohen, 2009, p. 15)

This makes for an important contrast to what Cohen calls *left liberal equality of opportunity*, which,

> Sets itself against the constraining effect of social circumstances...of birth and upbringing that constrain [opportunities] not by assigning an inferior *status* to their victims, but by causing them to labor and live under substantial disadvantages...When left-liberal equality of opportunity is fully achieved, people's fates are determined by their native talent and their choices, and, therefore, not at all by their social backgrounds. (Cohen, 2009, pp. 16–17)

[1] This period was bookmarked by his seminal article "On the Currency of Egalitarian Justice", *Ethics 99* (1989), pp. 906–944 and *Rescuing Justice and Equality* in (2009).

Both of these forms of equality of opportunity are familiar theoretical constructs that are often reflected in social policy and anti-discrimination law.

Cohen's innovation is to introduce a third form of equality of opportunity:

> Left-liberal equality of opportunity corrects for social disadvantage, but not for native, or *inborn,* disadvantage. What I would call *socialist* equality of opportunity treats the inequality that arises out of native differences as a further source of injustice, beyond that imposed by unchosen social backgrounds, since native differences are equally unchosen. (Cohen, 2009, p. 17)

His point is that left-liberals arbitrarily draw a line between disadvantages of class or other forms of social background and what is often now called the genetic lottery.[2] Logically, if who your parents are is a matter of luck, not choice, this warrants not just mitigating for class and other forms of social background, but also differences in talent. He explains,

> Socialist equality of opportunity seeks to correct for all unchosen disadvantages, disadvantages, that is, for which the agent cannot herself reasonably be held responsible, whether they be disadvantages that reflect social misfortune or disadvantages that reflect natural misfortune. When socialist equality of opportunity prevails, differences of outcome reflect nothing but difference of taste and choice, not differences in natural and social capacities and powers. (Cohen, 2009, pp. 17–18)

Here, Cohen is marrying in a novel way his familiar embrace of luck egalitarianism with a theory of equality of opportunity. But in doing so, he is allowing that some inequalities are permissible under socialism.

Specifically, Cohen allows that under socialist equality of opportunity, income and wealth inequalities arising from option luck are permissible and indeed likely. He notes,

[2] See e.g. Paige (2021).

> Socialist equality of opportunity tolerates inequality of benefit, where the inequality reflects the genuine choices of parties who are initially equally placed and who may therefore reasonably be held responsible for the consequence of those choices. (Cohen, 2009, p. 26)

The situation of inequality of benefit that Cohen tolerates in his preferred form of equality of opportunity involves option luck, which he explains in the following way:

> The paradigm case of option luck is a deliberate gamble. We start out equally placed, with $100 each, and we are relevantly identical in all respects, in character, in talents, and in circumstances. One of the features that we share is a penchant for gambling, so we flip a coin on the understanding that I give you $50 if it comes up heads, and you give me $50 if it comes up tails. I end up with $150 and you end up with $50, and no extra anythings to offset that monetary shortfall. This inequality is consistent with socialist equality of opportunity. (Cohen, 2009, pp. 30–31)

This "toleration" of inequality is a significant one. Imagine for example that Canada commits to socialist equality of opportunity along the lines Cohen envisions. Two identically situated Canadians have savings of $10,000 that they would like to invest (or gamble) on a non-Canadian stock market such as the NASDAQ. Let us suppose that both of them are choosing to buy shares in a semi-conductor chip company in 2015, one of them invests in NVDIA and the other invests in INTEL. The one who invested in NVDIA would have seen a benefit of more than $2 million over the past decade, the one who invested in INTEL would have suffered a loss of $3000 or so. In other words, because of option luck, one would be a multi-millionaire, the other impoverished.

For Cohen, socialists cannot "condemn" (Cohen, 2009, p. 34) on the grounds of justice the high stakes inequalities that result for our Canadian semi-conductor chip investors. Socialist equality of opportunity cannot justify for example a capital gains tax on the option luck profits of the NVDIA investor that would reduce the level of the inequality between the two investors or indeed redistribute some of the profits to other less lucky Canadians.

9.1 Constraints on the Equal Opportunity to Become Unequal

The example of the two semi-conductor investors exercising their option luck is an illustration of a well-known structural difficulty that equality of opportunity is in its essence a justification for inequalities.[3] Cohen's account of socialist equality of opportunity narrows when inequalities are justified, but it still provides a license nonetheless for significant inequalities that trace to option luck.

As I emphasized at the outset, Cohen does appeal to the "principle of community" as an independent constraint on option luck inequalities.

> Community is put under strain when large inequalities obtain. The sway of socialist equality of opportunity must therefore be tempered by a principle of community. "Community" can mean many things, but the requirement of community that is central here is that people care about, and, where necessary and possible, care for, one another, and, to, care that they care about one another…We cannot enjoy full community, you and I, if you make, and keep, say ten times as much money as I do, because my life will then labor under challenges that you will never face, challenges that you could help me to cope with, but do not, because you keep your money. (Cohen, 2009, pp. 34–35)

In Cohen's socialist camping trip allegory, he imagines an individual named Leslie who, like my example of the NVDIA investor, reaps an enormous benefit from an exercise of option luck, and wants to retain that benefit rather than share it with other campers. (I don't know what to think personally about the fact that Cohen names this camper Leslie!)

[3] There are frequent expressions of this difficulty: In John Schaar's very influential (1967) critique, equality of opportunity "is really a demand for an equal right and opportunity to become unequal…[I]t so arranges social conditions that each individual can go as high as his natural abilities will permit" (Schaar, 1967, pp. 238, 233). Likewise, Ronald Dworkin charges that equality of opportunity is fraudulent as an ideal, "fraudulent because in a market economy people do not have equal opportunity who are less able to produce what others want." (Dworkin, 1985, p. 207). The single most influential execution of this objection came from John Rawls: "Equality of opportunity means an equal chance to leave the less fortunate behind in the personal quest for influence and social position." (Rawls, 1971, p. 73. Rawls leaves this passage unchanged in the 1999 revised edition.)

For Cohen, the principle of socialist justice provides Leslie with the license to do so, but he thinks that if she is genuinely committed to the principle of community, she will share her option luck benefit.

Certainly, I agree with Cohen that inequalities threaten community—the classic empirical evidence comes from Richard Wilkinson in for example his book *Unhealthy Societies: The Afflictions of Inequality* (Wilkinson, 2002)—and that a concern for community warrants reducing inequalities of all sorts. But what I think is worthwhile bringing to the forefront—indeed critical—is why Cohen thinks that option luck situations provide Leslie with a license to "keep your money" in the first place, under any account of justice.

Before turning to in the next section to that question, I want to highlight that there are alternative forms of equality of opportunity for egalitarian socialists that inherently set constraints on inequalities of benefit, without a need to appeal to the additional principle of community like Cohen does. Although Cohen structures his case for socialism around the logic that what he calls socialist equality of opportunity is a better form than bourgeoise or left-liberal equality of opportunity, I think that there is a better form of equality of opportunity that can address option luck inequalities in a way that Cohen's form fails to.

Different forms of equality of opportunity are, I have argued at length elsewhere (Jacobs, 2004), an ideal for the normative regulation of competitions that distribute valuable benefit in society. In most accounts of equality of opportunity, it is possible to distinguish three dimensions of fairness that might be in play to guide this regulation. *Procedural fairness* reflects a concern with the basic rules of procedure that guide a competition including the determination of the winners. *Background fairness* reflects a concern that there is a level playing field for all competitors. *Stakes fairness* focuses on the inequalities in benefits or what is at stake in the competition. This third kind of fairness plays the role of constraining inequalities such as those that arise as a result of exercising option luck in the example of Leslie in Cohen's camping example or my example of the NVDIA semi-conductor chip investor versus the INTEL investor.

These three dimensions of equality of opportunity can be illustrated by considering the example of a boxing competition with prizes and status for winners and losers. Boxing matches characteristically are regulated by certain familiar rules—the so-called Queensberry Rules. Some of these rules reflect procedural fairness such as, for instance, not punching one's opponent below the waist, no head butting, no swinging after the bell goes to end the round, and so on. Likewise, fair matches do not begin with an agreed-upon winner; instead, the winner is determined by the rules such as who wins by a knock-out or scores the most points in the case of a decision fight. Considerations of procedural fairness in this sense are presumably quite familiar. But boxing matches typically respect another dimension of fairness, as well. In competitions such as the Olympics, boxers are classified based on their body weight and fight other boxers in the same class. Underlying this practice is the intuition that there is something fundamentally unfair about a match between a 125 pound featherweight boxer and a 200 pound heavyweight. Assuming that the heavy weight boxer wins a match between the two, that outcome is said to be unfair even if the boxer did not violate the rules of procedural fairness such as hitting the featherweight boxer after the bell ended the round. Background fairness reflects the concern that boxers enter a match on roughly equal terms with respect to body weight. Background fairness is met, in other words, when there is a level playing field for all competitors. The third dimension of fairness concerns the prizes, how the winner is determined, or what is at stake in the boxing match. The idea that the winner in a boxing match is determined by a knock-out or points (as opposed to say fighting until death) is part of this dimension. In for instance professional boxing, the stake prize is money and a title. The practice is to have the winner receive say 60% of the money (say \$600,000) and the loser 40% (\$400,000). The justification typically is that this is fairer than a winner-take-all prize of \$1,000,000. The dimension of fairness drawn upon here is what I mean by stakes fairness.

This three-dimensional form of equality of opportunity is an innovative advance on how the concept of equality of opportunity has been viewed in treatments of egalitarian justice and can be mapped on to the three forms of equality of opportunity Cohen identifies. The traditional view of equality of opportunity is one-dimensional—what Cohen calls bourgeoise equality of opportunity. This view focuses on procedural fairness. In the 1960s, a number of influential liberal political philosophers introduced a two-dimensional view of equality of opportunity, which Rawls calls fair equality of opportunity and Cohen calls left-liberal equality of opportunity. This two-dimensional view stressed not only procedural fairness but also background fairness. Of course, these ideas of procedural fairness and background fairness reflected in particular the profound influence of John Rawls's description of fair equality of opportunity (Rawls, 1971, pp. 73–76). The two-dimensional view of equality of opportunity constitutes a major advance over the one-dimensional view because it is sensitive to the extent to which the distribution of opportunities is partly a function of background socio-economic differences between individuals. In market societies where there are competitions for benefits, the two-dimensional view can have significant redistributive implications because in order to ensure background fairness, it is often necessary to redistribute some of society's scarce resources. The two-dimensional view continues to dominate perceptions of equality of opportunity.

The added dimension of stakes fairness, however, makes for a more comprehensive account of equality of opportunity. Stakes fairness reflects a concern with the distribution of benefits and burdens within a competition and what constitutes winning or losing. Part of the issue here is concerns whether it is fair to have, for instance, a winner-take-all scheme when people exercise option luck. There are three aspects of stakes fairness that inform equality of opportunity as a regulative ideal, which I shall elaborate upon in turn: 1) the concern that there should be constraints on the risks participants in competitions are exposed to; (2) the concern with what and how much is actually at stake in an individual competition; and (3) the concern with limiting the impact of the result of one competition on another.

Equality of opportunity expose individuals to risks in the course of their participating in the competition for benefits. Boxers risk injury, for example, in every boxing match. These risks are a part of the normal functioning of the Queensberry rules. And indeed virtually any other sport is similar, whether it is football, baseball, soccer, diving, or ice hockey. How great should the risks be in any competition including the job market and post-secondary education? Are there fairness constraints on the risks that individuals should be exposed to in order to compete? Would a fight to the death, for example, ever be fair? Likewise, does any competitor have the right to consent to risking a major (as opposed to a minor) physical assault? Stakes fairness is concerned with the regulation of these risks.

Another core idea of stakes fairness is the concern about what and how much is actually at stake in an individual competition regulated by a form of equality of opportunity. In our everyday lives, even if circumstances and unchosen disadvantages were levelled, extreme or even high stakes outcomes should still be limited. Imagine someone who makes some bad choices as a young adult. Should those choices, even if they were genuine at the time and not regretted, burden that person for the rest of their lives? An ideal society should inherently have opportunities for second chances, as a matter of justice, not just community. Hence, the analogy from prize fighting where it is the norm for professional boxers to share the money prize, the difference between the winner and loser being their proportion of the prize. This example expresses the insight that winner-take-all stakes for competitive benefits are rarely fair. Appeals to stakes fairness suggest that it is principally a regulatory device to prescribe a wider distribution of the benefit at stake in a competition than a simple winner-take-all scheme, and ensure a principled commitment to second- and third-chances..

With regard to the third aspect of stakes fairness, the fundamental idea is that winning or losing one competitive opportunity in civil society shouldn't affect one's prospects in a competition for another opportunity. For example, financial success shouldn't translate into better educational prospects for you or your children; ability to pay or any other similar measurement should not affect the educational opportunities an individual enjoys. In certain respects, this aspect of stakes fairness blurs the distinction between this dimension of fairness and background fairness; in effect, the concern can also be represented as one about the initial standing of individuals in a competition. But I use the language of stakes fairness because it seems to me that the most effective way to address the underlying concern here is by regulating the stakes in any given competition.

My obvious point of discussing the idea of stakes fairness as a dimension of equality of opportunity is to say in effect that if this were integrated into Cohen's form of socialist equality of opportunity, there would be as a principle of justice a constraint on the level and nature of the option luck inequalities that would be permissible under socialism. In the scenario of the NVDIA semi-conductor chip investor, the massive returns they receive could be readily subject to a fair capital gains tax that significantly reduces or eliminates the wealth inequality arising when people exercise option luck. Likewise benefits received by Leslie on Cohen's socialist camping trip would similarly be taxed appropriately by the group.

Luck Egalitarianism and Atomism.

In a seminal essay written almost fifty years ago, Charles Taylor coined the term atomism to describe an idea about distributive justice, rights and entitlement to benefits that he perceptively identified was ascending and gaining greater currency among political philosophers. Atomism in contemporary political theory, explained Taylor, tries "to defend in some sense the priority of the individual and his rights over society, or which present a purely instrumental view of society" (Taylor, 1985, p. 187). What is puzzling for Taylor about atomism is the failure to appreciate that individuals as rights-bearing agents develop their capacities within societies, and that this creates justice-based obligations to contribute to society that are operate in tandem with the recognition of rights. As Taylor explains, under atomism, "our obligation to belong to or sustain a society…is seen as derivative, as laid on us conditionally, through our consent, or through it being to our advantage." (Taylor, 1985, p. 188).

Stakes fairness and arguably also left-liberal equality of opportunity amount to rejections of atomism. The underlying reasoning is that individuals, no matter how talented they are, have an obligation to share with others the benefits that come from those talents and other exercise of option luck—this obligation to share is not a matter of choice, but rather is a requirement of justice. The semi-conductor chip investor in NVDIA has this obligation as would Leslie on Cohen's socialist camping trip. And arguably tax schemes like capital gain taxes reflect this believe about the requirement of justice.

In some respects, Cohen's articulation of socialist equality of opportunity, based on luck egalitarianism, seems not to reject atomism. As I emphasized above, Cohen held the view that justice does not require the NVDIA investor nor Leslie to share the benefits of their option luck.

Cohen's appeal to the principle of community does make the case for why the NVDIA investor and Leslie should share the benefits of option luck with others in their community. But there is an odd way in which Cohen thinks that this is a matter of choice and discretion, not a demand of justice.

Certainly, it is noteworthy to reflect on how Cohen's principle of community is consistent with, or can be squared with atomism. I doubt that they can be reconciled and that Cohen would embrace the principle of community over atomism, which leaves Cohen's views about option luck and luck egalitarianism without a strong theoretical foundation.

9.2 Conclusion

At the outset of this paper, I noted that Cohen had little to say about human rights, which is surprising for a democratic socialist. Someone may think that this neglect is not especially significant or impactful. But one of the insights I draw from Taylor's framing of atomism is that careful reflection about the human rights tradition leads to an appreciation of how the ascription of human rights to an individual creates for that person justice-based demands that are not grounded in choice or consent. And that this is a serious problem for socialists like Cohen who build their view of the demands of justice on luck egalitarianism.

References

Cohen, G. A. (1995). *Self-ownership, freedom, and equality*. Cambridge University Press.

Cohen, G. A. (2008). *Rescuing justice and equality*. Harvard University Press.

Cohen, G. A. (2009). *Why not socialism*. Princeton University Press.

Dworkin, R. (1985). *A matter of principle*. Harvard University Press.
Jacobs, L. A. (1993). *Rights and deprivation*. Oxford University Press; online 2023). https://academic.oup.com/book/53431
Jacobs, L. A. (2004). *Pursuing equal opportunities: The theory and practice of egalitarian justice*. Cambridge University Press.
MacIntyre, A. (1976). On democratic theory: Essays in retrieval by CB Macpherson. *Canadian Journal of Philosophy, VI*(2), 177–1181.
MacIntyre, A. (1981). *After virtue*. University of Notre Dame Press.
Paige, K. (2021). *The genetic lottery: Why DNA matters for social equality*. Princeton University Press.
Rawls, J. (1971). *A theory of justice*. Harvard University Press.
Schaar, J. H. (1967). Equality of opportunity and beyond. In J. Roland Pennock & J. W. Chapman (Eds.), *NOMOS IX: Equality*. Atherton Press.
Taylor, C. (1985). Atomism. In *Philosophy and the human sciences, philosophical papers 2*. Cambridge University Press.
Wilkinson, R. (2002). *Unhealthy societies: The afflictions of inequality*. Routledge.

Index

B. Burgis and M. McManus (eds.), *Analytical Marxism and Democratic Socialism in the 21st Century*, Palgrave Studies in Classical Liberalism,
https://doi.org/10.1007/978-3-032-02894-5

The manufacturer's authorised representative in the EU is Springer Nature Customer Service Centre GmbH, Europaplatz 3, 69115 Heidelberg, Germany. If you have any concerns regarding our products, please contact ProductSafety@springernature.com

Printed and bound by CPI Group (UK) Ltd, Croydon, CR0 4YY
21/09/2026
02219945-0004